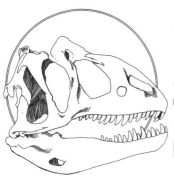

# 100 Greatest Science Discoveries of All Time

Kendall Haven

**LIBRARIES**
U N L I M I T E D

A Member of the Greenwood Publishing Group

Westport, Connecticut • London

**Library of Congress Cataloging-in-Publication Data**

Haven, Kendall F.
  100 greatest science discoveries of all time / Kendall Haven.
      p. cm.
  Includes bibliographical references and index.
  ISBN-13: 978-1-59158-265-6 (alk. paper)
  ISBN-10: 1-59158-265-2 (alk. paper)
  1. Discoveries in science. I. Title. II. Title: One hundred greatest
science discoveries of all time.
  Q180.55.D57H349   2007
  509—dc22       2006032417

British Library Cataloguing in Publication Data is available.

Library of Congress Catalog Card Number: 2006032417
ISBN: 978-1-59158-265-6

First published in 2007

Libraries Unlimited, 88 Post Road West, Westport, CT 06881
A Member of the Greenwood Publishing Group, Inc.
www.lu.com

Printed in the United States of America

The paper used in this book complies with the
Permanent Paper Standard issued by the National
Information Standards Organization  (Z39.48-1984).

10   9   8   7   6   5   4   3   2   1

# Contents

Acknowledgments . . . . . . . . . . . . . . . . . . . . . . . . . . . . . . . . . . . . . . . . . . . ix
Introduction . . . . . . . . . . . . . . . . . . . . . . . . . . . . . . . . . . . . . . . . . . . . . . . xi
*How to Use this Book* . . . . . . . . . . . . . . . . . . . . . . . . . . . . . . . . . . . . . . xv

Levers and Buoyancy . . . . . . . . . . . . . . . . . . . . . . . . . . . . . . . . . . . . . . . . 3
The Sun Is the Center of the Universe . . . . . . . . . . . . . . . . . . . . . . . . . . 5
Human Anatomy . . . . . . . . . . . . . . . . . . . . . . . . . . . . . . . . . . . . . . . . . . . . 7
The Law of Falling Objects . . . . . . . . . . . . . . . . . . . . . . . . . . . . . . . . . . 9
Planetary Motion . . . . . . . . . . . . . . . . . . . . . . . . . . . . . . . . . . . . . . . . . . 11
Jupiter's Moons . . . . . . . . . . . . . . . . . . . . . . . . . . . . . . . . . . . . . . . . . . . 13
Human Circulatory System . . . . . . . . . . . . . . . . . . . . . . . . . . . . . . . . . 15
Air Pressure . . . . . . . . . . . . . . . . . . . . . . . . . . . . . . . . . . . . . . . . . . . . . . 17
Boyle's Law . . . . . . . . . . . . . . . . . . . . . . . . . . . . . . . . . . . . . . . . . . . . . . 19
The Existence of Cells . . . . . . . . . . . . . . . . . . . . . . . . . . . . . . . . . . . . . 21
Universal Gravitation . . . . . . . . . . . . . . . . . . . . . . . . . . . . . . . . . . . . . . 23
Fossils . . . . . . . . . . . . . . . . . . . . . . . . . . . . . . . . . . . . . . . . . . . . . . . . . . . 25
Distance to the Sun . . . . . . . . . . . . . . . . . . . . . . . . . . . . . . . . . . . . . . . . 27
Bacteria . . . . . . . . . . . . . . . . . . . . . . . . . . . . . . . . . . . . . . . . . . . . . . . . . . 29
Laws of Motion . . . . . . . . . . . . . . . . . . . . . . . . . . . . . . . . . . . . . . . . . . . 31
Order in Nature . . . . . . . . . . . . . . . . . . . . . . . . . . . . . . . . . . . . . . . . . . . 33
Galaxies . . . . . . . . . . . . . . . . . . . . . . . . . . . . . . . . . . . . . . . . . . . . . . . . . 36
The Nature of Electricity . . . . . . . . . . . . . . . . . . . . . . . . . . . . . . . . . . . 38
Oceans Control Global Weather . . . . . . . . . . . . . . . . . . . . . . . . . . . . . . 40
Oxygen . . . . . . . . . . . . . . . . . . . . . . . . . . . . . . . . . . . . . . . . . . . . . . . . . . 43
Photosynthesis . . . . . . . . . . . . . . . . . . . . . . . . . . . . . . . . . . . . . . . . . . . . 45
Conservation of Matter . . . . . . . . . . . . . . . . . . . . . . . . . . . . . . . . . . . . . 47
The Nature of Heat . . . . . . . . . . . . . . . . . . . . . . . . . . . . . . . . . . . . . . . . 49
Erosion of the Earth . . . . . . . . . . . . . . . . . . . . . . . . . . . . . . . . . . . . . . . 51
Vaccinations . . . . . . . . . . . . . . . . . . . . . . . . . . . . . . . . . . . . . . . . . . . . . . 53
Infrared and Ultraviolet . . . . . . . . . . . . . . . . . . . . . . . . . . . . . . . . . . . . 55
Anesthesia . . . . . . . . . . . . . . . . . . . . . . . . . . . . . . . . . . . . . . . . . . . . . . . 57
Atoms . . . . . . . . . . . . . . . . . . . . . . . . . . . . . . . . . . . . . . . . . . . . . . . . . . . 59
Electrochemical Bonding . . . . . . . . . . . . . . . . . . . . . . . . . . . . . . . . . . . 61
The Existence of Molecules . . . . . . . . . . . . . . . . . . . . . . . . . . . . . . . . . 63
Electromagnetism . . . . . . . . . . . . . . . . . . . . . . . . . . . . . . . . . . . . . . . . . 65
First Dinosaur Fossil . . . . . . . . . . . . . . . . . . . . . . . . . . . . . . . . . . . . . . . 67
Ice Ages . . . . . . . . . . . . . . . . . . . . . . . . . . . . . . . . . . . . . . . . . . . . . . . . . 69
Calories (Units of Energy) . . . . . . . . . . . . . . . . . . . . . . . . . . . . . . . . . . 71
Conservation of Energy . . . . . . . . . . . . . . . . . . . . . . . . . . . . . . . . . . . . 73

Doppler Effect . . . . . . . . . . . . . . . . . . . . . . . . . . . . . . . . . . . . . . . . . . . . 75

Germ Theory . . . . . . . . . . . . . . . . . . . . . . . . . . . . . . . . . . . . . . . . . . . . . 77

The Theory of Evolution . . . . . . . . . . . . . . . . . . . . . . . . . . . . . . . . . . . 79

Atomic Light Signatures. . . . . . . . . . . . . . . . . . . . . . . . . . . . . . . . . . . . 81

Electromagnetic Radiation/Radio Waves . . . . . . . . . . . . . . . . . . . . . . 83

Heredity . . . . . . . . . . . . . . . . . . . . . . . . . . . . . . . . . . . . . . . . . . . . . . . . 86

Deep-Sea Life. . . . . . . . . . . . . . . . . . . . . . . . . . . . . . . . . . . . . . . . . . . . 88

Periodic Chart of Elements. . . . . . . . . . . . . . . . . . . . . . . . . . . . . . . . . . 90

Cell Division. . . . . . . . . . . . . . . . . . . . . . . . . . . . . . . . . . . . . . . . . . . . . 92

X-Rays . . . . . . . . . . . . . . . . . . . . . . . . . . . . . . . . . . . . . . . . . . . . . . . . . 95

Blood Types . . . . . . . . . . . . . . . . . . . . . . . . . . . . . . . . . . . . . . . . . . . . . 97

Electron . . . . . . . . . . . . . . . . . . . . . . . . . . . . . . . . . . . . . . . . . . . . . . . . 99

Virus . . . . . . . . . . . . . . . . . . . . . . . . . . . . . . . . . . . . . . . . . . . . . . . . . . 101

Mitochondria . . . . . . . . . . . . . . . . . . . . . . . . . . . . . . . . . . . . . . . . . . . 103

Radioactivity. . . . . . . . . . . . . . . . . . . . . . . . . . . . . . . . . . . . . . . . . . . . 105

Atmospheric Layers . . . . . . . . . . . . . . . . . . . . . . . . . . . . . . . . . . . . . . 107

Hormones . . . . . . . . . . . . . . . . . . . . . . . . . . . . . . . . . . . . . . . . . . . . . . 109

$E = mc^2$ . . . . . . . . . . . . . . . . . . . . . . . . . . . . . . . . . . . . . . . . . . . . . . 111

Relativity . . . . . . . . . . . . . . . . . . . . . . . . . . . . . . . . . . . . . . . . . . . . . . 114

Vitamins . . . . . . . . . . . . . . . . . . . . . . . . . . . . . . . . . . . . . . . . . . . . . . . 117

Radioactive Dating . . . . . . . . . . . . . . . . . . . . . . . . . . . . . . . . . . . . . . . 119

Function of Chromosomes . . . . . . . . . . . . . . . . . . . . . . . . . . . . . . . . . 121

Antibiotics . . . . . . . . . . . . . . . . . . . . . . . . . . . . . . . . . . . . . . . . . . . . . 124

Fault Lines . . . . . . . . . . . . . . . . . . . . . . . . . . . . . . . . . . . . . . . . . . . . . 126

Superconductivity. . . . . . . . . . . . . . . . . . . . . . . . . . . . . . . . . . . . . . . . 128

Atomic Bonding . . . . . . . . . . . . . . . . . . . . . . . . . . . . . . . . . . . . . . . . . 131

Isotopes. . . . . . . . . . . . . . . . . . . . . . . . . . . . . . . . . . . . . . . . . . . . . . . . 133

Earth's Core and Mantle. . . . . . . . . . . . . . . . . . . . . . . . . . . . . . . . . . . 136

Continental Drift. . . . . . . . . . . . . . . . . . . . . . . . . . . . . . . . . . . . . . . . . 138

Black Holes . . . . . . . . . . . . . . . . . . . . . . . . . . . . . . . . . . . . . . . . . . . . . 140

Insulin. . . . . . . . . . . . . . . . . . . . . . . . . . . . . . . . . . . . . . . . . . . . . . . . . 142

Neurotransmitters . . . . . . . . . . . . . . . . . . . . . . . . . . . . . . . . . . . . . . . . 144

Human Evolution . . . . . . . . . . . . . . . . . . . . . . . . . . . . . . . . . . . . . . . . 146

Quantum Theory. . . . . . . . . . . . . . . . . . . . . . . . . . . . . . . . . . . . . . . . . 148

Expanding Universe . . . . . . . . . . . . . . . . . . . . . . . . . . . . . . . . . . . . . . 150

Uncertainty Principle . . . . . . . . . . . . . . . . . . . . . . . . . . . . . . . . . . . . . 153

Speed of Light . . . . . . . . . . . . . . . . . . . . . . . . . . . . . . . . . . . . . . . . . . 155

Penicillin. . . . . . . . . . . . . . . . . . . . . . . . . . . . . . . . . . . . . . . . . . . . . . . 158

Antimatter. . . . . . . . . . . . . . . . . . . . . . . . . . . . . . . . . . . . . . . . . . . . . . 160

Neutron. . . . . . . . . . . . . . . . . . . . . . . . . . . . . . . . . . . . . . . . . . . . . . . . 163

Cell Structure . . . . . . . . . . . . . . . . . . . . . . . . . . . . . . . . . . . . . . . . . . . 165

The Function of Genes . . . . . . . . . . . . . . . . . . . . . . . . . . . . . . . . . . . . 167

Ecosystem. . . . . . . . . . . . . . . . . . . . . . . . . . . . . . . . . . . . . . . . . . . . . . 169

Weak and Strong Force . . . . . . . . . . . . . . . . . . . . . . . . . . . . . . . . . . . 171

Metabolism. . . . . . . . . . . . . . . . . . . . . . . . . . . . . . . . . . . . . . . . . . . . . 174

Coelacanth . . . . . . . . . . . . . . . . . . . . . . . . . . . . . . . . . . . . . . . . . . . . . . . . . 176
Nuclear Fission. . . . . . . . . . . . . . . . . . . . . . . . . . . . . . . . . . . . . . . . . . . . . . 178
Blood Plasma . . . . . . . . . . . . . . . . . . . . . . . . . . . . . . . . . . . . . . . . . . . . . . . 181
Semiconductor Transistor. . . . . . . . . . . . . . . . . . . . . . . . . . . . . . . . . . . . . . 183
The Big Bang . . . . . . . . . . . . . . . . . . . . . . . . . . . . . . . . . . . . . . . . . . . . . . . 185
Definition of Information . . . . . . . . . . . . . . . . . . . . . . . . . . . . . . . . . . . . . . 188
Jumpin' Genes . . . . . . . . . . . . . . . . . . . . . . . . . . . . . . . . . . . . . . . . . . . . . . 190
Fusion. . . . . . . . . . . . . . . . . . . . . . . . . . . . . . . . . . . . . . . . . . . . . . . . . . . . . 192
Origins of Life . . . . . . . . . . . . . . . . . . . . . . . . . . . . . . . . . . . . . . . . . . . . . . 194
DNA . . . . . . . . . . . . . . . . . . . . . . . . . . . . . . . . . . . . . . . . . . . . . . . . . . . . . . 196
Seafloor Spreading . . . . . . . . . . . . . . . . . . . . . . . . . . . . . . . . . . . . . . . . . . . 199
The Nature of the Atmosphere . . . . . . . . . . . . . . . . . . . . . . . . . . . . . . . . . . 201
Quarks . . . . . . . . . . . . . . . . . . . . . . . . . . . . . . . . . . . . . . . . . . . . . . . . . . . . 203
Quasars and Pulsars . . . . . . . . . . . . . . . . . . . . . . . . . . . . . . . . . . . . . . . . . 205
Complete Evolution . . . . . . . . . . . . . . . . . . . . . . . . . . . . . . . . . . . . . . . . . . 208
Dark Matter . . . . . . . . . . . . . . . . . . . . . . . . . . . . . . . . . . . . . . . . . . . . . . . . 211
The Nature of Dinosaurs . . . . . . . . . . . . . . . . . . . . . . . . . . . . . . . . . . . . . . 213
Planets Exist Around Other Stars . . . . . . . . . . . . . . . . . . . . . . . . . . . . . . . . 215
Accelerating Universe . . . . . . . . . . . . . . . . . . . . . . . . . . . . . . . . . . . . . . . . 218
Human Genome . . . . . . . . . . . . . . . . . . . . . . . . . . . . . . . . . . . . . . . . . . . . . 220

References . . . . . . . . . . . . . . . . . . . . . . . . . . . . . . . . . . . . . . . . . . . . . . . . . . 223
Appendix 1: Discoveries by Scientific Field . . . . . . . . . . . . . . . . . . . . . . . 229
Appendix 2: Scientists . . . . . . . . . . . . . . . . . . . . . . . . . . . . . . . . . . . . . . . . 233
Appendix 3: The Next 40 . . . . . . . . . . . . . . . . . . . . . . . . . . . . . . . . . . . . . . 237
Index . . . . . . . . . . . . . . . . . . . . . . . . . . . . . . . . . . . . . . . . . . . . . . . . . . . . . . 239

# Acknowledgments

I owe a great deal of thanks to those who have helped me research and shape these entries. The librarians at the Sonoma County Public Library and those at the Sonoma State Charles Schultz Library have been invaluable in helping me locate and review the many thousands of references I used for this work. I owe a special thanks to Roni Berg, the love of my life, for her work in both shaping these individual entries and in creating the 100 fun facts you will read in this book. Finally, I owe a great thank you to Barbara Ittner, the Libraries Unlimited editor who steadfastly supported and encouraged me to create this book and whose wisdom and insights shaped it and are reflected on every page.

# Introduction

Discovery! The very word sends tingles surging up your spine. It quickens your pulse. Discoveries are the moments of "Ah, ha! I understand!" and of "Eureka! I found it!"

Everyone longs to discover *something*—anything! A discovery is finding or observing something new—something unknown or unnoticed before. It is noticing what was always there but had been overlooked by all before. It is stretching out into untouched and uncharted regions. Discoveries open new horizons, provide new insights, and create vast fortunes. Discoveries mark the progress of human civilizations. They advance human knowledge.

Courtroom juries try to discover the truth. Anthropologists discover artifacts from past human civilizations and cultures. People undergoing psychotherapy try to discover themselves.

When we say that Columbus "discovered" the New World, we don't mean that he created it, developed it, designed it, or invented it. The New World had always been there. Natives had lived on it for thousands of years before Columbus's 1492 arrival. They knew the Caribbean Islands long before Columbus arrived and certainly didn't need a European to discover the islands for them. What Columbus did do was make European societies aware of this new continent. He was the first European to locate this new land mass and put it on the maps. That made it a discovery.

Discoveries are often unexpected. Vera Rubin discovered cosmic dark matter in 1970. She wasn't searching for dark matter. In fact, she didn't known that such a thing existed until her discovery proved that it was there. She even had to invent a name (dark matter) for it after she had discovered its existence.

Sometimes a discovery is built upon previous work by other scientists, but more often not. Some discoveries are the result of long years of research by the discovering scientist. But just as often, they are not. Discoveries often come suddenly and represent the beginning points for new fields of study or new focuses for existing scientific fields.

Why study discoveries? Because discoveries chart the direction of human development and progress. Today's discoveries will shape tomorrow's world. Major discoveries define the directions science takes, what scientists believe, and how our view of the world changes over time. Einstein's 1905 discovery of relativity radically altered twentieth-century physics. Discoveries chart the path and progress of science just as floating buoy markers reveal the course of a twisting channel through a wide and shallow bay.

Discoveries often represent radically new concepts and ideas. They create virtually all of the sharp departures from previous knowledge, life, and thinking. These new scientific discoveries are as important to our evolution as are the evolutionary changes to our DNA that have allowed us to physically adapt to our changing environments.

This book briefly describes the 100 greatest science discoveries of all time, the discoveries that have had the greatest impact on the development of human science and thinking. Let me be clear about exactly what that means:

**Greatest**: "Of highest importance; much higher in some quality or degree of understanding" (Webster's New College Dictionary).

**Science**: Any of the specific branches of scientific knowledge (physical sciences, earth sciences, and life sciences) that derive knowledge from systematic observation, study, and experimentation.

**Discovery**: The first time something is seen, found out about, realized, or known.

**All time**: The recorded (written) history of human civilizations.

This book, then, describes the process of finding out, of realizing key scientific information for the 100 science discoveries of the highest importance over the course of recorded human history. These are the biggest and most important of all of the thousands of science discoveries. These are the science discoveries that represent the greatest efforts by the best and brightest in the world of science.

There are many areas of human development and many kinds of important discoveries not included here—for example, discoveries in art, culture, exploration, philosophy, society, history, or religion. I also excluded science discoveries that cannot be attributed to the work of one individual or to a small group of collaborators. Global warming, as an example, is a major research focus of our time. Its discovery may be critical to millions—if not billions—of human lives. However, no one individual can be credited with the discovery of global warming. At a minimum, 30 researchers spread over 25 years each had a hand in making this global discovery. So it is not included in my list of 100.

You will meet many of the giants of science in this book. Many—but certainly not all. There are many who have made major contributions to the history and thought of science without making one specific discovery that qualifies as one of the 100 greatest. Many of the world's greatest thinkers and discoverers are not here because their discoveries do not qualify as *science* discoveries.

Discoveries are not normally sought or made in response to existing practical needs, as are inventions. Discoveries expand human knowledge and understanding. Often, it takes decades (or even centuries) for scientists to understand and appreciate discoveries that turn out to be critical. Gregor Mendel's discovery of the concept of heredity is a good example. No one recognized the importance of this discovery for more than 50 years—even though we now regard it as the founding point for the science of genetics. Einstein's theory of relativity was instantly recognized as a major discovery. However, a century later, scientists still struggle to understand what it means and how to use it as we inch farther into space.

That would not be the case with a great invention. The process of invention focuses on the creation of practical devices and products. Inventors apply knowledge and understanding to solve existing, pressing problems. Great inventions have an immediate and practical use.

Not so with discoveries. Einstein's theory of relativity produced no new products, practices, or concepts that affect our daily life. Neither did Kepler's discovery of the elliptical orbits of the planets around the sun. The same is true of Alfred Wegener's discovery that the continents drift. Yet each represents a great and irreplaceably important advance in our understanding of our world and of the universe.

I had three main purposes in shaping and writing this book:

1. To present key scientific discoveries and show their impact on our thinking and understanding.

2. To present each discovery within the continuum of scientific progress and development.

3. To show the process of conducting scientific exploration through the context of these discoveries.

It is interesting to note that the scientists who are associated with these 100 greatest science discoveries have more traits and characteristics in common than do those associated with the 100 greatest science inventions (see my book by that title, Libraries Unlimited, 2005). The scientists listed in this book—those who have made major science discoveries—in general excelled at math as students and received advanced degrees in science or engineering.

As a group they were fascinated by nature and the world around them. They felt a strong passion for their fields of science and for their work. They were often already established professionals in their fields when they made their grand discoveries. Their discoveries tend to be the result of dedicated effort and creative initiative. They got excited about some aspect of their scientific field and worked hard, long hours with dedication and inspiration. These are impressive men and women we can hold up as model scientists, both fortunate in their opportunities and to be emulated in how they took advantage of those opportunities and applied both diligence and honesty in their pursuit of their chosen fields.

It is also amazing to consider how recent many of these discoveries are that we take for granted and consider to be common knowledge. Seafloor spreading was only discovered 50 years ago, the existence of other galaxies only 80 years ago, the existence of neutrons only 70 years ago. Science only discovered the true nature and behavior of dinosaurs 30 years ago and of nuclear fusion only 50 years ago. The concept of an ecosystem is only 70 years old, That of metabolism is also only 70 years old. Yet already each of these concepts has woven itself into the tapestry of common knowledge for all Americans.

I had to devise some criteria to compare and rank the many important science discoveries since I had literally thousands of discoveries to choose from. Here are the seven criteria I used:

1. Does this discovery represent truly new thinking, or just a refinement and improvement of some existing concept?

2. What is the extent to which this discovery has altered and reshaped scientific direction and research? Has this discovery changed the way science views the world in a fundamental way? Has it radically altered or redirected the way scientists think and act?

3. What is the importance of this discovery to the development of that specific field of science?

4. Has this discovery had long-term effects on human development? Has its impact filtered down to our daily lives?

5. Is this a discovery within a recognized field of science? Is it a *science* discovery?

6. Am I adequately representing the breadth and diversity of the many fields, subfields, and specialties of science?

7. Can this discovery be correctly credited to one individual and to one event or to one prolonged research effort?

There are many worthy discoveries and many worthy scientists that did not make the final cut to be represented here. All of them are worthy of study and of acclaim. Find your own favorites and research them and their contributions (see Appendix 3 for additional suggestions).

Several entries include two discoveries because they are closely linked and because neither alone qualifies as one of the 100 greatest. However, considered collectively, they take on an importance far greater than their individual impact would suggest.

Enjoy these stories. Revel in the wisdom and greatness of these discoveries. Search for your own favorites. Then research them and create your own discovery stories to share!

# How to Use This Book

This book provides a wealth of information on—obviously—science discoveries, but also on the process of doing science, and glimpses into the lives of the many fascinating people who have advanced our scientific knowledge.

Use the book as a reference for science units and lessons focused on different aspects of, or fields of science. Use it to introduce units on discoveries, or on the process of doing science. Use it as a reference for science biography research. Use it as an introduction to the process of discovery and the process of conducting scientific study. Use it for fun reading.

Each entry is divided into four sections. An introductory section defines the discovery and lists its name, year of discovery, and discovering scientist. This is followed by a brief justification for placing this discovery on the greatest 100 list ("Why Is This One of the 100 Greatest?").

The body of each entry ("How Was It Discovered?") focuses on how the discovery was made. These sections provide a look at the process of science and will help students appreciate the difficulty of, the importance of, and the process of scientific discovery. Following this discussion, I have included a Fun Fact (an intriguing fact related to the subject of the discovery) and a few selected references. More general references are listed at the back of the book.

Following the 100 discovery entries, I have included three appendixes and a list of general references. The list of the 100 discoveries by their field of science (Appendix 1), an alphabetical list of all mentioned scientists (Appendix 2), and a list of "The Next 40" (Appendix 3). This is a list of 40 important discoveries that just missed inclusion on my 100 Greatest list and is an important source list for additional discoveries for students to research and discover for themselves.

# 100

## Greatest
## Science
## Discoveries
## of All Time

# Levers and Buoyancy

## Year of Discovery: 260 B.C.

> **What Is It?** The two fundamental principles underlying all physics and engineering.
>
> **Who Discovered It?** Archimedes

## Why Is This One of the 100 Greatest?

The concepts of buoyancy (water pushes up on an object with a force equal to the weight of water that the object displaces) and of levers (a force pushing down on one side of a lever creates a lifting force on the other side that is proportional to the lengths of the two sides of the lever) lie at the foundation of all quantitative science and engineering. They represent humanity's earliest breakthroughs in understanding the relationships in the physical world around us and in devising mathematical ways to describe the physical phenomena of the world. Countless engineering and scientific advances have depended on those two discoveries.

## How Was It Discovered?

In 260 B.C. 26-year-old Archimedes studied the two known sciences—astronomy and geometry—in Syracuse, Sicily. One day Archimedes was distracted by four boys playing on the beach with a driftwood plank. They balanced the board over a waist-high rock. One boy straddled one end while his three friends jumped hard onto the other. The lone boy was tossed into the air.

The boys slid the board off-center along their balancing rock so that only one-quarter of it remained on the short side. Three of the boys climbed onto the short, top end. The fourth boy bounded onto the rising long end, crashing it back down to the sand and catapulting his three friends into the air.

Archimedes was fascinated. And he determined to understand the principles that so easily allowed a small weight (one boy) to lift a large weight (three boys).

Archimedes used a strip of wood and small wooden blocks to model the boys and their driftwood. He made a triangular block to model their rock. By measuring as he balanced different combinations of weights on each end of the lever (*lever* came from the Latin word meaning "to lift"), Archimedes realized that levers were an example of one of Euclid's proportions at work. The force (weight) pushing down on each side of the lever had to be proportional to the lengths of board on each side of the balance point. He had discovered the mathematical concept of levers, the most common and basic lifting system ever devised.

Fifteen years later, in 245 B.C., Archimedes was ordered by King Hieron to find out whether a goldsmith had cheated the king. Hieron had given the smith a weight of gold and asked him to fashion a solid-gold crown. Even though the crown weighed exactly the same as the original gold, the king suspected that the goldsmith had wrapped a thin layer of gold around some other, cheaper metal inside. Archimedes was ordered to discover whether the crown was solid gold without damaging the crown itself.

It seemed like an impossible task. In a public bathhouse Archimedes noticed his arm floating on the water's surface. A vague idea began to form in his mind. He pulled his arm completely under the surface. Then he relaxed and it floated back up.

He stood up in the tub. The water level dropped around the tub's sides. He sat back down. The water level rose.

He lay down. The water rose higher, and he realized that he felt lighter. He stood up. The water level fell and he felt heavier. Water had to be pushing up on his submerged body to make it feel lighter.

He carried a stone and a block of wood of about the same size into the tub and submerged them both. The stone sank, but felt lighter. He had to push the wood down to submerge it. That meant that water pushed up with a force related to the amount of water displaced by the object (the object's size) rather than to the object's weight. How heavy the object felt in the water had to relate to the object's *density* (how much each unit volume of it weighed).

That showed Archimedes how to answer the king's question. He returned to the king. The key was *density*. If the crown was made of some other metal than gold, it could weigh the same but would have a different density and thus occupy a different volume.

The crown and an equal weight of gold were dunked into a bowl of water. The crown displaced more water and was thus shown to be a fake.

More important, Archimedes discovered the principle of buoyancy: Water pushes up on objects with a force equal to the amount of water the objects displace.

 **Fun Facts:** When Archimedes discovered the concept of buoyancy, he leapt form the bath and shouted the word he made famous: "Eureka!" which means "I found it!" That word became the motto of the state of California after the first gold rush miners shouted that they had found gold.

# More to Explore

Allen, Pamela. *Mr. Archimedes Bath*. London: Gardeners Books, 1998.

Bendick, Jeanne. *Archimedes and the Door to Science*. New York: Bethlehem Books, 1995.

Gow, Mary. *Archimedes: Mathematical Genius of the Ancient World*. Berkeley Heights, NJ: Enslow Publishers, 2005.

Heath, Tom. *The Works of Archimedes: Edited in Modern Notation*. Dover, DE: Adamant Media Corporation, 2005.

Stein, Sherman. *Archimedes: What Did He Do Besides Cry Eureka?* Washington, DC: The Mathematical Association of America, 1999.

Zannos, Susan. *The Life and Times of Archimedes*. Hockessin, DE: Mitchell Lane Publishers, 2004.

# The Sun Is the Center of the Universe

## Year of Discovery: A.D. 1520

> **What Is It?** The sun is the center of the universe and the earth rotates around it.
>
> **Who Discovered It?** Nicholaus Copernicus

## Why Is This One of the 100 Greatest?

Copernicus measured and observed the planets and stars. He gathered, compiled, and compared the observations of dozens of other astronomers. In so doing Copernicus challenged a 2,000-year-old belief that the earth sat motionless at the center of the universe and that planets, sun, and stars rotated around it. His work represents the beginning point for our understanding of the universe around us and of modern astronomy.

He was also the first to use scientific observation as the basis for the development of a scientific theory. (Before his time logic and thought had been the basis for theory.) In this way Copernicus launched both the field of modern astronomy and modern scientific methods.

## How Was It Discovered?

In 1499 Copernicus graduated from the University of Bologna, Italy; was ordained a priest in the Catholic Church; and returned to Poland to work for his uncle, Bishop Waczenrode, at the Frauenburg Cathedral. Copernicus was given the top rooms in a cathedral tower so he could continue his astronomy measurements.

At that time people still believed a model of the universe created by the Greek scientist, Ptolemy, more than 1,500 years earlier. According to Ptolemy, the earth was the center of the universe and never moved. The sun and planets revolved around the earth in great circles, while the distant stars perched way out on the great spherical shell of space. But careful measurement of the movement of planets didn't fit with Ptolomy's model.

So astronomers modified Ptolemy's universe of circles by adding more circles within circles, or epi-circles. The model now claimed that each planet traveled along a small circle (epi-circle) that rolled along that planet's big orbital circle around the earth. Century after century, the errors in even *this* model grew more and more evident. More epi-circles were added to the model so that planets moved along epi-circles within epi-circles.

Copernicus hoped to use "modern" (sixteenth-century) technology to improve on Ptolemy's measurements and, hopefully, eliminate some of the epi-circles.

For almost 20 years Copernicus painstakingly measured the position of the planets each night. But his tables of findings still made no sense in Ptolemy's model.

Over the years, Copernicus began to wonder what the movement of the planets would look like from another moving planet. When his calculations based on this idea more accurately predicted the planets' actual movements, he began to wonder what the motion of the planets would look like if the *earth* moved. Immediately, the logic of this notion became apparent.

Each planet appeared at different distances from the earth at different times throughout a year. Copernicus realized that this meant Earth could not lie at the center of the planets' circular paths.

From 20 years of observations he knew that only the sun did not vary in apparent size over the course of a year. This meant that the distance from Earth to the sun had to always remain the same. If the earth was not at the center, then the sun had to be. He quickly calculated that if he placed the sun at the universe's center and had the earth orbit around it, he could completely eliminate all epi-circles and have the known planets travel in simple circles around the sun.

But would anyone believe Copernicus's new model of the universe? The whole world—and especially the all-powerful Catholic Church—believed in an Earth-centered universe.

For fear of retribution from the Church, Copernicus dared not release his findings during his lifetime. They were made public in 1543, and even then they were consistently scorned and ridiculed by the Church, astronomers, and universities alike. Finally, 60 years later, first Johannes Kepler and then Galileo Galilei proved that Copernicus was right.

 **Fun Facts:** Approximately one million Earths can fit inside the sun. But that is slowly changing. Some 4.5 pounds of sunlight hit the earth each second.

# More to Explore

Crowe, Michael. *Theories of the World from Antiquity to the Copernican Revolution.* New York: Dover, 1994.

Dreyer, J. *A History of Astronomy from Thales to Kepler.* New York: Dover, 1998

Fradin, Dennis. *Nicolaus Copernicus: The Earth Is a Planet.* New York: Mondo Publishing, 2004.

Goble, Todd. *Nicolaus Copernicus and the Founding of Modern Astornomy.* Greensboro, NC: Morgan Reynolds, 2003.

Knight, David C. *Copernicus: Titan of Modern Astronomy.* New York: Franklin Watts, 1996

Vollman, William. *Uncentering the Earth: Copernicus and the Revolutions of the Heavenly Spheres.* New York: W. W. Norton, 2006.

# Human Anatomy

## Year of Discovery: 1543

> **What Is It?** The first scientific, accurate guide to human anatomy.
>
> **Who Discovered It?** Andreas Vesalius

## Why Is This One of the 100 Greatest?

The human anatomy references used by doctors through the year A.D. 1500 were actually based mostly on animal studies, more myth and error than truth. Andreas Vesalius was the first to insist on dissections, on exact physiological experiment and direct observation—scientific methods—to create his anatomy guides. His were the first reliable, accurate books on the structure and workings of the human body.

Versalius's work demolished the long-held reliance on the 1,500-year-old anatomical work by the early Greek, Galen, and marked a permanent turning point for medicine. For the first time, actual anatomical fact replaced conjecture as the basis for medical profession.

## How Was It Discovered?

Andreas Vesalius was born in Brussels in 1515. His father, a doctor in the royal court, had collected an exceptional medical library. Young Vesalius poured over each volume and showed immense curiosity about the functioning of living things. He often caught and dissected small animals and insects.

At age 18 Vesalius traveled to Paris to study medicine. Physical dissection of animal or human bodies was not a common part of accepted medical study. If a dissection *had* to be performed, professors lectured while a barber did the actual cutting. Anatomy was taught from the drawings and translated texts of Galen, a Greek doctor whose texts were written in 50 B.C.

Vesalius was quickly recognized as brilliant but arrogant and argumentative. During the second dissection he attended, Vesalius snatched the knife from the barber and demonstrated both his skill at dissection and his knowledge of anatomy, to the amazement of all in attendance.

As a medical student, Vesalius became a ringleader, luring his fellow students to raid the boneyards of Paris for skeletons to study and graveyards for bodies to dissect. Vesalius regularly braved vicious guard dogs and the gruesome stench of Paris's mound of Monfaucon (where the bodies of executed criminals were dumped) just to get his hands on freshly killed bodies to study.

In 1537 Vesalius graduated and moved to the University of Padua (Italy), where he began a long series of lectures—each centered on actual dissections and tissue experiments. Students and other professors flocked to his classes, fascinated by his skill and by the new reality he uncovered—muscles, arteries, nerves, veins, and even thin structures of the human brain.

This series culminated in January 1540, with a lecture he presented to a packed theater in Bologna, Italy. Like all other medical students, Versalius had been trained to believe in Galen's work. However, Vesalius had long been troubled because so many of his dissections revealed actual structures that differed from Galen's descriptions.

In this lecture, for the first time in public, Vesalius revealed his evidence to discredit Galen and to show that Galen's descriptions of curved human thighbones, heart chambers, segmented breast bones, etc., better matched the anatomy of apes than humans. In his lecture, Vesalius detailed more than 200 discrepancies between actual human anatomy and Galen's descriptions. Time after time, Vesalius showed that what every doctor and surgeon in Europe relied on fit better with apes, dogs, and sheep than the human body. Galen, and every medical text based on his work, were wrong.

Vesalius stunned the local medical community with this lecture. Then he secluded himself for three years preparing his detailed anatomy book. He used master artists to draw what he dissected—blood vessels, nerves, bones, organs, muscles, tendons, and brain.

Vesalius completed and published his magnificent anatomy book in 1543. When medical professors (who had taught and believed in Galen their entire lives) received Vesalius's book with skepticism and doubt, Vesalius flew into a rage and burned all of his notes and studies in a great bonfire, swearing that he would never again cut into human tissue.

Luckily for us, his published book survived and became the standard anatomy text for over 300 years.

 **Fun Facts:** The average human brain weighs three pounds and contains 100 *billion* brain cells that connect with each other through *500* trillion dendrites! No wonder it was hard for Vesalius to see individual neurons.

# More to Explore

O'Malley, C. *Andreas Vesalius of Brussels.* Novato, CA: Jeremy Norman Co., 1997.

Persaud, T. *Early History of Human Anatomy: From Antiquity to the Beginning of the Modern Era.* London: Charles C. Thomas Publishers, 1995.

Saunders, J. *The Illustrations from the Works of Andreas Vesalius of Brussels.* New York: Dover, 1993.

Srebnik, Herbert. *Concepts in Anatomy.* New York: Springer, 2002.

Tarshis, Jerome. *Andreas Vesalius: Father of Modern Anatomy.* New York: Dial Press, 1999.

Vesalius, Andreas. *On the Fabric of the Human Body.* Novato, CA: Jeremy Norman, 1998.

# The Law of Falling Objects

## Year of Discovery: 1598

---

**What Is It?** Objects fall at the same speed regardless of their weight.

**Who Discovered It?** Galileo Galilei

---

## Why Is This One of the 100 Greatest?

It seems a simple and obvious discovery. Heavier objects don't fall faster. Why does it qualify as one of the great discoveries? Because it ended the practice of science based on the ancient Greek theories of Aristotle and Ptolemy and launched modern science. Galileo's discovery brought physics into the Renaissance and the modern age. It laid the foundation for Newton's discoveries of universal gravitation and his laws of motion. Galileo's work was an essential building block of modern physics and engineering.

## How Was It Discovered?

Galileo Galilei, a 24-year-old mathematics professor at the University of Pisa, Italy, often sat in a local cathedral when some nagging problem weighed on his mind. Lamps gently swung on long chains to illuminate the cathedral. One day in the summer of 1598, Galileo realized that those lamps always swung at the same speed.

He decided to time them. He used the pulse in his neck to measure the period of each swing of one of the lamps. Then he timed a larger lamp and found that it swung at the same rate. He borrowed one of the long tapers alter boys used to light the lamps and swung both large and small lamps more vigorously. Over many days he timed the lamps and found that they always took exactly the same amount of time to travel through one complete arc. It didn't matter how big (heavy) the lamp was or how big the arc was.

Heavy lamps fell through their arc at the same rate as lighter lamps. Galileo was fascinated. This observation contradicted a 2,000-year-old cornerstone of beliefs about the world.

He stood before his class at the University of Pisa, Italy, holding bricks as if weighing and comparing them—a single brick in one hand and two bricks that he had cemented together in the other. "Gentlemen, I have been watching pendulums swing back and forth. And I have come to a conclusion. Aristotle is wrong."

The class gasped, "Aristotle? Wrong?!" The first fact every schoolboy learned in beginning science was that the writings of the ancient Greek philosopher, Aristotle, were the foundation of science. One of Aristotle's central theorems stated that heavier objects fall faster because they weigh more.

Galileo climbed onto his desk, held the bricks at eye level, and let them fall. Thud! Both bricks crashed to the floor. "Did the heavier brick fall faster?" he demanded.

The class shook their heads. No, it had not. They landed together.

"Again!" cried Galileo. His students were transfixed as Galileo again dropped the bricks. Crash! "Did the heavy brick fall faster?" No, again the bricks landed together. "Aristotle is wrong," declared their teacher to a stunned circle of students.

But the world was reluctant to hear Galileo's truth. On seeing Galileo's brick demonstration, friend and fellow mathematician Ostilio Ricci admitted only that "*This* double brick falls at the same rate as *this* single brick. Still, I cannot so easily believe Aristotle is wholly wrong. Search for another explanation."

Galileo decided that he needed a more dramatic, irrefutable, and public demonstration. It is believed (though not substantiated) that, for this demonstration, Galileo dropped a ten-pound and a one-pound cannonball 191 feet from the top of the famed Leaning Tower of Pisa. Whether he actually dropped the cannonballs or not, the science discovery had been made.

 **Fun Facts:** Speaking of falling objects, the highest speed ever reached by a woman in a speed skydiving competition is 432.12 kph (268.5 mph). Italian daredevil Lucia Bottari achieved this record-breaking velocity above Bottens, Switzerland, on September 16, 2002, during the annual Speed Skydiving World Cup.

# More to Explore

Aldrain, Buzz. *Galileo for Kids: His Life and Ideas*. Chicago: Chicago Review Press, 2005.

Atkins, Peter, *Galileo's Finger: The Ten Great Ideas of Science*. New York: Random House, 2004.

Bendick, Jeanne. *Along Came Galileo*. San Luis Obispo, CA: Beautiful Feet Books, 1999.

Drake, Stillman. *Galileo*. New York: Hill and Wang, 1995.

Fisher, Leonard. *Galileo*. New York: Macmillan, 1998.

Galilei, Galileo. *Galileo on the World Systems: A New Abridged Translation and Guide*. Berkeley: University of California Press, 1997.

MacHamer, Oeter, ed. *The Cambridge Companion to Galileo*. New York: Cambridge University Press, 1998.

MacLachlan, James. *Galileo Galilei: First Physicist*. New York: Oxford University Press, 1997.

Sobel, Dava. *Galileo's Daughter*. New York: Walker & Co., 1999.

# Planetary Motion

## Year of Discovery: 1609

> **What Is It?** The planets orbit the sun not in perfect circles, but in ellipses.
>
> **Who Discovered It?** Johannes Kepler

## Why Is This One of the 100 Greatest?

Even after Copernicus simplified and corrected the structure of the solar system by discovering that the sun, not the earth, lay at the center of it, he (like all astronomers before him) assumed that the planets orbited the sun in perfect circles. As a result, errors continued to exist in the predicted position of the planets.

Kepler discovered the concept of the ellipse and proved that planets actually follow slightly elliptical orbits. With this discovery, science was finally presented with an accurate pictures of the position and mechanics of the solar system. After 400 years of vastly improved technology, our image of how planets move is still the one Kepler created. We haven't changed or corrected it one bit, and likely never will.

## How Was It Discovered?

For 2,000 years, astronomers placed the earth at the center of the universe and assumed that all heavenly bodies moved in perfect circles around it. But predictions using this system never matched actual measurements. Scientists invented epi-circles—small circles that the planets actually rolled around that, themselves, rolled around the great circular orbits for each planet. Still there were errors, so scientists created epi-circles on the epi-circles.

Copernicus discovered that the sun lay at the center of the solar system, but still assumed that all planets traveled in perfect circles. Most epi-circles were eliminated, but errors in planetary plotting continued.

Johannes Kepler was born in Southern Germany in 1571, 28 years after the release of Copernicus's discovery. Kepler suffered through a troubled upbringing. His aunt was burned at the stake as a witch. His mother almost suffered the same fate. The boy was often sick and had bad eyesight that glasses could not correct. Still, Kepler enjoyed a brilliant—but again troubled—university career.

In 1597 he took a position as an assistant to Tycho Brahe, famed German astronomer. For decades Tycho had been measuring the position of the planets (especially Mars) with far greater precision than any other European astronomer. When Tycho died in 1601 he left all his notes and tables of planetary readings to Kepler.

Kepler rejected the epi-circle on epi-circle model of how planets moved and decided to work out an orbit for Mars that best fit Tycho's data. It was still dangerous to suggest that the sun lay at the center of the solar system. The all-powerful Catholic Church had burned Friar Giordano Bruno at the stake for believing Copernicus. No other scientist had dared come forth to support Copernicus's radical notion. Still, Kepler was determined to use Copernicus's organization for the universe and Tycho's data to make sense of the planets.

Kepler tried many ideas and mathematical approaches that didn't work. His bad eyesight prevented him from making his own astronomical sightings. He was forced to rely entirely on Tycho's existing measurements. In bitter frustration, he was finally driven to consider what was—at the time—unthinkable: planetary orbits that weren't perfect circles. Nothing else explained Tycho's readings for Mars.

Kepler found that ellipses (elongated circles) fit far better with the accumulated readings. Yet the data *still* didn't fit. In desperation, Kepler was forced to consider something else that was also unthinkable at that time: maybe the planets didn't orbit the sun at a constant speed.

With these two revolutionary ideas Kepler found that elliptical orbits fit perfectly with Tycho's measured planetary motion. Elliptical orbits became Kepler's first law. Kepler then added his Second Law: each planet's speed altered as a function of its distance from the sun. As a planet flew closer, it flew faster.

Kepler published his discoveries in 1609 and then spent the next 18 years calculating detailed tables of planetary motion and position for all six known planets. This was also the first practical use of logarithms, invented by Scotsman John Napier during the early years of Kepler's effort. With these tables of calculations (which exactly matched measured planetary positions) Kepler proved that he had discovered true planetary motion.

 **Fun Facts:** Pluto was called the ninth planet for 75 years, since its discovery in 1930. Pluto's orbit is the least circular (most elliptical) of all planets. At its farthest, it is 7.4 billion km from the sun. At its nearest it is only 4.34 billion km away. When Pluto is at its closest, its orbit actually slips inside that of Neptune. For 20 years out of every 248, Pluto is actually closer to the sun than Neptune is. That occurred from 1979 to 1999. For those 20 years Pluto was actually the *eighth* planet in our solar system and Neptune was the ninth!

# More to Explore

Casper, Max. *Kepler.* New York: Dover, 1993.

Dreyer, J. *A History of Astronomy from Thales to Kepler.* New York: Dover, 1993.

Huff, Toby. *The Rise of Early Modern Science.* New York: Cambridge University Press, 1993.

North, John. *The Norton History of Astronomy and Cosmology.* New York: Norton, 1995.

Stephenson, Bruce. *Kepler's Physical Astronomy.* Princeton, NJ: Princeton University Press, 1997.

# Jupiter's Moons

## Year of Discovery: 1610

**What Is It?** Other planets (besides Earth) have moons.

**Who Discovered It?** Galileo Galilei

## Why Is This One of the 100 Greatest?

Galileo discovered that other planets have moons and thus extended human understanding beyond our own planet. His careful work with the telescopes he built launched modern astronomy. His discoveries were the first astronomical discoveries using the telescope.

Galileo proved that Earth is not unique among planets of the universe. He turned specks of light in the night sky into fascinating spherical objects—into *places*—rather than pinpricks of light. In so doing, he proved that Polish astronomer Nicholaus Copernicus had been right when he claimed that the sun was the center of the solar system.

With his simple telescope Galileo single-handedly brought the solar system, galaxy, and greater universe within our grasp. His telescope provided vistas and understanding that did not exist before and could not exist without the telescope.

## How Was It Discovered?

This was a discovery made possible by an invention—the telescope. Galileo saw his first telescope in late 1608 and instantly recognized that a more powerful telescope could be the answer to the prayers of every astronomer. By late 1609 Galileo had produced a 40-power, two-lens telescope. That 1609 telescope was the first practical telescope for scientific use.

A paper by Johannes Kepler describing the orbits of the planets convinced Galileo to believe the theory of Polish astronomer Nicholaus Copernicus, who first claimed that the sun was the center of the universe, not the earth. Believing Copernicus was a dangerous thing to do. Friar Giordano Bruno had been burned at the stake for believing Copernicus. Galileo decided to use his new telescope to prove that Copernicus was right by more accurately charting the motion of the planets.

Galileo first turned his telescope on the moon. There he clearly saw mountains and valleys. He saw deep craters with tall, jagged rims slicing like serrated knives into the lunar sky. The moon that Galileo saw was radically different from the perfectly smooth sphere that Aristotle and Ptolemy said it was (the two Greek astronomers whose teachings still formed the basis of all science in 1610). Both the all-powerful Catholic Church and every university and scientist in Europe believed Aristotle and Ptolemy.

In one night's viewing of the moon's surface through his telescope, Galileo proved Aristotle wrong—again. The last time Galileo's observations had contradicted Aristotle's teachings, Galileo had been fired from his teaching position for being right when he proved that all objects fall at the same rate regardless of their weight.

Galileo next aimed his telescope at Jupiter, the biggest planet, planning to carefully chart its motion over several months. Through his telescope (the name is a combination of the Greek words for "distant" and "looking") Galileo saw a magnified view of the heavens no human eye had ever seen. He saw Jupiter clearly, and, to his amazement, he found moons circling the giant planet. Aristotle had said (and all scientists believed) that Earth was the only planet in the universe that had a moon. Within days, Galileo discovered four of Jupiter's moons. These were the first discovered moons other than our own.

Aristotle was wrong again.

Still, old beliefs do not die easily. In 1616 the Council of Cardinals forbade Galileo ever again to teach or promote Copernicus's theories. Many senior church officials refused to look through a telescope, claiming it was a magician's trick and that the moons were in the telescope.

When Galileo ignored their warning, he was summoned to Rome by the Church's all-powerful Inquisition. A grueling trial followed. Galileo was condemned by the Church and forced to publicly recant his views and findings. He was placed under house arrest for the rest of his life, dying in 1640 without hearing even one voice other than his own proclaim that his discoveries were true. The Church did not rescind the condemnation of Galileo and his discoveries until October 1992, 376 years after they incorrectly condemned him.

 **Fun Facts:** Galileo would have been astonished to learn that Jupiter resembles a star in composition. In fact, if it had been about 80 times more massive, it would have been classified as a star rather than a planet.

# More to Explore

Aldrain, Buzz. *Galileo for Kids: His Life and Ideas.* Chicago: Chicago Review Press, 2005.

Atkins, Peter, *Galileo's Finger: the Ten Great Ideas of Science.* New York: Random House, 2004.

Bendick, Jeanne. *Along Came Galileo.* San Luis Obispo, CA: Beautiful Feet Books, 1999.

Drake, Stillman. *Galileo.* New York: Hill and Wang, 1995.

Fisher, Leonard. *Galileo.* New York: Macmillan, 1998.

Galilei, Galileo. *Galileo on the World Systems: A New Abridged Translation and Guide.* Berkeley: University of California Press, 1997.

MacHamer, Oeter, ed. *The Cambridge Companion to Galileo.* New York: Cambridge University Press, 1998.

MacLachlan, James. *Galileo Galilei: First Physicist.* New York: Oxford University Press, 1997.

Sobel, Dava. *Galileo's Daughter.* New York: Walker & Co., 1999.

# Human Circulatory System

## Year of Discovery: 1628

**What Is It?** The first complete understanding of how arteries, veins, heart, and lungs function to form a single, complete circulatory system.

**Who Discovered It?** William Harvey

## Why Is This One of the 100 Greatest?

The human circulatory system represents the virtual definition of life. No system is more critical to our existence. Yet only 400 years ago, no one understood our circulatory system. Many seriously thought that the thumping inside the chest was the voice of the conscience trying to be heard. Most thought that blood was created in the liver and consumed by the muscles. Some still thought that arteries were filled with air.

William Harvey discovered the actual function of the major elements of the circulatory system (heart, lungs, arteries, and veins) and created the first complete and accurate picture of human blood circulation. Harvey was also the first to use the scientific method for biological studies. Every scientist since has followed his example. Harvey's 1628 book represents the beginning of modern physiology.

## How Was It Discovered?

Through the sixteenth century, doctors relied on the 1,500-year-old writings of the Greek physician Galen, who said that food was converted into blood in the liver and was then consumed by the body for fuel. Most agreed that the blood that flowed through arteries had no connection with the blood that flowed through veins.

William Harvey was born in 1578 in England and received medical training at Oxford. He was invited to study at Padua University in Italy, the acknowledged medical center of Europe.

When Harvey returned to England in 1602, he married the daughter of Queen Elizabeth's doctor, was appointed a physician in the court of King James I, and was then appointed personal physician to King Charles I in 1618.

While serving the English kings, Harvey focused his studies on veins and arteries. He conducted extensive experiments with animals and human corpses. During these dissections, he discovered the series of flap valves that exist throughout the veins. He was not the first to find these valves, but he *was* the first to note that they always directed blood flow toward the heart. Blood flowed in veins only *from* the arms, legs, and head back *to* the heart.

He began a series of animal experiments in which he tied off a single artery or vein to see what happened. Sometimes he clamped an artery and later released it to see where this surge of blood would go. He did the same with veins, clamping a vein and then releasing it. Sometimes he clamped both vein and artery and then released one at a time. These experiments proved that arteries and veins were connected into a single circulatory system and that blood always flowed from arteries to veins.

Harvey turned to the heart itself and soon realized that the heart acted as a muscle and pushed blood *out* to lungs and *out* into arteries. Following blood as it flowed through various animals, Harvey saw that blood was not consumed, but circulated over and over again through the system, carrying air and nourishment to the body.

By 1625 Harvey had discovered an *almost* complete picture of the circulatory system. He faced two problems. First, he couldn't figure out how blood got from an artery across to a vein, even though his experiments proved that it did. (Harvey had no microscope and so couldn't see blood vessels as small as capillaries. By 1670—three years after Harvey's death—Italian Marcello Malpighi had discovered capillaries with a microscope, thus completing Harvey's circulatory system.)

The second problem Harvey faced was his fear of mob reactions, Church condemnation when he said that the heart was just a muscular pump and not the house of the soul and consciousness, and the press (scribes). He was afraid he'd lose his job with the king. In 1628 Harvey found a small German publisher to publish a thin (72-page) summary of his work and discoveries. He published it in Latin (the language of science), hoping no one in England would read it.

News of Harvey's book raced across Europe and made him instantly notorious. He lost many patients, who were shocked by his claims. But Harvey's science was careful and accurate. By 1650 Harvey's book had become the accepted textbook on the circulatory system.

 **Fun Facts:** Americans donate over 16 million pints of blood each year. That's enough blood to fill a swimming pool 20 feet wide, 8 feet deep, and one-third of a mile long!

# More to Explore

Curtis, R. *Great Lives: Medicine*. New York: Charles Scribner's Sons Books for Young Readers, 1993.

Harvey, William. *On the Motion of the Heart and Blood in Animals*. Whitefish, MT: Kessinger Publishing, 2005.

Power, D'Arcy. *William Harvey: Master of Medicine*. Whitefish, MT: Kessinger, 2005.

Shackleford, Joel. *William Harvey and the Mechanics of the Heart*. New York: Oxford University Press, 2003.

Wyatt, Hervey. *William Harvey: 1578 to 1657*. Whitefish, MT: Kessinger, 2005.

Yount, Lisa. *William Harvey: Discoverer of How Blood Circulates*. Berkeley Heights, NJ: Enslow, 1998.

# Air Pressure

## Year of Discovery: 1640

---

**What Is It?** Air (the atmosphere) has weight and presses down on us.

**Who Discovered It?** Evangelista Torricelli

---

## Why Is This One of the 100 Greatest?

It is a simple, seemingly obvious notion: air has weight; the atmosphere presses down on us with a real force. However, humans don't feel that weight. You aren't aware of it because it has always been part of your world. The same was true for early scientists, who never thought to consider the weight of air and atmosphere.

Evangelista Torricelli's discovery began the serious study of weather and the atmosphere. It launched our understanding of the atmosphere. This discovery helped lay the foundation for Newton and others to develop an understanding of gravity.

This same revelation also led Torricelli to discover the concept of a vacuum and to invent the barometer—the most basic, fundamental instrument of weather study.

## How Was It Discovered?

On a clear October day in 1640, Galileo conducted a suction-pump experiment at a public well just off the market plaza in Florence, Italy. The famed Italian scientist lowered a long tube into the well's murky water. From the well, Galileo's tube draped up over a wooden cross-beam three meters above the well's wall, and then down to a hand-powered pump held by two assistants: Evangelista Torricelli, the 32-year-old the son of a wealthy merchant and an aspiring scientist, and Giovanni Baliani, another Italian physicist.

Torricelli and Baliani pumped the pump's wooden handlebar, slowly sucking air out of Galileo's tube, pulling water higher into the tube. They pumped until the tube flattened like a run-over drinking straw. But no matter how hard they worked, water would not rise more than 9.7 meters above the well's water level. It was the same in every test.

Galileo proposed that—somehow—the weight of the water column made it collapse back to that height.

In 1643, Torricelli returned to the suction pump mystery. If Galileo was correct, a heavier liquid should reach the same critical weight and collapse at a lower height. Liquid mercury weighted 13.5 times as much as water. Thus, a column of mercury should never rise any higher than 1/13.5 the height of a water column, or about 30 inches.

Torricelli filled a six-foot glass tube with liquid mercury and shoved a cork into the open end. Then he inverted the tube and submerged the corked end in a tub of liquid mercury before he pulled out the stopper. As he expected, mercury flowed out of the tube and into the tub. But not *all* of the mercury ran out.

Torricelli measured the height of the remaining mercury column—30 inches, as expected. Still, Torricelli suspected that the mystery's true answer had something to do with the vacuum he had created above his column of mercury.

The next day, with wind and a cold rain lashing at the windows, Torricelli repeated his experiment, planning to study the vacuum above the mercury. However, on this day the mercury column only rose to a height of 29 inches.

Torricelli was perplexed. He had expected the mercury to rise to the same height as yesterday. What was different? Rain beat on the windows as Torricelli pondered this new wrinkle.

What was different was the atmosphere, the weather. Torricelli's mind latched onto a revolutionary new idea. Air, itself, had weight. The real answer to the suction pump mystery lay not in the weight of the liquid, nor in the vacuum above it, but in the weight of the atmosphere pushing down around it.

Torricelli realized that the weight of the air in the atmosphere pushed down on the mercury in the tub. That pressure forced mercury up into the tube. The weight of the mercury in the *tube* had to be exactly equal to the weight of the atmosphere pushing down on the mercury in the *tub*.

When the weight of the atmosphere changed, it would push down either a little bit more or a little bit less on the mercury in the tub and drive the column of mercury in the tube either a little higher or a little lower. Changing weather must change the weight of the atmosphere.

Torricelli had discovered atmospheric pressure and a way to measure and study it.

 **Fun Facts:** Home barometers rarely drop more than 0.5 inch of mercury as the weather changes from fair to stormy. The greatest pressure drop ever recorded was 2.963 inches of mercury, measured inside a South Dakota tornado in June 2003.

# More to Explore

Asimov, Isaac. *Asimov's Chronology of Science and Discovery.* New York: Harper & Row, 1989.

Clark, Donald. *Encyclopedia of Great Inventors and Discoveries.* London: Marshall Cavendish Books, 1991.

Haven, Kendall. *Marvels of Science.* Englewood, CO: Libraries Unlimited, 1994.

Macus, Rebecca. *Galileo and Experimental Science.* New York: Franklin Watts, 1991.

Middleton, W. E. *The History of the Barometer.* New Brunswick, NJ: Johns Hopkins University Press, 2003.

# Boyle's Law

## Year of Discovery: 1650

> **What Is It?** The volume of a gas is inversely proportional to the force squeezing it.
>
> **Who Discovered It?** Robert Boyle

## Why Is This One of the 100 Greatest?

The concept Robert Boyle discovered (now called Boyle's Law) laid the foundation for all quantitative study and chemical analysis of gasses. It was the first quantitative formula to describe the behavior of gasses. Boyle's Law is so basic to understanding chemistry that it is taught to every student in beginning chemistry classes.

A genius experimenter, Boyle also proved that gasses were made of atoms—just like solids. But in a gas, the atoms are spread far apart and disconnected so that they can be squeezed tighter. Through these experiments Boyle helped convince the scientific world that atoms existed—an issue still debated 2,000 years after their existence was first proposed by Democritus in 440 B.C.

## How Was It Discovered?

Robert Boyle was the son of an earl and a member of the British Scientific Society. During a 1662 society meeting, Robert Hooke read a paper describing a French experiment on the "springiness of air." The characteristics of air were of great interest to scientists in the seventeenth century.

French scientists built a brass cylinder fitted tightly with a piston. Several men pushed down hard on the piston, compressing the air trapped below. Then they let go. The piston sprang back up, but not all the way back up. No matter how often the French tried this experiment, the piston never bounced all the way back up.

The French claimed this proved that air was not perfectly springy. Once compressed, it stayed slightly compressed.

Robert Boyle claimed that the French experiment proved nothing. Their piston, he said, was too tight to bounce all the way back up. Others argued that, if they made the piston looser, air would leak around the edges and ruin the experiment.

Boyle promised to create a perfect piston that was neither too tight nor too loose. He also claimed that his perfect piston would prove the French wrong.

Two weeks later Robert Boyle stood before the society with a large glass tube that he had shaped into a lopsided "U." One side of the "U" rose over three feet high and was skinny. The other side was short and fat. The short side was sealed at the top. The tall, skinny side was open.

Boyle poured liquid mercury into his tube until it covered the bottom of the "U" and rose just a little in both sides. A large pocket of air was trapped above this mercury in the short fat side. A piston, Boyle explained, was *any* devise that compressed air. Since his used mercury to compress air, there would be no friction to affect the results—as had been true in the French experiment.

Boyle recorded the glass piston's weight and etched a line in the glass where mercury met the trapped air pocket. Boyle trickled liquid mercury down the long neck of the tall side of his piston until he had filled the neck. Mercury now rose well over halfway up the short side. The trapped air had been squeezed to less than half of its original volume by the weight and force of mercury.

Boyle drew a second line on the short chamber to mark the new level of mercury inside—marking the compressed volume of trapped air.

He then drained mercury through a valve at the bottom of the "U" until the glass piston and mercury weighed exactly the same as they had at the beginning. The mercury level returned to its exact starting line. The trapped air had sprung back exactly to where it started. Air *was* perfectly springy. The French were wrong. Boyle was right.

Robert Boyle continued the experiments with his funny glass piston and noticed something quite remarkable. When he doubled the pressure (weight of mercury) on a trapped body of air, he halved its volume. When he tripled the pressure, the air's volume was reduced to one-third. The change in volume of air when compressed was always proportional to the change in the pressure squeezing that air. He created a simple mathematical equation to describe this proportionality. Today we call it "Boyle's Law." No other concept has been more useful in understanding and using gasses to serve the needs of humankind.

 **Fun Facts:** Oceanographer Sylvia Earle set the women's depth record for solo diving (1,000 meters or 3,281 feet). According to the concept Boyle discovered, pressure at that depth is over 100 times what it is at the surface!

# More to Explore

Boyle, Robert. *The Skeptical Chemist*. New York: Dover, 2003.

Hall, Marie. *Robert Boyle on Natural Philosophy*. Bloomington: Indiana University Press, 1995.

Hunter, Michael. *Robert Boyle Reconsidered*. New York: Cambridge University Press, 2003.

Irwin, Keith. *The Romance of Chemistry*. New York: Viking Press, 1996.

Tiner, John. *Robert Boyle: Trailblazer of Science*. Fenton, MI: Mott Media, 1999.

Wojcik, Jan. *Robert Boyle and the Limits of Reason*. New York: Cambridge University Press, 2003.

# The Existence of Cells

## Year of Discovery: 1665

> **What Is It?** The cell is the basic building block of all living organisms.
>
> **Who Discovered It?** Robert Hooke

## Why Is This One of the 100 Greatest?

The cell is the basic unit of anatomy. Countless millions of cells build living plants and animals. The functions of a body can be studied by studying individual cells. Just as the discovery of the molecule and atom allowed scientists to better understand chemical substances, Hooke's discovery of the cell has allowed biologists to better understand living organisms.

Hooke's work with a microscope opened the public's eyes to the microscopic world just as Galileo's work with the telescope opened their eyes to a vast and wondrous universe. Hooke's work and discoveries mark the moment when microscopy came of age as a scientific discipline.

## How Was It Discovered?

Robert Hooke was a most interesting fellow. Weak and sickly as a child, Hooke's parents never bothered to educate him because they didn't think he would survive. When Hooke was still alive at age 11, his father began a halfhearted, homeschool education. When Hooke was 12, he watched a portrait painter at work and decided, "I can do that." Some initial sketches showed that he was good at it.

The next year Hooke's father died, leaving Hooke a paltry inheritance of only £100. Hooke decided to use the money to apprentice himself to a painter, but quickly learned that the paint fumes gave him terrible headaches.

He used his money instead to enter Westminster school. On one of his first days there, Hooke listened to a man play the school organ and thought, "I can do that." Hooke soon proved that he was good at it and learned both to play and to serve as a choirmaster.

Unfortunately, the new English puritanical government banned such frivolity as church choirs and music. Hook's money had been wasted. Not knowing what else to do, Hooke hired himself out as a servant to rich science students at nearby Oxford University. Hooke was fascinated with science and again thought, "I can do that." As it turns out, he was exceptionally good at it. His servitude at Oxford (mostly to Robert Boyle) was the start of one of the most productive science careers in English history. Hooke soon developed an excellent reputation as a builder and as an experimenter.

Microscopes were invented in the late 1590s. By 1660 only a few had been built that were able to magnify objects 100 times normal size. As microscopes became more powerful, they maintained focus on only a tiny sliver of space and were increasingly more difficult to focus and to use.

Hooke was hired onto the staff of the Royal Society (an early English scientific organization) in 1660 and soon began a long series of microscopic studies. By 1662 he had helped design a 300-power microscope, which he used to examine the microscopic structure of common objects. Using this microscope and his artistic talent, Hooke created the first detailed studies of the microscopic world, rendering with lifelike accuracy the contours of a fly's compound eyes, the structure of a feather, and a butterfly's wing. He also drew and identified a series of microscopic bugs.

In 1664 Hooke turned his microscope onto a thin sheet of dried cork and found it to be composed of a tightly packed pattern of tiny rectangular holes. Actually, cork has large, open cells. That's why Hooke was able to see them at all. The cells of other plants and animal tissue he studied were all too small to be seen through his microscopes.

Hooke called these holes *cells* (the Latin word for small chambers that stand in a row—as in prison cells). These cells were empty because the cork was dead. Hooke correctly suspected that, while living, these had been filled with fluid.

The name "cell" stuck. More important, the concept galvanized biologists. The living world was constructed of countless tiny cells stacked together like bricks in a wall. The entire field of biology shifted toward a study of cell structure and cell function.

 **Fun Facts:** Cell biology is the only science in which multiplication means the same thing as division.

# More to Explore

Dyson, James. *A History of Great Inventions*. New York: Carroll & Graf Publishers, 2001.

Headstrom, Richard. *Adventures with a Microscope*. Mineola, NY: Dover Publications, 1997.

Inwood, Stephen. *The Forgotten Genius: The Biography of Robert Hooke*. San Francisco: MacAdam/Cage Publishing, 2005.

Jardine, Lisa. *The Curious Life of Robert Hooke*. New York: HarperPerennial, 2005.

Oxlade, Chris. *The World of Microscopes*. New York: Usborne Books, 1999.

Suplee, Curt. *Milestones of Science*. Washington, DC: National Geographic Society, 2000.

Yenne, Bill. *100 Inventions That Shaped World History*. New York: Bluewood Books, 1998.

# Universal Gravitation

## Year of Discovery: 1666

> **What Is It?** Gravity is the attractive force exerted by all objects on all other objects.
>
> **Who Discovered It?** Isaac Newton

## Why Is This One of the 100 Greatest?

By the early seventeenth century, many forces had been identified: friction, gravity, air resistance, electrical, forces people exerted, etc. Newton's mathematical concept of gravity was the first step in joining these seemingly different forces into a single, unified concept. An apple fell; people had weight; the moon orbited Earth—all for the same reason. Newton's law of gravity was a giant, simplifying concept.

Newton's concept of, and equations for, gravity stand as one of the most used concepts in all science. Most of our physics has been built upon Newton's concept of universal gravitation and his idea that gravity is a fundamental property of all matter.

## How Was It Discovered?

In 1666, Isaac Newton was a 23-year-old junior fellow at Trinity College in Cambridge. With his fair complexion and long blond hair, many thought he still looked more like a boy. His small, thin stature and shy, sober ways reinforced that impression. His intense eyes and seemingly permanent scowl pushed people away.

In London, the bubonic plague ravaged a terrified population. Universities were closed, and eager academics like Isaac Newton had to bide their time in safe country estates waiting for the plague to loosen its death grip on the city. It was a frightening time.

In his isolation, Newton was obsessed with a question: What held the moon circling the earth, and what held the earth in a captive orbit around the sun? Why didn't the moon fall down to the earth? Why didn't the earth fall down to the sun?

In later years Newton swore that this story actually happened. As he sat in the orchard at his sister's estate, he heard the familiar soft "thunk" of an apple falling to the grass-carpeted ground, and turned in time to see a second apple fall from an overhanging branch and bounce once before settling gently into the spring grass. It was certainly not the first apple Isaac Newton had ever seen fall to the ground, nor was there anything at all unusual about its short fall. However, while it offered no answers to the perplexed young scientist, the falling apple did present Isaac with an important new question, "The apple falls to Earth while the moon does not. What's the difference between the apple and the moon?"

Next morning, under a clearing sky, Newton saw his young nephew playing with a ball. The ball was tied to a string the boy held tight in his fist. He swung the ball, slowly at first, and then faster and faster until it stretched straight out.

With a start Newton realized that the ball was exactly like the moon. Two forces acted on the ball—its motion (driving it outward) and the pull of a string (holding it in). *Two* forces acted on the moon. Its motion and the pull of gravity—the same pull (force) that made the apple fall.

For the first time, Newton considered the possibility that gravity was a universal attractive force instead of a force that applied only to planets and stars. His deep belief in alchemy and its concept of the attraction of matter led him to postulate that gravitational attraction force did not just apply to heavenly objects, but to *all* objects with any mass. Gravity pulled apples to earth, made rain fall, and held planets in their orbits around the sun.

Newton's discovery of the concept of universal gravitation was a major blow to the prevalent belief that the laws of nature on Earth were different from those that ruled the heavens. Newton showed that the machinery that ruled the universe and nature is simple.

Newton developed universal gravitation as a property of all matter, not just of planets and stars. Universal gravitation and its mathematical expression lie at the foundation of all modern physics as one of the most important principles in all science.

 **Fun Facts:** The Flower of Kent is a large green variety of apple. According to the story, this is the apple Isaac Newton saw falling to ground from its tree, inspiring his discovery of universal gravitation.

# More to Explore

Christianson, Gale. *Isaac Newton and the Scientific Revolution.* New York: Oxford University Press, 1996.

Gale, Christeanson. *In the Presence of the Creator: Isaac Newton and His Times.* New York: Collier Macmillan, 1994.

Gleick, James. *Isaac Newton.* New York: Vintage , 2004

Koestler, Arthur. *The Sleepwalkers: A History of Man's Changing Vision of the Universe.* London: Hutchinson & Co., 1999.

Maury, Jean. *Newton: The Father of Modern Astronomy.* New York: Harry Abrams, 1996.

Peteson, Ivars. *Newton's Clock.* New York: W. H. Freeman, 1995.

White, Michael. *Isaac Newton: The Last Sorcerer.* Jackson, TN: Perseus Books, 1999.

# Fossils

## Year of Discovery: 1669

---

**What Is It?** Fossils are the remains of past living organisms.

**Who Discovered It?** Nicholas Steno

---

## Why Is This One of the 100 Greatest?

The only way we can learn about the ancient past is to examine fossil remains of now extinct plants and animals and try to re-create that long-gone life and environment. Scientists can only do this if they correctly interpret the fossil remains that are dug from ancient rock layers.

That process began with Nicholas Steno. He provided the first true definition of the word "fossil" and the first understanding of the origin and nature of fossils. Steno's work represents the beginning of our modern process of dating and studying fossils and the development of modern geology.

## How Was It Discovered?

For 2,000 years, *anything* dug from the earth was called a fossil. By the middle ages, *fossil* had come to be used for only those things made of stone that were dug from the earth and that looked remarkably like living creatures. Many thought these fossils were God's practice attempts to create living things. Some claimed they were the Devil's attempts to imitate God. Some believed they were the remains of drowned animals from Noah's flood. No one thought them to be of scientific value.

Nicholas Steno was born Niels Stensen in 1638 in Copenhagen, Denmark. He changed his name to its Latinized form in 1660 when he moved first to Paris and then to Italy to study medicine. Steno was a student of Galileo's experimental and mathematical approach to science and focused his studies on human muscular systems and on using math and geometry to show how muscles contracted and moved bones and the skeleton. Steno gained considerable fame in Italy for these anatomical studies.

In October 1666, two fishermen caught what was described as "a huge shark" near the town of Livorno, Italy. Because of its enormous size, Duke Ferdinand ordered that its head to be sent to Steno for study. Steno dutifully dissected the head, focusing on the musculature of the shark's deadly jaw.

However, when he examined the shark's teeth under a microscope, Steno was struck by their resemblance to certain stone fossils called *glossopetrae*, or "tongue stones," that were found in rock layers throughout the coastal hills. *Glossopetrae* had been found and known since the early Roman Empire. The famed Roman author Pliny the Elder thought they were part of the moon that fell from the sky. As Steno compared his monstrous shark teeth with *glossopetrae* samples, he suspected that *glossopetrae* not only *resembled* sharks' teeth, they *were* sharks' teeth.

Italian scientists scoffed that *glossopetrae* couldn't be from a sea creature because they were often found miles from the sea. Steno argued that they must have been deposited in shallow water or mud when the ancient shark died and that these areas had somehow been lifted up to become dry land. Others countered that *glossopetrae* couldn't be teeth since sharks' teeth were not made of stone.

Steno expanded his study to include fossils that resembled bones and bone fragments. When he viewed these under the microscope he was convinced that they, too, had originally been bones, not stones. After months of study, Steno used the then new "corpuscular theory of matter" (a forerunner of atomic theory) to argue that time and chemical action could alter the composition of teeth and bones into stone.

Steno published his discovery and supporting evidence in 1669. In addition to proving that fossils were really the ancient bones of living creatures, Steno investigated how these bones came to lie in the middle of rock layers. Through this work he discovered the process of sedimentation and of creating sedimentary rock layers. For this discovery Steno is also credited with founding modern geology.

At the height of his scientific career, Steno was ordained a Catholic priest and completely abandoned science because he said that science was incompatible with the teachings of the Church. Luckily, his discoveries remained to advance and benefit science.

 **Fun Facts:** When we think of fossils, we think of giant dinosaurs. But, the world's largest rodent fossil remains were discovered in northern South America in 2003. The fossil remains of this giant rodent weighed 1,500 pounds (700 kilograms) and dated back some eight million years.

# More to Explore

Archer, Michael. *Fossil Hunters: The Job of Paleontologists.* New York: Scholastic, 1999.

Lutz, Frank. *Nicholas Steno.* New York: Dover, 1995.

Mayor, Adrienne. *The First Fossil Hunters.* Princeton, NJ: Princeton University Press, 2001.

Sternberg, Charles. *The Life of a Fossil Hunter.* Bloomington: Indiana University Press, 1999.

# Distance to the Sun

## Year of Discovery: 1672

**What Is It?** The first accurate calculation of the distance from the earth to the sun, of the size of the solar system, and even of the size of the universe.

**Who Discovered It?** Giovanni Cassini

## Why Is This One of the 100 Greatest?

Our understanding of the universe depends on two foundations—our ability to measure the distances to faraway stars, and our ability to measure the chemical composition of stars. The discovery that allowed scientists to determine the composition of stars is described in the 1859 entry on spectrographs. The distance to the sun has always been regarded as the most important and fundamental of all galactic measurements. Cassini's 1672 measurement, however, was the first to accurately estimate that distance.

Cassini's discovery also provided the first shocking hint of the truly immense size of the universe and of how small and insignificant Earth is. Before Cassini, most scientists believed that stars were only a few *million* miles away. After Cassini, scientists realized that even the closest stars were billions (if not trillions) of miles away!

## How Was It Discovered?

Born in 1625, Giovanni Cassini was raised and educated in Italy. As a young man he was fascinated by astrology, not astronomy, and gained widespread fame for his astrological knowledge. Hundreds sought his astrological advice even though he wrote papers in which he proved that there was no truth to astrological predictions.

In 1668, after conducting a series of astronomical studies in Italy that were widely praised, Cassini was offered a position as the director of the Paris Observatory. He soon decided to become a French citizen and changed his name to Jean Dominique Cassini.

With an improved, high-powered telescope that he carefully shipped from Italy, Cassini continued a string of astronomical discoveries that made him one of the world's most famous scientists. These discoveries included the rotational periods of Mars and Saturn, and the major gaps in the rings of Saturn—still called the Cassini gaps.

Cassini was also the first to suspect that light traveled at a finite speed. Cassini refused to publish his evidence, and later even spent many years trying to disprove his own theory. He was a deeply religious man and believed that light was of God. Light therefore had to be perfect and infinite, and not limited by a finite speed of travel. Still, all of his astronomical work supported his discovery that light traveled at a fixed and finite speed.

Because of his deep faith in the Catholic Church, Cassini also believed in an Earth-centered universe. By 1672, however, he had become at least partially convinced by the early writing of Kepler and by Copernicus's careful arguments to consider the possibility that the sun lay at the center.

This notion made Cassini decide to try to calculate the distance from the earth to the sun. However, it was difficult and dangerous to make direct measurements of the sun (one could go blind). Luckily, Kepler's equations allowed Cassini to *calculate* the distance from the earth to the sun if he could *measure* the distance from the earth to any planet.

Mars was close to Earth and well-known to Cassini. So he decided to use his improved telescopes to measure the distance to Mars. Of course he couldn't *actually* measure that distance. But if he measured the angle to a spot on Mars at the same time from two different points on Earth, then he could use these angles and the geometry of triangles to calculate the distance to Mars.

To make the calculation work, he would need to make that baseline distance between his two points on Earth both large and precisely known. He sent French astronomer Jean Richer to Cayenne in French Guiana off the north cost of South America. Cassini stayed in Paris.

On the same August night in 1672, at exactly the same moment, both men measured the angle to Mars and placed it exactly against the background of distant stars. When Richer returned to Paris with his readings, Cassini was able to calculate the distance to Mars. He then used Kepler's equations to discover that the distance to the sun had to be 87 million miles (149.6 million km). Modern science has found that Cassini's calculation was only 7 percent off the true distance (just over 93 million miles).

Cassini went on to calculate the distances to other planets and found that Saturn lay a staggering 1,600,000,000 (1.6 billion) miles away! Cassini's discoveries of distance meant that the universe was millions of times bigger than anyone had dreamed.

 **Fun Facts:** The sun's diameter is 1.4 million km (875,000 miles). It is approximately 109 times wider than the earth.

# More to Explore

Brush, Stephen. *The History of Modern Astronomy*. New York: Garland, 1997.

Core, Thomas. *The Distance from the Sun to the Earth*. New York: Dover, 2002.

Hinks, Arthur. *New Measurements of the Distance to the Sun*. London: Taylor and Francis, 1995.

Sellers, David. *The Transit of Venus: The Quest to Find the True Distance to the Sun*. New York: Magavelda Press, 2001.

# Bacteria

## Year of Discovery: 1680

> **What Is It?** Microscopic organisms exist that cannot be seen by the human eye.
>
> **Who Discovered It?** Anton van Leeuwenhoek

## Why Is This One of the 100 Greatest?

Just as Galileo used his telescope to open the human horizon to the planets and stars of space, so van Leeuwenhoek used his microscope to open human awareness to the microscopic world that was invisibly small and that no one had even dreamed existed. He discovered protozoa, bacteria, blood cells, sperm, and capillaries. His work founded the science of microbiology and opened tissue studies and plant studies to the microscopic world. He completed human understanding of the circulatory system.

## How Was It Discovered?

Anton van Leeuwenhoek was born in 1632 in Delft, Holland. With no advanced schooling, he was apprenticed as a cloth merchant and assumed that buying and selling cloth would be his career.

But van Leeuwenhoek was curious about the world and interested in mathematics. Completely self-taught, he learned enough math to moonlight as a surveyor and read what he could about the natural world around him. He never learned any language other than Dutch, so he was never able to read any of the scientific papers and research (all written in Latin or French).

Microscopes existed in Holland by 1620. Christian Huygens and Robert Hooke were the first two scientists to make scientific use of microscopes. Both designed and built two-lens microscopes (two ground glass lenses inside a thin metal barrel).

In 1657 van Leeuwenhoek looked through his first microscope and was fascinated. He tried a two-lens microscope, but was disappointed by its distortion and low resolution. When he built his first microscope, he used a highly curved single lens to gain greater magnification.

By 1673 van Leeuwenhoek had built a 270-power microscope that was able to see objects only one-one-millionth of a meter in length. Van Leeuwenhoek remained very secretive about his work and never allowed others to see his microscopes or setup.

29

Van Leeuwenhoek started his microscopic studies with objects he could mount on the point of a pin—a bee's mouth parts, fleas, human hairs, etc. He described and drew what he saw in precise detail. By 1674 he had developed the ability to focus on a flat dish and turned his attention to liquids—water drops, blood cells, etc.

Those 1674 studies were where he made his great discovery. He discovered a host of microscopic protozoa (bacteria) in every water drop. He had discovered microscopic life, invisible to the human eye.

Van Leeuwenhoek expanded his search for these unseeably small creatures and found them everywhere: on human eyelashes, on fleas, in dust, and on skin. He drew and described these tiny creatures with excellent, precise drawings.

Each drawing often took days to complete. As an amateur, Van Leeuwenhoek had to work at his science in the evenings and early morning hours when not at work. Embarrassed by his lack of language skills and by his poor spelling (even in Dutch), van Leeuwenhoek felt hesitant to publish any articles about his wondrous findings.

Beginning in 1676, he agreed to send letters and drawings to the Royal Society of London. They had them translated into English. That extensive collection of letters (written and collected over many decades) formed the first and best map of the microscopic world. What van Leeuwenhoek observed shattered many scientific beliefs of the day and put him decades—if not centuries—ahead of other researchers.

He was the first to claim that bacteria cause infection and disease. (No one else believed it until Pasteur proved it in 1856.) Van Leeuwenhoek saw that vinegar killed bacteria and said that it would clean wounds. Again, it was two centuries before his belief became standard medical practice.

It was also 200 years before anyone built a better microscope. But with his marvelous microscope, van Leeuwenhoek discovered the critically important microscopic world.

 **Fun Facts:** In 1999 scientists discovered the largest bacterium ever. The organism can grow to as large as .75 mm across—about the size of the period at the end of this sentence. The newfound bacterium is 100 times larger than the previous record holder. For comparison, if the newly discovered bacterium was the size of a blue whale, the average bacterium would be the size of a newborn mouse.

# More to Explore

Dobell, Clifford. *Anthony van Leeuwenhoek and His "Little Animals."* New York: Dover, 1990.

Ralston, Alma. *The Cleere Observer: A Biography of Antony van Leeuwenhoek.* New York: Macmillan, 1996.

Ruestow, E. *The Microscope in the Dutch Republic: The Shaping of Discovery.* New York: Cambridge University Press, 1996.

Schierbeek, A. *Measuring the Invisible World: The Life and Works of Anthony van Leeuwenhoek.* London: Abelard-Schuman, 1999.

Yount, Lisa. *Antony van Leeuwenhoek: First to See Microscopic Life.* Beecher, IL: Sagebrush, 2001.

# Laws of Motion

## Year of Discovery: 1687

> **What Is It?** The fundamental relationships of matter, force, and motion upon which are built all physical science and engineering.
>
> **Who Discovered It?** Isaac Newton

## Why Is This One of the 100 Greatest?

Newton's three laws of motion form the very the foundation of physics and engineering. They are the underlying theorems that our physical sciences are built upon, just as Euclid's basic theorems form the foundation of our modern geometry. For the creation of these laws, combined with his discovery of gravity and his creation of calculus, Newton is considered the preeminent scientific intellect of the last millennium.

## How Was It Discovered?

Ever since Johannes Kepler's 1609 discovery that planets travel in elliptical (not circular) orbits around the sun, scientists had been frantically trying to mathematically explain these orbits. Robert Hooke and John Halley both tried. But neither could make the mathematics work.

Born in 1642 in Lincolnshire, England, 60 miles from Cambridge, Isaac Newton was a difficult child. His father died three months before Isaac's birth. Isaac never liked his stepfather and was left to be raised by his grandparents. But Newton felt no affection toward anyone—not his mother, not his grandparents, nor even his half-brother and sister. He often threatened to hit them and to burn down the house. He was a discipline problem in school.

Only one man, William Ayscough, recognized Isaac's brilliance and potential and arranged for Newton to study at Trinity College (part of Cambridge University). Being poor and unable to pay the large tuition, Newton worked as a servant to other students to pay for room and board. Newton was always solitary and secretive. Others said he was surly and argumentative.

In 1665 Cambridge closed when the plague struck London. Newton retired to his sister's country estate. There he felt frustrated by the isolation and by a lack of mathematical tools to describe the changing forces and motions he wanted to understand. He was determined to master the forces that made things move (or not move).

Newton studied writings by Galileo and Aristotle as well as the more recent works by Kepler and Halley. He gathered the scattered and often contradictory observations and theories developed since the time of the early Greeks. He studied and refined them, searching for common truths and for errors. Newton was amazingly good at sifting through this mountain of ideas for the few that held truth.

Newton was not much of an experimenter. He thought about problems, conducting mind experiments as did Einstein. Newton thought about things intently for a long time until he formed the answers he needed. In his own words, he "kept the subject constantly before him and waited until the first dawnings opened little by little into full light."

Solving the mystery of the forces that create motion quickly became an obsession with Newton. He focused his attention on Galileo's laws of falling bodies and on Kepler's laws about the motion of planets. He often went without sleep or food, to the edge of physical breakdown.

Newton developed his three laws of motion in early 1666. They were the essential building blocks for his creation of calculus and his discovery of gravity. However, Newton did not publish these laws until Halley coaxed him to write *Principia* 20 years later.

In 1684 Jean Picard produced the first accurate figures for the size and mass of Earth. This finally gave Newton the numbers he needed to prove that his laws of motion combined with his equation for gravity correctly predicted the actual orbits of the planets. Even after completing this mathematical proof, Newton only published *Principia* in 1687 because Halley begged and cajoled him to—mostly because Robert Hooke claimed (falsely) to have developed universal laws of motion himself. *Principia* became one of the most revered and most used publications in the history of science.

 **Fun Facts:** For every motion, there is a force. Gary Hardwick of Carlsbad, California, created enough force to set a skateboard speed record (standing position) of 100.66 km/h (62.55 mph) at Fountain Hills, Arizona, on September 26, 1998.

# More to Explore

Boorstin, Daniel. *The Discoverers: A History of Man's Search to Know His World and Himself.* New York: Random House, 1997.

Christianson, Gale. *Isaac Newton and the Scientific Revolution.* New York: Oxford University Press, 1996.

Gale, Christeanson. *In the Presence of the Creator: Isaac Newton and His Times.* New York: Collier Macmillan, 1994.

Gleick, James. *Isaac Newton.* New York: Vintage, 2004.

Maury, Jean. *Newton: The Father of Modern Astronomy.* New York: Harry Abrams, 1996.

Peteson, Ivars. *Newton's Clock.* New York: W. H. Freeman, 1995.

Westfall, Richard. *The Life of Isaac Newton.* New York: Cambridge University Press, 1997.

White, Michael. *Isaac Newton: The Last Sorcerer.* Jackson, TN: Perseus Books, 1999.

# Order in Nature

> **What Is It?** All living plants and animals can be grouped and organized into a simple hierarchy.
>
> **Who Discovered It?** Carl Linnaeus

## Why Is This One of the 100 Greatest?

Until the eighteenth century, nature was viewed as a wild profusion of life. Carl Linnaeus discovered order and organization in that seeming randomness. His system for naming, grouping, and conceptually organizing plants and animals provided insights into botany, biology, ecosystems, and biological structure that scientists still rely on almost 300 years later.

For his discovery, Carl Linnaeus is called the father of modern taxonomy. ("Taxonomy" is Greek for "naming in order.") The proof of his influence over, and importance to, modern science can be seen in two ways. First, all of science still uses his system and still uses Latin names for existing and new species as Linnaeus did—the last vestige of that ancient language once the universal language of science. Every newly discovered species is immediately classified and named according to Linnaeus's system. Second, every biologist has used Linnaeus's system to organize, understand, identify, and refer to every plant and animal species.

Linnaeus was the first to identify humans as *homo sapiens* and place humans in the greater flow of life as part of the primate order. His classification system was the origin of the concept of a "tree of life" since every living thing belonged to a species, genus, family, class, order, and phyla and to the plant or animal kingdom—analogous to the twigs, branches, and trunk of a tree.

## How Was It Discovered?

Carl Linnaeus hated disorder. He claimed he could never understand anything that was not systematically ordered. Born in Sweden in 1707, he was supposed to become a priest like his father. But Carl showed little aptitude for, and no interest in, the priesthood and was finally allowed to switch to medicine.

He entered the University of Lund's School of Medicine in 1727 but spent more time in the university's small botanical garden than in class. Linnaeus had been fascinated by plants and flowers since he was a small child. In 1728 Linnaeus transferred to the University of Uppsala (partly because they had bigger botanical gardens). There he read a paper by French botanist Sebastian Vaillant that claimed (it was considered shockingly revolution-

33

ary at the time) that plants reproduced sexually and had male and female parts that corresponded to the sexual organs of animals.

The idea appealed to Linnaeus. As an obsessive cataloger, he had always detested the notion that each of the thousands of plants he saw in botanical gardens were individual and separate species. Linnaeus began to wonder if he could use the differences in plants' reproductive parts as a means of classifying and ordering the vast array and profusion of plants. His dream of bringing order to the chaos of nature was born.

Glib, cordial, and with a natural talent for ingratiating himself with rich and powerful supporters, Linnaeus was able to arrange financial support for a series of expeditions across different areas of Sweden to study and catalog plant species. He spent months tramping across the countryside listing, describing, and studying every plant he found. His expeditions were always the picture of perfect order. He started each day's hike precisely at 7:00 in the morning. Linnaeus stopped for a meal break at 2:00 P.M. He paused for a rest and lecture break at 4:00 P.M.

During these expeditions, Linnaeus focused his studies on the reproductive systems of each plant he found. Soon he discovered common characteristics of male and female plant parts in many species that he could group into a single category. He lumped these categories together into larger groups that were, again, combined with other groups into yet larger classifications. He found that plants fit neatly into groups based on a few key traits and that order did exist in the natural world.

By 1735 he had described more than 4,000 species of plants and published his classification system in a book, *Systema Naturae*. This system described the eight levels Linnaeus finally built into his system: species, genus, family, order, Class, Subphylum, Phylum, and Kingdom. This system—based solely on the sexual elements of plants and (later) animals—was controversial with the public. But botanists found it easy to use and appealing.

Linnaeus's system spread quickly across Europe and was often drawn as a tree, with giant branches being classes, down to the tiniest twigs of species. From these drawings came the concept of a "Tree of Life."

Linnaeus spent the next 30 years touring Europe adding new plants to his system. In 1740 he added animal species into his system. By 1758 he had described and classified 4,400 animal species and more than 7,700 plant species.

In 1758, with the tenth edition of his book, he introduced the binomial (two-name) system of naming each plant and animal by species and genus. With that addition, Linnaeus's system was complete. He had discovered both that order existed in the natural world and a system for describing that order—a system still very much alive and in use today.

 **Fun Facts:** The world's most massive living tree is General Sherman, the giant sequoia (Sequoiadendron giganteum) growing in the Sequoia National Park in California. It stands 83.82m (274.9 ft.) tall and has a diameter of 11.1 m (36 ft., 5 in.). This one tree is estimated to contain enough wood to make five billion matches—one for almost every person on Earth.

# More to Explore

Anderson, Margaret. *Carl Linnaeus: Father of Classification.* Berkeley Heights, NJ: Enslow, 2001.

Dickenson, Alice. *Carl Linnaeus.* New York: Franklin Watts, 1995.

Fara, Patricia. *Sex, Botany, and Empire: The Story of Carl Linnaeus and Joseph Banks.* New York: Columbia University Press, 2004.

Hagberg, Knut. *Carl Linnaeus.* New York: Dutton, 1992.

Stoutenburg, Adrien. *Beloved Botanist: The Story of Carl Linnaeus.* New York: Scribner, 1994.

Tore, Frangsmyr, ed. *Linnaeus: The Man and His Work.* Berkeley: University of California Press, 2001.

# Galaxies

**What Is It?** Our sun is not the center of the universe but is rather part of a giant, disc-shaped cluster of stars that floats through space.

**Who Discovered It?** Thomas Wright and William Herschel

## Why Is This One of the 100 Greatest?

The discovery that stars are clumped into galaxies represents the first advance in efforts to describe the actual shape of the universe and the distribution of stars in it. Wright's theory of galaxies was the first astronomical work to place our sun not in the center of the universe, but in a tightly packed cluster of stars that Wright called a galaxy. This discovery led science a giant step forward in its efforts to understand the vast universe of which our sun and Earth represent only tiny and very ordinary specks. Twenty-five years later, Herschel conducted careful observational studies that proved Wright was right.

## How Was It Discovered?

For thousands of years scientist believed that the universe consisted of a vast spherical shell of stars, with Earth at its center. Nothing existed in the immense void between Earth and that shell of stars except the few planets and the sun.

By the mid-1600s, most scientists acknowledged that the sun, not the earth, sat at the center of the spherical universe. Some prominent scientists (Christian Huygens, for example) believed that stars were really holes in the black sphere of space where light from a luminous region of perpetual day beyond shined through.

Two men's discoveries combined to establish the existence of dense clusters of stars called galaxies. Born in 1711, Englishman Thomas Wright taught mathematics and navigation but was a passionate amateur astronomer. As had many astronomers before him, Wright observed that the stars were not evenly spread across the sky. A seeming cloud of faint stars was densely packed along the band called the Milky Way.

This bothered Wright. He believed that God had created a universe of perfect order. That should mean that stars were neatly and evenly—perfectly—spaced across the heavens. Wright could not accept that the heavens were not perfect and so began to play with schemes for the placement of stars to make them really be uniform in their placement even though they *appeared* not to be.

Wright considered that the stars might be spread along the surfaces of a field of giant bubbles. If we were packed along one of those rings of stars, looking *along* the ring would cause us to see more stars than if we looked straight out from it. He then considered the rings of Saturn and proposed that the stars might be packed into wide rings or a thin disk. If we were *in* that disc, it would account for the uneven distribution of stars we saw—even if the stars were really evenly spaced across that disk.

In 1750 Wright published a book, *An Original Theory on New Hypothesis of the Universe*, in which he proposed this theory. He was the first to use the word *galaxy* to describe a giant cluster of stars. Five years later, famed astronomer and mathematician Immanuel Kant proposed a similar arrangement of the stars into a giant disk-shaped cluster.

English astronomer William Hershel (born in 1738) read with interest Wright's theory. In 1785 Herschel decided to use statistical methods to count the stars. He surely couldn't count them all. So he randomly picked 683 small regions of the sky and set about counting the stars in each region using a 48-inch telescope—considered a giant scope at the time. Herschel quickly realized that the number of stars per unit area of sky rose steadily as he approached the Milky Way and spiked in regions in the Milky Way. (The number of stars per unit area of sky reached a minimum in directions at right angles to the Milky Way.)

This made Herschel think of Wright's and Kant's theories. Hershel concluded that his counting results could only be explained if most of the stars were compacted into a lens-shaped mass and that the sun was buried in this lens. Herschel was the first to add statistical measurement to Wright's discovery of the existence and shape of galaxies.

 **Fun Facts:** The central galaxy of the Abell 2029 galaxy cluster, 1,070 million light years distant in Virgo, has a diameter of 5,600,000 light years, 80 times the diameter of our own Milky Way galaxy.

# More to Explore

Greenstein, George. *Portraits of Discovery: Profiles in Scientific Genius.* New York: John Wiley & Sons, 1997.

Hubbard, Elbert. *William Hershel.* Whitefish, MT: Kessinger, 2001.

Roan, Carl. *The Discovery of the Galaxies.* San Francisco: Jackdaw Publications, 2000.

Taschek, Karen. *Death Stars, Weird Galaxies, and a Quasar-Spangled Universe.* Albuquerque: University of New Mexico Press, 2006.

Whitney, Charles Allen. *Discovery of Our Galaxy.* Iowa City: Iowa State Press, 1997.

# The Nature of Electricity

Year of Discovery: 1752

**What Is It?** All forms of electricity are the same.

**Who Discovered It?** Benjamin Franklin

## Why Is This One of the 100 Greatest?

Electricity is one of our greatest energy resources and one of the few natural energy sources. Franklin's electricity experiments were the first scientific ventures into the nature and use of electricity and uncovered its true nature. They set the stage for much of the scientific and engineering development in the nineteenth century and for the explosion of electrical development—batteries, motors, generators, lights, etc.

## How Was It Discovered?

All that was known about electricity in the mid-eighteenth century was that there were two kinds of it: playful static and deadly lightning. Benjamin Franklin was the first scientist to begin serious electrical experiments (in 1746). He was also the first to suspect that static and lightning were two forms of the same thing.

Franklin had been experimenting with Leyden jars—large glass jars, partially filled with water and wrapped with tin foil both inside and out. A rod extended through an insulating cork out the top of the jar to a metal knob. Once a Leyden jar was charged with a hand crank, anyone who grabbed the knob got a resounding shock.

Franklin found ways to more than double the amount of electricity his Leyden jars carried, and he invented a way to connect them in series so that they could, collectively, carry an almost deadly punch.

During a 1752 demonstration for friends, Franklin accidentally touched a Leyden jar's knob. With a sharp crack, a sizzling blue arc leapt from jar to Franklin's hand. He shot back half a dozen feet and crashed to the floor. Franklin realized that that jolt looked exactly like a mini-lightning bolt.

He decided to prove that static and lightning were the same by designing a Leyden jar–like electric circuit to let electricity flow from clouds just as it did into a jar.

Franklin's "circuit" was made of a thin metal wire fixed to a kite (to gather electricity from the clouds) and tied to a twine kite string. Electricity would flow down the twine to a large iron key tied to the bottom. Franklin tied the other end of the key to a nonconducting silk ribbon that he would hold. Thus, electricity would be trapped in the key, just as it was in a Leyden jar.

When an afternoon storm brewed up dark and threatening a few weeks later, Franklin rushed to launch his kite. The wind howled and the clouds boiled. A cold rain pounded down about Franklin's upturned collar. The kite twisted and tore at the air like a rampaging bull.

Then it happened. No, a lightning bolt did not strike the kite, as has often been reported. And a good thing, too. A French scientist was killed a few months later by a lightning strike when he tried to repeat Franklin's experiment. No, what happened that stormy afternoon was that the twine began to glow a faint blue. The twine's fibers lifted and bristled straight out. Franklin could almost see electricity trickling down the twine as if electricity were liquid.

Franklin reached out a cautious hand closer and closer to the key. And pop! A spark leapt to his knuckle and shocked him—just like a Leyden jar.

Lightning and static *were* all the same, fluid electricity!

The practical outcome of this experiment was Franklin's invention of the lightning rod, credited with saving thousands of houses and lives over the next 100 years. More important, Franklin's work inspired experiments by Volta, Faraday, Oersted, and others in early part of the nineteenth century that further unraveled electricity's nature.

 **Fun Facts:** Popeye uses spinach to power his muscles. Now scientists are looking to spinach as a power source for supplying electricity. Chemical substances extracted from spinach are among the ingredients needed to make a solar cell that converts light into electricity.

# More to Explore

Brands, H. W. *Benjamin Franklin: The Original American.* New York: Barnes & Noble, 2004.

Fradin, Dennis. *Who Was Benjamin Franklin?* New York: Penguin Young Readers' Group, 2002.

Isaacson, Walter. *Benjamin Franklin: An American Life.* New York: Simon & Schuster, 2003.

McCormick, Ben. *Ben Franklin: America's Original Entrepreneur.* New York: McGraw-Hill, 2005.

Morgan, Edmund. *Benjamin Franklin.* New Haven, CT: Yale University Press, 2003.

Sandak, Cass. *Benjamin Franklin.* New York: Franklin Watts, , 1996.

Skousen, Mark, ed. *Completed Autobiography of Benjamin Franklin.* Washington, DC: Regnery Publishing, 2005.

Wright, Esmond. *Franklin of Philadelphia.* Cambridge, MA: Harvard University Press, 1996.

# Oceans Control Global Weather

## Year of Discovery: 1770

**What Is It?** By pumping massive amounts of heat through the oceans, vast ocean currents control weather and climate on land.

**Who Discovered It?** Benjamin Franklin

## Why Is This One of the 100 Greatest?

The Atlantic Ocean's Gulf Stream is the most important of our world's ocean currents. It is a major heat engine, carrying massive amounts of warm water north to warm Europe. It has directed the patterns of ocean exploration and commerce and may be a major determinant of the onset of ice ages. Finally, it is the key to understanding global circulation patterns and the interconnectedness of the world's oceans, weather, and climates.

American statesman, inventor, and scientist Benjamin Franklin conducted the first scientific investigation of the Gulf Stream and discovered its importance to Earth's weather and climate. His work launched scientific study of ocean currents, ocean temperature, the interaction of ocean current with winds, and the effect of ocean currents on climate. Franklin's discoveries mark the beginnings of modern oceanographic science.

## How Was It Discovered?

Benjamin Franklin set out to map the Gulf Stream in order to speed transatlantic shipping. He wound up discovering that ocean currents are a major controlling factor of global climate and weather.

Ocean surface currents were noted by early Norse sailors as soon as they sailed the open Atlantic. Columbus and Ponce de Leon described the Gulf Stream current along the coast of Florida and in the strait between Florida and Cuba. Others noted North Atlantic currents over the next hundred years. However, no one charted these currents, recorded them on maps, or connected the individual sightings into a grand, oceanwide system of massive currents.

In 1769 British officials in Boston wrote to London complaining that the British packets (small navy ships that brought passengers and mail to the colonies) took two weeks longer in their trans-Atlantic crossing than did American merchant ships. Benjamin Franklin, an American representative in London at the time, heard this report and refused to believe it.

**40**

Packet ships rode higher in the water, were faster ships, and were better crewed than heavy Rhode Island merchant ships.

Franklin mentioned the report to a Rhode Island merchant captain off-loading cargo in London. This captain said it was absolutely true and happened because Rhode Island whalers had taught American merchant captains about the Gulf Stream, a 3 mph current that spread eastward from New York and New England toward England. American captains knew to curve either north or south on westward trips to avoid fighting this powerful current.

When Franklin checked, the Gulf Stream didn't appear on any maps, nor did it appear in any of the British Navy shipping manuals. Franklin began interviewing merchant and whaling captains, recording on maps and charts their experience with the Gulf Stream current. Whalers, especially, knew the current well because whales tended to congregate along its edges.

By 1770 Franklin had prepared detailed maps and descriptions of this current. British Navy and merchant captains, however, didn't believe him and refused to review his information. By 1773 rising tensions between England and the colonies made Franklin withhold his new findings from the British.

Franklin began taking regular water temperature readings on every Atlantic Ocean crossing. By 1783 he had made eight crossings, carefully plotting the exact course his ship took each time and marking his temperature readings on the ship's map.

On his last voyage from France to America, Franklin talked the ship's captain into tracking the edge of the Gulf Stream current. This slowed the voyage as the ship zigzagged back and forth using the warm water temperature inside the Gulf Stream and the colder water temperature outside it to trace the current's boundary.

The captain also allowed Franklin to take both surface and subsurface (20 and 40 fathoms) temperature readings. Franklin was the first to consider the depth (and thus the volume) of an ocean current.

Franklin discovered that the Gulf Stream poured masses of warm water (heat) from the tropical Caribbean toward northern Europe to warm its climate. He began to study the interaction between wind and current and between ocean currents and weather. Through the brief papers he wrote describing the Gulf Stream data he had collected, Franklin brought science's attention and interest to ocean currents and their effect on global climate.

Franklin's description of the Gulf Stream was the most detailed available until German scientist Alexander von Humbolt published his 1814 book about the Gulf Stream based on his measurements from more than 20 crossings. These two sets of studies represent the beginnings of modern oceanographic study.

 **Fun Facts:** The Gulf Stream is bigger than the combined flow of the Mississippi, the Nile, the Congo, the Amazon, the Volga, the Yangtze, and virtually every other major river in the world.

# More to Explore

Brands, H. W. *Benjamin Franklin: The Original American.* New York: Barnes & Noble, 2004.

Fradin, Dennis. *Who Was Benjamin Franklin?* New York: Penguin Young Readers' Group, 2002.

Isaacson, Walter. *Benjamin Franklin: An American Life.* New York: Simon & Schuster, 2003.

McCormick, Ben. *Ben Franklin: America's Original Entrepreneur.* New York: McGraw-Hill, 2005.

Morgan, Edmund. *Benjamin Franklin.* New Haven, CT: Yale University Press, 2003.

Sandak, Cass. *Benjamin Franklin.* New York: Franklin Watts, 1996.

Skousen, Mark, ed. *Completed Autobiography of Benjamin Franklin.* Washington, DC: Regnery Publishing, 2005.

Wright, Esmond. *Franklin of Philadelphia.* Cambridge, MA: Harvard University Press, 1996.

# Oxygen

## Year of Discovery: 1774

> **What Is It?** The first gas separated and identified as a unique element.
>
> **Who Discovered It?** Joseph Priestley

## Why Is This One of the 100 Greatest?

Priestley's discovery of oxygen sparked a chemical revolution. He was the first person to isolate a single gaseous element in the mixture of gasses we call "air." Before Priestley's discovery, scientific study had focused on metals. By discovering that air wasn't a uniform thing, Priestley created a new interest in the study of gasses and air.

Because oxygen is a central element of combustion, Priestley's discovery also led to an understanding of what it means to burn something and to an understanding of the conversion of matter into energy during chemical reactions.

Finally, Priestley established a simple but elegant and effective process for conducting analysis of new gasses and gaseous elements. What did it look like? Would it burn (first a candle and then wood splinters)? Would it keep a mouse alive? Was it absorbed by water?

## How Was It Discovered?

Reverend Joseph Priestley was more fascinated by air than by his church duties. Air was one of the four traditional elements (with fire, water, and earth). But Priestley felt driven to find out what air was made of.

Other scientists wrote of creating new gasses that bubbled up during chemical reactions. Some had described these as "wild gasses" that built up enough pressure to explode glass jars or to triple the rate at which wood burned. But none had successfully isolated and studied these new gasses.

Priestley's imagination soared. He felt compelled to seek out and study these wild, untamed gasses.

In early 1774 Priestley decided the only way to isolate and study these new gasses was to trap them under water in an upside down (inverted), water-filled glass jar in which there was no air.

He decided to begin by burning solid *mercurius calcinatus* and studying the gas that reaction had been reported to create.

On August 1, 1774, Priestley used a powerful magnifying lens to focus sunlight on a bottle of powdered *mercurius calcinatus.* A cork stopper sealed this bottle with a glass tube leading from it to a washtub full of water, where water-filled glass jars stood inverted on a wire mesh stand. Priestley's glass tube ended just under the open mouth of one of these bottles so that whatever gas he produced would bubble up into, and be trapped in, that glass jar.

As his powdered mercury compound heated, clear bubbles began to drift up from the end of the glass tube. The jar began to fill. Priestley filled three bottles with the gas and was thus the first human to successfully trap this mysterious gas. But what was it?

Priestley carefully raised one bottle out of the water. He held a lit candle beneath its mouth. The dim glow around the candle's wick erupted into a brilliant ball of fire. As reported, this strange gas *did* force substances to burn fiercely.

Priestley placed a new jar, filled with ordinary air, upside down on the wire stand next to a second jar of his mystery gas. He placed a mouse in each jar, and waited. The mouse in ordinary air began to struggle for breath in 20 minutes. The mouse in his second jar of this strange gas breathed comfortably for over 40 minutes!

There seemed only one name for this amazing gas: "pure air." Priestley carefully raised a jar of "pure air" out of his tub. He jammed his own nose into its wide mouth. His heart began to beat faster. He closed his eyes, gathered his courage, and breathed in as deeply as he could.

Joseph felt nothing odd from this breath. He tried a second breath and felt happy and filled with energy. Priestley's breath felt particularly light and easy for some time afterward. It took another scientist, Antoine Lavoisier in Paris, to give Priestley's "pure air" the name we know it by today: "oxygen."

 **Fun Facts:** Without oxygen, biological death begins to occur within three minutes. Free-diving World Champion Pipin Ferreras holds the world record for holding his breath: 8 minutes, 58 seconds.

# More to Explore

Bowden, Mary, ed. *Joseph Priestley: Radical Thinker.* Philadelphia: Chemical Heritage Foundation, 2005.

Conley, Kate. *Joseph Priestley and the Discovery of Oxygen.* Hockessin, DE: Mitchell Lane, 2003.

Crowther, J. G. *Scientists of the Industrial Revolution: Joseph Black, James Watt, Joseph Priestley, and Henry Cavendish.* New York: Dufour Editions, 1996.

Gibbs, Frank. *Joseph Priestley.* New York: Doubleday, 1997.

Irwin, Keith. *The Romance of Chemistry.* New York: Viking Press, 1996.

Partington, James. *A Short Course in Chemistry.* New York: Dover, 1999.

Schofield, Robert. *The Enlightenment of Joseph Priestley.* University Park: Pennsylvania State University Press, 1997.

# Photosynthesis

## Year of Discovery: 1779

> **What Is It?** Plants use sunlight to convert carbon dioxide in the air into new plant matter.
>
> **Who Discovered It?** Jan Ingenhousz

## Why Is This One of the 100 Greatest?

Photosynthesis is the process that drives plant production all across Earth. It is also the process that produces most of the oxygen that exists in our atmosphere for us to breathe. Plants and the process of photosynthesis are key elements in the critical (for humans and other mammals) planetary oxygen cycle.

When Jan Ingenhousz discovered the process of photosynthesis, he vastly improved our basic understanding of how plants function on this planet and helped science gain a better understanding of two important atmospheric gasses: oxygen and carbon dioxide. Modern plant engineering and crop sciences owe their foundation to Jan Ingenhousz's discovery.

## How Was It Discovered?

Jan Ingenhousz was born in Breda in the Netherlands in 1730. He was educated as a physician and settled down to start his medical practice back home in Breda.

In 1774 Joseph Priestley discovered oxygen and experimented with this new, invisible gas. In one of these tests, Priestley inserted a lit candle into a jar of pure oxygen and let it burn until all oxygen had been consumed and the flame went out. Without allowing any new air to enter the jar, Priestley placed mint sprigs floating in a glass of water in the jar to see if the mint would die in this "bad" air. But the mint thrived. After two months, Priestley placed a mouse in the jar. It also lived—proving that the mint plant had restored oxygen to the jar's air. But this experiment didn't always work. Priestley admitted that it was a mystery and then moved on to other studies.

In 1777, Ingenhousz read about Priestley's experiments and was fascinated. He could focus on nothing else and decided to investigate and explain Priestley's mystery.

Over the next two years, Ingenhousz conducted 500 experiments trying to account for every variable and every possible contingency. He devised two ways to trap the gas that a plant produced. One was to enclose the plant in a sealed chamber. The other was to submerge the plant.

Ingenhousz used both systems, but found it easier to collect and study the gas collected underwater as tiny bubbles. Every time he collected the gas that a plant gave off, he tested it to see if it would support a flame (have oxygen) or if it would extinguish a flame (be carbon dioxide).

Ingenhousz was amazed at the beauty and symmetry of what he discovered. Humans inhaled oxygen and exhaled carbon dioxide. Plants did just the opposite—sort of. Plants in *sunlight* absorbed human waste carbon dioxide and produced fresh oxygen for us to breathe. Plants in deep shade or at night (in the dark), however, did just the opposite. They acted like humans, absorbing oxygen and producing carbon dioxide.

After hundreds of tests, Ingenhousz determined that plants produced far more oxygen than they absorbed. Plants immersed in water produced a steady stream of tiny oxygen bubbles when in direct sunlight. Bubble production stopped at night. Plants left for extended periods in the dark gave off a gas that extinguished a flame. When he placed the same plant in direct sunlight, it produced a gas that turned a glowing ember into a burning inferno. The plant again produced oxygen.

Ingenhousz showed that this gas production depended on sunlight. He continued his experiments and showed that plants did not produce new mass (leaf, stem, or twig) by absorbing matter from the ground (as others believed). The ground did not lose mass as a plant grew. Ingenhousz showed that new plant *growth* must come from sunlight. Plants captured carbon from carbon dioxide in the air and converted it into new plant matter in the presence of sunlight.

Ingenhousz had discovered the process of *photosynthesis*. He proved that plants created new mass "from the air" by fixing carbon with sunlight. In 1779 he published his results in *Experiments Upon Vegetables*. The name *photosynthesis* was created some years later and comes from the Greek words meaning "to be put together by light."

 **Fun Facts:** Some species of bamboo have been found to grow at up to 91 cm (3 ft.) per day. You can almost watch them grow!

# More to Explore

Allen, J. F., et al., eds. *Discoveries in Photosynthesis*. New York: Springer-Verlag, 2006.

Asimov, Isaac. *How Did We Find Out About Photosynthesis?* New York: Walker & Co., 1993.

Forti, G. *Photosynthesis Two Centuries After Its Discovery*. New York: Springer-Verlag, 1999.

Ingenhousz, Jan. *Jan Ingenhousz: Plant Physiologist*. London: Chronica Botanica, 1989.

# Conservation of Matter

## Year of Discovery: 1789

> **What Is It?** The total amount of matter (mass) always remains the same no matter what physical or chemical changes take place.
>
> **Who Discovered It?** Antoine Lavoisier

## Why Is This One of the 100 Greatest?

Lavoisier was the first chemist to believe in *measurement* during and after experiments. All chemists before had focused on *observation* and *description* of the reactions during an experiment. By carefully measuring the weight of each substance, Lavoisier discovered that matter is neither created nor destroyed during a chemical reaction. It may change from one form to another, but it can always be found, or accounted for. Scientists still use this principle every day and call it "conservation of matter."

Lavoisier's work also established the foundation and methods of modern chemistry. He did much work with gasses, gave oxygen its name (Joseph Priestley discovered oxygen but called it "pure air") , and discovered that oxygen makes up 20 percent of the atmosphere. Lavoisier is considered the father of modern chemistry.

## How Was It Discovered?

In the spring of 1781, Frenchman Antoine Lavoisier's wife, Marie, translated a paper by English scientist Robert Boyle into French. The paper described an experiment with tin during which Boyle had noted an unexplained weight change when the tin was heated. Boyle, like most scientists, was content to assume that the extra weight had been "created" during his chemical experiment.

Lavoisier scoffed at the notion of mysterious creation or loss of mass (weight) during reactions. He was convinced that chemists' traditional experimental approach was inadequate. During experiments chemists carefully *observed* and *described* changes in a substance. Lavoisier claimed it was far more important to record what could be measured. Weight was one property he could always measure.

Lavoisier decided to repeat Boyle's experiment, carefully measure weight, and discover the source of the added weight. Antoine carried a small sheet of tin to his delicate balancing scales and recorded its weight. Next he placed the tin in a heat-resistant glass flask and sealed its lid to contain the entire reaction within the flask.

He weighed the flask (and the tin inside) before heating it over a burner. A thick layer of calx (a light gray tarnish) formed on the tin as it heated—as Boyle had described in his paper.

Lavoisier turned off the burner, let the flask cool, and then reweighed it. The flask had not changed weight. He pried off the flask's lid. Air rushed in, as if into a partial vacuum. Antoine removed and weighed the calx-covered tin. It had gained two grams of weight (as had Boyle's).

Lavoisier deduced that the weight had to have come from the air inside the flask and that was why new air rushed into the flask when he opened it. The tin gained two grams as it mixed with air to form calx. When he opened the lid, two grams of new air rushed in to replace the air that had been absorbed into calx.

He repeated the experiment with a larger piece of tin. However, still only two grams of air were absorbed into calx. He ran the experiment again and measured the volume of air that was absorbed into calx—20 percent of the total air inside the flask.

He concluded that only 20 percent of air was capable of bonding with tin. He realized that this 20 percent of air must be the "pure air" Priestley had discovered in 1774, and Lavoisier named it "oxygen."

Through further experiments Lavoisier realized that he had proved something far more important. Boyle thought weight, or matter, was "created" during experiments. Lavoisier had proved that matter was neither created nor lost during a chemical reaction. It always came from someplace and went to someplace. Scientists could always find it if they measured carefully.

The all-important concept of conservation of matter had been discovered. However, Lavoisier didn't release this principle until he published his famed chemistry textbook in 1789.

 **Fun Facts:** The Furnace Constellation (Fornax) was created to honor the famous French chemist Antoine Lavoisier, who was guillotined during the French Revolution in 1794.

# More to Explore

Donovan, Arthur. *Antoine Lavoisier: Science Administration and Revolution*. New York: Cambridge University Press, 1996.

Grey, Vivian. *The Chemist Who Lost His Head*. Coward, McCann & Geoghegan, New York, 1982.

Holmes, Lawrence. *Antoine Lavoisier: The Next Crucial Year or the Source of His Quantitative Method of Chemistry*. Collingdale, PA: Diane Publishing Co., 1998.

Kjelle, Marylou. *Antoine Lavoisier: Father of Chemistry*. Hockessin, DE: Mitchell Lane, 2004.

Riedman, Sarah. *Antoine Lavoisier: Scientist and Citizen*. Scarborough, ON: Nelson, 1995.

Susac, Andrew. *The Clock, the Balance, and the Guillotine: The Life of Antoine Lavoisier*. New York: Doubleday, 1995.

Yount, Lisa. *Antoine Lavoisier: Founder of Modern Chemistry*. Berkeley Heights, NJ: Enslow, 2001.

# The Nature of Heat

## Year of Discovery: 1790

> **What Is It?** Heat comes from friction, not from some internal chemical property of each substance.
>
> **Who Discovered It?** Count Rumford

## Why Is This One of the 100 Greatest?

Scientists believed that heat was an invisible, weightless liquid called *caloric*. Things that were hot were stuffed with caloric. Caloric flowed from hot to cold. They also believed that fire (combustion) came from another invisible substance called *phlogiston*, a vital essence of combustible substances. As a substance burned, it lost phlogiston to air. The fire ended when all phlogiston had been lost.

These erroneous beliefs kept scientists from understanding the nature of heat and of oxidation (including combustion), and stalled much of the physical sciences. Benjamin Thompson, who called himself Count Rumford, shattered these myths and discovered the principle of friction. This discovery opened the door to a true understanding of the nature of heat.

## How Was It Discovered?

In 1790, 37-year-old Count Rumford was serving the King of Bavaria as a military advisor. As part of his duties he was in charge of the king's cannon manufacturing.

Born in Massachusetts as Benjamin Thompson, Rumford had served as a British spy during the American Revolutionary War. Then he spied on the British for the Prussians. In 1790 he fled to Bavaria and changed his name to Count Rumford.

The cannon manufacturing plant was a deafeningly noisy warehouse. On one side, metal wheel rims and mounting brackets were hammered into shape around wooden wheels and cannon carriages. Steam rose from hissing vats as glowing metal plates were cooled in slimy water.

On the other side of the warehouse, great cannons were forged. Molten metal poured into huge molds—many 12 feet long and over 4 feet across. Spinning drills scraped and gouged out the inside of each cannon barrel.

Drill bits grew dangerously hot. Streams of water kept them from melting. Hissing steam billowed out of the cannon barrels toward the ceiling, where it condensed and dripped like rain onto the workers below.

On one visit, Rumford recognized that great quantities of heat flowed into the air and water from those cannon barrels. At that time scientists believed that, as a substance grew hotter, more caloric squeezed into it. Eventually caloric overflowed and spilled out in all directions to heat whatever it touched.

Rumford wondered how so much caloric (heat) could pour out of the metal of one cannon barrel—especially since the cannon barrels felt cold when the drilling started.

Rumford decided to find out how much caloric was in each barrel and where that caloric was stored. He fashioned a long trough to catch all the water pouring out of a cannon barrel while it was being drilled so he could measure its increase in temperature.

He also directed that extra hoses be sprayed on the drilling to prevent the formation of steam. Rumford didn't want any caloric escaping as steam he couldn't capture and measure.

Drilling began with a great screeching. Hoses sprayed water onto the drill bits. The metal began to glow. A torrent of heated water eight inches deep tumbled down the narrow, foot-wide trough and past the Count and his thermometers.

Rumford was thrilled. More caloric flowed out of that cannon barrel than he could have imagined in even his wildest dreams. And still the hot water continued to flow past him, all of it heated to more than 50 degrees celsius.

Eventually the Count's face soured. Something was very wrong. The metal cannon barrel had already lost more than enough heat (caloric) to turn it into a bubbling pool of liquid metal many thousands of degrees hot. It seemed impossible for so much caloric to have existed in the metal.

Count Rumford watched the borers go back to work and realized that what he saw was *motion*. As drill bits ground against the cannon's metal, their *motion* as they crashed against the surface of the metal must create heat. *Movement* was being converted into *heat!*

Today we call it *friction*, and know it is one of the primary sources of heat. But in 1790, no one believed Count Rumford's new theory of friction heat, and they held onto the notion of caloric for another 50 years.

 **Fun Facts:** Friction with air molecules is what burns up meteors as they plunge into the atmosphere. That same friction forced NASA to line the bottom of every space shuttle with hundreds of heat-resistant ceramic tiles. Failure of one of those tiles led to the explosion of the *Columbia* in 2004.

## More to Explore

Brown, Sanborn. *Benjamin Thompson, Count Rumford*. Boston: MIT Press, 1996.

———. *Collected Works of Count Rumford*. Cambridge, MA: Harvard University Press, 1994.

———. *Count Rumford: Physicist Extraordinary*. Westport, CT: Greenwood, 1995.

Ellis, George. *Memoir of Benjamin Thompson,* Count Rumford. Somerset, PA: New Library Press, 2003.

van den Berg, J. H. *Two Principal Laws of Thermodynamics: A Cultural and Historical Exploration*. Pittsburgh: Duquesne University Press, 2004.

# Erosion of the Earth

## Year of Discovery: 1792

> **What Is It?** The earth's surface is shaped by giant forces that steadily, slowly act to build it up and wear it down.
>
> **Who Discovered It?** James Hutton

## Why Is This One of the 100 Greatest?

In the eighteenth century scientists still believed that Earth's surface had remained unchanged until cataclysmic events (the great flood of Noah's ark fame was the most often sited example) radically and suddenly changed the face of our planet. They tried to understand the planet's surface structures by searching for those few explosive events. Attempts to study the earth, its history, its landforms, and its age based on this belief led to wildly inaccurate guesses and misinformation.

James Hutton discovered that the earth's surface continually and slowly changes, evolves. He discovered the processes that gradually built up and wore down the earth's surface. This discovery provided the key to understanding our planet's history and launched the modern study of earth sciences.

## How Was It Discovered?

In the 1780s, 57-year-old, more-or-less retired physician and farmer (and amateur geologist) James Hutton decided to try to improve on the wild guesses about the age of the earth that had been put forth by other scientists. Hutton decided to study the rocks of his native Scotland and see if he could glean a better sense of Earth's age by studying the earth's rocks.

Lanky Hutton walked with long pendulum-like strides across steep, rolling green hills. Soon he realized that the existing geological theory—called *catastrophism*—couldn't possibly be right. Catastrophism claimed that all of the changes in the earth's surface were the result of sudden, violent (catastrophic) changes. (Great floods carved out valleys in hours. Great wrenchings shoved up mountains overnight.) Hutton realized that no catastrophic event could explain the rolling hills and meandering river valleys he hiked across and studied.

It was one thing to say that an existing popular theory was wrong. But it was quite another to *prove* that it was wrong or to suggest a replacement theory that better explained Earth's actual surface. Hutton's search broadened as he struggled to discover what forces actually formed the hills, mountains, valleys, and plains of Earth.

Late that summer Hutton stopped at a small stream tumbling out of a steep canyon. Without thinking, he bent down and picked up a handful of tiny pebbles and sand from the streambed. As he sifted these tiny rocks between his fingers, he realized that these pebbles had drifted down this small stream, crashing and breaking into smaller pieces as they went. They used to sit somewhere up higher on the long ridge before him.

This stream was carrying dirt and rock from hilltop to valley floor. This stream was re-shaping the entire hillside—slowly, grain by grain, day by day. Not catastrophically as geologists claimed.

The earth, Hutton realized, was shaped slowly, not overnight. Rain pounding down on hills pulled particles of dirt and rock down into streams and then down to the plains. Streams gouged out channels, gullies, and valleys bit by bit, year by year.

The wind tore at hills in the same way. The forces of nature were everywhere tearing down the earth, leveling it out. Nature did this not in a day, but over countless centuries of relentless, steady work by wind and water.

Then he stopped. If that were true, why hadn't nature already leveled out the earth? Why weren't the hills and mountains worn down? There must be a second force that builds up the land, just as the forces of nature tear it down.

For days James Hutton hiked and pondered. What built up the earth? It finally hit him: the heat of Earth's core built up hills and mountains by pushing outward.

Mountain ranges were forced up by the heat of the earth. Wind and rain slowly wore them back down. With no real beginning and no end, these two great forces struggled in dynamic balance over eons, the real time scale for geologic study.

With that great discovery, James Hutton forever changed the way geologists would look at the earth and its processes, and he completely changed humankind's sense of the scale of time required to bring about these changes.

 **Fun Facts:** Millions of years ago flowing water eroded the surface of Mars, leaving behind the gullies, banks, and dry riverbeds scientists have found there. Now Mar's atmosphere is too thin to support liquid water. A cup of water on Mars would instantly vaporize and vanish, blown away by the solar winds.

# More to Explore

Baxter, Stephen. *Ages in Chaos : James Hutton and the Discovery of Deep Time*. New York: Forge Books, 2004.

Geologic Society of London. *James Hutton—Present and Future*. London: Geologic Society of London, 1999.

Gould, Stephen. *Time's Arrow, Time's Cycle: Myth and Metaphor in the Discovery of Geological Time*. Cambridge, MA: Harvard University Press, 1997.

Hutton, James. *Theory of the Earth*. Whitefish, MT: Kessinger Publishing, 2004.

McIntyre, Donald. *James Hutton: The Founder of Modern Geology*. Edinburgh, Scotland: National Museum of Scotland, 2002.

Repcheck, Jack. *The Man Who Found Time: James Hutton and the Discovery of Earth's Antiquity*. Jackson, TN: Perseus Books Group, 2003.

# Vaccinations

## Year of Discovery: 1798

> **What Is It?** Humans can be protected from disease by injecting them with mild forms of the very disease they are trying to avoid.
>
> **Who Discovered It?** Lady Mary Wortley Montagu and Edward Jenner

## Why Is This One of the 100 Greatest?

Have you had smallpox? Polio? Typhoid? Probably not.

However, such infectious diseases used to plague humankind. The word *plague* comes from one of these killer diseases—the bubonic plague. Throughout the fourteenth and fifteenth centuries, the plague killed nearly half of the population of Europe.

Smallpox killed over 100,000 people a year for a century and left millions horribly scarred and disfigured. The influenza epidemic of 1918 killed 25 million worldwide. Polio killed thousands in the early twentieth century and left millions paralyzed.

One simple discovery not only stopped the spread of each of these diseases, it virtually eradicated them. That discovery was vaccinations. Vaccinations have saved millions of lives and have prevented unimaginable amounts of misery and suffering. American children are now regularly vaccinated for as many as 15 diseases.

## How Were Vaccinations Discovered?

Twenty-four-year-old Lady Mary Wortley Montagu, a well-known English poet, traveled to Turkey with her husband in 1712 when he became the British ambassador. Lady Mary noticed that native populations in Turkey didn't suffered from smallpox, the dread disease that had left her scarred and pockmarked and that killed tens of thousands in England each year.

She soon learned that elderly tribal women performed what was called "ingrafting." Previous British travelers had dismissed the practice as a meaningless tribal ritual. Lady Mary suspected that this annual event held the secret to their immunity from smallpox.

Village families would decide if anyone in the family should have smallpox that year. An old woman arrived carrying a nutshell full of infected liquid. She would open one of the volunteer's veins with a needle dipped in the liquid, as the family sang and chanted. The infected person stayed in bed for two to three days with a mild fever and a slight rash. He or she was then as well as before, never getting a serious case of smallpox. Mary wondered if English populations could be protected by ingrafting.

Upon her return to England in 1713, Lady Mary lectured about the potential of ingrafting. She was dismissed as an untrained and "silly" woman. In early 1714 Caroline, Princess of Wales, heard one of Lady Mary's talks and approved Lady Mary's ingrafting of convicts and orphans.

Lady Mary collected the puss from smallpox blisters of sick patients and injected small amounts of the deadly liquid into her test subjects. The death rate of those she inoculated was less than one-third that of the general public, and five times as many of her subjects got mild, non-scarring cases.

However, there was a problem with ingrafting. Inoculations with live smallpox viruses were dangerous. Some patients died from the injections that were supposed to protect them.

Enter Edward Jenner, a young English surgeon, in 1794. Living in a rural community, Jenner noticed that milkmaids almost never got smallpox. However, virtually all milkmaids *did* get cowpox, a disease that caused mild blistering on their hands. Jenner theorized that cowpox must be in the same family as smallpox and that getting mild cowpox was like ingrafting and made a person immune to the deadly smallpox.

He tested his theory by injecting 20 children with liquid taken from the blisters of a milkmaid with cowpox. Each infected child got cowpox. Painful blisters formed on their hands and arms, lasting several days.

Two months later, Jenner injected live smallpox into each of his test children. If Jenner's theory was wrong, many of these children would die. However, none of his test children showed any sign of smallpox.

Jenner invented the word "*vaccination*" to describe his process when he announced his results in 1798. *Vacca* is the Latin word for cow; *vaccinia* is Latin for cowpox.

 **Fun Facts:** The World Health Organization declared smallpox eradicated in 1979, and the President George H. Bush said that since then authorities have not detected a single natural case of the disease in the world.

## More to Explore

Asimov, Isaac. *Asimov's Chronology of Science and Discovery*. New York: Harper & Row, 1989.

Clark, Donald. *Encyclopedia of Great Inventors and Discoveries*. London: Marshall Cavendish Books, 1993.

Dyson, James. *A History of Great Inventions*. New York: Carroll & Graf Publishers, 2001.

Haven, Kendall, and Donna Clark. *100 Most Popular Scientists for Young Adults*. Englewood, CO: Libraries Unlimited, 1999.

Vare, Ethlie Ann, and Greg Ptacek. *Mothers of Invention*. New York: William Morrow, 1989.

Yenne, Bill. *100 Inventions That Shaped World History*. New York: Bluewood Books, 1993.

# Infrared and Ultraviolet

## Years of Discovery: 1800 and 1801

> **What Is It?** Energy is radiated by the sun and other stars outside of the narrow visible spectrum of colors.
>
> **Who Discovered It?** Frederick Herschel (IR) and Johann Ritter (UV)

## Why Is This One of the 100 Greatest?

Infrared and ultraviolet radiation are key parts of our scientific development over the past 200 years. Yet until 1800 it never occurred to anyone that radiation could exist outside the narrow band that human eyes detect. The discovery of infrared and ultraviolet light expanded science's view beyond the visible light to the whole radiation spectrum, from radio waves to gamma rays.

Infrared (IR) radiation has been key to many astronomical discoveries. In addition, earth science uses IR to measure heat in studies of everything from ocean temperatures to forest health. IR sensors power burglar alarms, fire alarms, and police and fire infrared detectors. Biologists have discovered that many birds and insects detect IR radiation with their eyes. Ultraviolet light (UV) led to a better understanding of solar radiation and to high-energy parts of the spectrum, including X-rays, microwaves, and gamma rays.

## How Was It Discovered?

Frederick Herschel was born in Hanover, Germany, in 1738. As a young man, he grew into a gifted musician and astronomer. It was Herschel who discovered the planet Uranus in 1781, the first new planet discovered in almost 2,000 years.

In late 1799 Herschel began a study of solar light. He often used color filters to isolate parts of the light spectrum for these studies and noted that some filters grew hotter than others. Curious about this heat in solar radiation, Herschel wondered if some colors naturally carried more heat than others.

To test this idea, Herschel built a large prism. In a darkened room, he projected the prism's rainbow light spectrum onto the far wall and carefully measured the temperature inside each of these separate colored light beams.

Herschel was surprised to find that the temperature rose steadily from violet (coolest) to a maximum in the band of red light. On a sudden impulse, Herschel placed a thermometer in the dark space right next to the band of red light (just beyond the light spectrum).

This thermometer should have stayed cool. It was not in any direct light. But it didn't. This thermometer registered the most heat of all.

55

Herschel was amazed. He guessed that the sun radiated heat waves along with light waves and that these invisible heat rays refract slightly less while traveling through a prism than do light rays. Over the course of several weeks, he tested heat rays and found that they refracted, reflected, bent, etc., exactly like light. Because they appeared below red light, Herschel named them infrared (meaning below red).

Johann Ritter was born in 1776 in Germany and became a natural science philosopher. His central beliefs were that there was unity and symmetry in nature and that all natural forces could be traced back to one prime force, *Urkraft*.

In 1801, Ritter read about Herschel's discovery of infrared radiation. Ritter had worked on sunlight's effect on chemical reactions and with electrochemistry (the effect of electrical currents on chemicals and on chemical reactions). During this work he had tested light's effect on silver chloride and knew that exposure to light turned this chemical from white to black. (This discovery later became the basis for photography.)

Ritter decided to duplicate Herschel's experiment, but to see if all colors darkened silver chloride at the same rate. He coated strips of paper with silver chloride. In a dark room he repeated Herschel's set up. But instead of measuring temperature in each color of the rainbow spectrum projected on wall, Ritter timed how long it took for strips of silver chloride paper to turn black in each color of the spectrum.

He found that red hardly turned the paper at all. He also found that violet darkened paper the fastest.

Again mimicking Herschel's experiment, Ritter placed a silver chloride strip in the dark area just beyond the band of violet light. This strip blackened the fastest of all! Even though this strip was not exposed to visible light, *some* radiation had acted on the chemicals to turn them black.

Ritter had discovered radiation beyond violet (ultraviolet) just as Herschel had discovered that radiation existed below the red end of the visible spectrum (infrared).

 **Fun Facts:** A TV remote control uses infrared light to adjust the volume or change the channel.

# More to Explore

Herschel, Frederick. *Preliminary Discourse on the Study of Natural Philosophy*. Dover, DE: Adamant Media, 2001.

————. *Treatise on Astronomy*. Dover, DE: Adamant Media, 2001.

Herschel, John. *Aspects of the Life and Thought of Sir John Frederick Herschel*. New York: Arno Press, 1994.

Kaufl, Hans. *High Resolution Infrared Spectroscopy in Astronomy*. New York: Springer-Verlag, 2003.

Robinson, Michael. *Ripples in the Cosmos*. Collingdale, PA: Diane Publishing, 2000.

# Anesthesia

## Year of Discovery: 1801

> **What Is It?** A medication used during surgery that causes loss of awareness of pain in patients.
>
> **Who Discovered It?** Humphry Davy

## Why Is This One of the 100 Greatest?

Anesthesia created safe surgery and made many medical and dental operations practical and plausible. The trauma suffered by patients from the pain of an operation was often so dangerous that it kept doctors from attempting many surgical procedures. That pain also kept many severely ill patients from seeking medical help.

Anesthesia eliminated much of the pain, fear, anxiety, and suffering for medical and dental patients during most procedures and gave the medical profession a chance to develop and refine the procedures that would save countless lives.

Anesthesiology is now a major medical specialty and an important position in every operating room. While it is probable that new drugs and new types of anesthesia will be developed in the coming decades, this important aspect of medicine will be with us forever.

## How Was It Discovered?

The word *anesthesia*, from the Greek words meaning "lack of sensation," was coined by Oliver Wendell Holmes (father of the supreme court chief justice by the same name) in 1846. However, the concept of anesthesia is millennia old. Ancient Chinese doctors developed acupuncture techniques that blocked the transmission of pain sensations to the brain. Ancient Romans and Egyptians used mandrake (the root of the mandragora plant) to induce unconsciousness. European doctors in the middle ages also favored mandrake. Inca shamans chewed coca leaves and spit the juice (cocaine) into wounds and cuts to numb their patients' pain.

Three nineteenth-century scientists each laid claim to the medical discovery of modern anesthesia. None of them deserves the credit because Humphry Davy had already earned that distinction.

Scottish obstetrician Sir Young Simpson was the first to experiment with chloroform. He observed that patients who inhaled a few breaths of the gas (a wad of cotton soaked in chloroform was placed under the nose) quickly became relaxed and calm, and were soon unconscious. His use of the drug drew no attention until, in 1838, Queen Victoria asked for Simpson and his chloroform for the birth of her seventh child.

Chloroform's greatest use came during the American Civil War. Southern cotton was often traded in England for medicines—including chloroform—that became a staple of battlefield operating tents for Southern doctors. After the war, chloroform continued to enjoy some popularity—especially in the South—until synthetic drugs were developed in the early twentieth century.

Georgia physician Crawford Long was the first to use ether during an operation. In 1842 he removed a neck tumor from James Venable, a local judge. The operation went perfectly and the judge felt no pain. But Long never bothered to publicize his success.

Two years later Boston dentist Horace Wells took up the notion of using ether to dull operation pain. Wells mistakenly turned off the gas too soon. His patient sat up and screamed. The crowd of observing doctors scoffed and called Well's claims for ether a hoax.

One year later (1845), Boston dentist William Morton gave ether another try. Morton's operation went flawlessly. Only after Morton's second successful public operation with ether, and only after he had published several articles touting the glories of ether, did doctors across America—and then Europe—turn to ether as their primary anesthetic.

However, none of these men was the first to discover modern medical anesthesia. In 1801, English scientist Humphry Davy was experimenting with gasses when he combined nitrogen and oxygen to produce nitrous oxide. Davy tested the resulting colorless gas and eventually took several deep breaths. He reported a soaring euphoria that soon passed into an uncontrollable outburst of laughter and sobbing until he passed out (it made him unconscious).

Davy named the stuff laughing gas and noted its tendency to make him unaware of pain. Davy recommended it for use as an anesthetic during medical and dental procedures. Even though doctors took no note of his discovery, Davy's work is the first scientific identification and testing of an anesthetic.

 **Fun Facts:** The common phrase "biting the bullet" dates from the days before anesthetics were available on the battlefield. Biting on the soft lead of a bullet absorbed the pressure of the bite without damaging a soldier's teeth.

# More to Explore

Asimov, Isaac. *Asimov's Chronology of Science and Discovery.* New York: Harper & Row, 1989.

Dyson, James. *A History of Great Inventions.* New York: Carroll & Graf Publishers, 2001.

Fradin, Dennis. *We Have Conquered Pain: The Discovery of Anesthesia.* New York: Simon & Schuster Children's, 1996.

Fullmer, June. Y*oung Humphry Davy: The Making of an Experimental Chemist.* Philadelphia: American Philosophical Society, 2000.

Galas, Judith. *Anesthetics: Surgery Without Pain.* New York: Thomson Gale, 1995.

Knight, David. *Humphry Davy: Science and Power.* New York: Cambridge University Press, 1998.

Lace, William. *Anesthetics.* New York: Lucent Books, 2004.

Radford, Ruby. *Prelude to Fame: Crawford Long's Discovery of Anaesthesia.* Atlanta, GA: Geron-X, 1990.

# Atoms

## Year of Discovery: 1802

---

**What Is It?** An atom is the smallest particle that can exist of any chemical element.

**Who Discovered It?** John Dalton

## Why Is This One of the 100 Greatest?

The modern worlds of chemistry and physics depend on knowing and studying the universe of atoms. But no one could actually *see* an atom until the invention of the electron microscope in 1938. Centuries before that, atoms were well known and were an important part of chemistry and physics research. It was John Dalton who defined the atom, allowing scientists to being serious study at the atomic level. An atom is the smallest particle of any element and the basic building block of matter. All chemical compounds are built from combinations of atoms.

Since atoms are the key to understanding chemistry and physics, Dalton's discovery of the atom ranks as one of the great turning points for science. Because of this discovery, Dalton is often called the father of modern physical science.

## How Was It Discovered?

In the fifth century B.C., Leucippus of Miletus and Democritus of Abdera theorized that each form of matter could be broken into smaller and smaller pieces. They called that smallest particle that could no longer be broken into smaller pieces an *atom*. Galileo and Newton both used the term *atom* in the same general way. Robert Boyle and Antoine Lavoisier were the first to use the word *element* to describe one of the newly discovered chemical substances. All of this work, however, was based on general philosophical theory, not on scientific observation and evidence.

John Dalton was born in 1766 near Manchester, England, and received a strict Quaker upbringing. With little formal education, he spent 20 years studying meteorology and teaching at religious, college-level schools. Near the end of this period, Dalton joined, and presented a variety of papers to, the Philosophical Society. These included papers on the barometer, the thermometer, the hygrometer, rainfall, the formation of clouds, evaporation, atmospheric moisture, and dew point. Each paper presented new theories and advanced research results.

Dalton quickly became famous for his innovative thinking and shifted to science research full time. In 1801 he turned his attention from the study of atmospheric gasses to chemical combinations. Dalton had no experience or training in chemistry. Still, he plowed confidently into his studies.

By this time almost 50 chemical elements had been discovered—metals, gasses, and nonmetals. But scientists studying chemistry were blocked by a fundamental question they couldn't answer: How did elements actually combine to form the thousands of compounds that could be found on Earth? For example, how did hydrogen (a gas) combine with oxygen (another gas) to form water (a liquid)? Further, why did exactly one gram of hydrogen always combine with exactly eight grams of oxygen to make water—never more, never less?

Dalton studied all of the chemical reactions he could find (or create), trying to develop a general theory for how the fundamental particle of each element behaved. He compared the weights of each chemical and the likely atomic structure of each element in each compound. After a year of study, Dalton decided that these compounds were defined by simple numerical ratios by weight. This decision allowed him to deduce the number of particles of each element in various well-known compounds (water, ether, etc.).

Dalton theorized that each element consisted of tiny, indestructible particles that were what combined with other elements to form compounds. He used the old Greek word, *atom*, for these particles. But now it had a specific chemical meaning.

Dalton showed that all atoms of any one element were identical so that any of them could combine with the atoms of some other element to form the known chemical compounds. Each compound had to have a fixed number of atoms of each element. Those fixed ratios never changed. He deduced that compounds would be made of the minimum number possible of atoms of each element. Thus water wouldn't be $H_4O_2$ because $H_2O$ was simpler and had the same ratio of hydrogen and oxygen atoms.

Dalton was the first to use letter symbols (H, O, etc.) to represent the various elements. Scientists readily accepted Dalton's theories and discoveries, and his concepts quickly spread across all Western science. We still use his concept of an atom today.

 **Fun Facts:** The smallest atom is the hydrogen atom, with just one electron circling a single proton. The largest naturally occurring atom is the uranium atom, with 92 electrons circling a nucleus stuffed with 92 protons and 92 neutrons. Larger atoms have been artificially created in the lab but do not occur naturally on earth.

## More to Explore

Greenway, Frank. *John Dalton and the Atom.* Ithaca, NY: Cornel University Press, 1997.

Lewis, Spencer. *The Mystery of John Dalton and His Alchemy Laws.* Whitefish, MT: Kessinger, 2005.

Millington, J. *John Dalton.* London: AMS Press, 1996.

Patterson, Elizabeth. *John Dalton and the Atomic Theory: The Biography of a Natural Philosopher.* New York: Doubleday, 1996.

Smith, Robert. *Memoir of John Dalton and History of the Atomic Theory Up to His Time.* Dover, DE: Adamant Media, 2005.

Smyth, A. L. *John Dalton: 1766–1844.* New York: Dover, 1998.

# Electrochemical Bonding

## Year of Discovery: 1806

> **What Is It?** Molecular bonds between chemical elements are electrical in nature.
>
> **Who Discovered It?** Humphry Davy

## Why Is This One of the 100 Greatest?

Davy discovered that the chemical bonds between individual atoms in a molecule are electrical in nature. We now know that chemical bonds are created by the sharing or transfer of electrically charged particles—electrons—between atoms. In 1800, the idea that chemistry somehow involved electricity was a radical discovery.

Davy's discovery started the modern field of electrochemistry and redefined science's view of chemical reactions and how chemicals bond together. Finally, Davy used this new concept to discover two new (and important) elements: sodium and potassium.

## How Was It Discovered?

Humphry Davy was born in 1778 along the rugged coast of Cornwall, England. He received only minimal schooling and was mostly self-taught. As a young teenager, he was apprenticed to a surgeon and apothecary. But the early writings of famed French scientist Antoine Lavoisier sparked his interest in science.

In 1798 Davy was offered a chance by wealthy amateur chemist Thomas Beddoes to work in Bristol, England, at a new lab Beddoes built and funded. Davy was free to pursue chemistry-related science whims. He experimented with gases in 1799, thinking that the best way to test these colorless creations was to breathe them. He sniffed nitrous oxide ($N_2O$) and passed out, remembering nothing but feeling happy and powerful. After he reported its effect, the gas quickly became a popular party drug under the name "laughing gas." Davy used nitrous oxide for a wisdom tooth extraction and felt no pain. Even though he reported this in an article, it was another 45 years before the medical profession finally used nitrous oxide as its first anesthetic.

Davy also experimented with carbon dioxide. He breathed it and almost died from carbon dioxide poisoning. A born showman, movie-star handsome, and always fashionably dressed, Davy delighted in staging grand demonstrations of each experiment and discovery for thrilled audiences of public admirers.

In 1799, Italian Alessandro Volta invented the battery and created the world's first man-made electrical current. By 1803, Davy had talked Beddoes into building a giant "Voltaic Pile" (battery) with 110 double plates to provide more power.

Davy turned his full attention to experimenting with batteries. He tried different metals and even charcoal for the two electrodes in his battery and experimented with different liquids (water, acids, etc.) for the liquid (called an electrolyte) that filled the space around the battery's plates.

In 1805 Davy noticed that a zinc electrode oxidized while the battery was connected. That was a *chemical* reaction taking place in the presence of an electrical current. Then he noticed other chemical reactions taking place on other electrodes. Davy realized that the battery (electric current) was *causing* chemical reactions to happen.

As he experimented with other electrodes, Davy began to realize the electrical nature of chemical reactions. He tried a wide variety of materials for the two electrodes and different liquids for the electrolyte.

In a grand demonstration in 1806, Davy passed a strong electric current through pure water and showed that he produced only two gasses—hydrogen and oxygen. Water molecules had been torn apart by an electric current. This demonstration showed that an electrical force could tear apart chemical bonds. To Davy this meant that the original chemical bonds had to be electrical in nature or an electric current couldn't have ripped them apart.

Davy had discovered the basic nature of chemical bonding. Chemical bonds were somehow electrical. This discovery radically changed the way scientists viewed the formation of molecules and chemical bonds.

Davy continued experiments, passing electrical currents from electrode to electrode through almost every material he could find. In 1807 he tried the power of a new battery with 250 zinc and copper plates on caustic potash and isolated a new element that burst into brilliant flame as soon as it was formed on an electrode. He named it *potassium*. A month later he isolated *sodium*. Davy had used his grand discovery to discover two new elements.

 **Fun Facts:** A popular use of electrochemical bonding is in cookware. The process unites the anodized surface with the aluminum base, creating a nonporous surface that is 400 percent harder than aluminum.

# More to Explore

Bowers, Brian, ed. *Curiosity Perfectly Satisfied: Faraday's Travels in Europe 1813–1815*. Philadelphia: Institute of Electrical Engineers, 1996.

Davy, John, ed. *Collected Works of Sir Humphry Davy*. Dorset, England: Thoemmes Continuum, 2001.

Fullmer, June. *Young Humphry Davy: The Making of an Experimental Chemist*. Philadelphia: American Philosophical Society, 2000.

Golinski, Jan. *Science as Public Culture: Chemistry and Enlightenment in Britain, 1760–1820*. New York: Cambridge University Press, 1999.

Knight, David. *Humphry Davy: Science and Power*. Ames, IA: Blackwell Publishers, 1995.

# The Existence of Molecules

## Year of Discovery: 1811

---

> **What Is It?** A molecule is a group of attached atoms. An atom uniquely identi-
> fies one of the 100+ chemical elements that make up our planet. Bonding a
> number of different atoms together makes a molecule, which uniquely
> identifies one of the many thousands of substances that can exist.
>
> **Who Discovered It?** Amedeo Avogadro

## Why Is This One of the 100 Greatest?

If atoms are the basic building block of each element, then molecules are the basic building blocks of each substance on Earth. Scientists were stalled by their inability to accurately imagine—let alone detect—particles as small as an atom or a molecule. Many had theorized that some tiny particle (that they called an atom) was the smallest possible particle and the basic unit of each element. However, the substances around us were not made of individual elements. Scientists were at a loss to explain the basic nature of substances.

Avogadro's discovery created a basic understanding of the relationship between all of the millions of substances on Earth and the few basic elements. It adjusted existing theory to conclude that every liter of gas (at the same temperature and pressure) had exactly the same number of molecules in it. This discovery allowed scientists to make critical calculations with and about gasses and allowed scientists to understand the nature of all substances. Avogadro's discovery (and the related Avogadro's Number) have become one of the cornerstones of organic and inorganic chemistry as well as the basis for the gas laws and much of the development of quantitative chemistry.

## How Was It Discovered?

In the spring of 1811, 35-year-old college professor Amedeo Avogadro sat in his classroom scowling at two scientific papers laid out on his desk. Avogadro taught natural science classes at Vercelli College in the Italian mountain town of Turin. Twenty-five students sat each day and listened to Professor Avogadro lecture, discuss, and quiz them on whatever aspects of science caught his fancy.

This day he read these two papers to his class, claimed that he saw an important mystery in them, and challenged his students to find it.

**63**

In the two papers, the English chemist, Dalton, and the French chemist, Gay-Lussac, each described an experiment in which they combined hydrogen and oxygen atoms to create water. Both reported that it took exactly two liters of gaseous hydrogen atoms to combine with exactly one liter of oxygen atoms to produce exactly two liters of gaseous water vapor. Dalton claimed that this experiment proved that water is the combination of two atoms of hydrogen and one atom of oxygen. Gay-Lussac also claimed it proved that a liter of any gas had to contain exactly the same number of atoms as a liter of any other gas, no matter what gas it was.

These studies were heralded as major breakthroughs for chemical study. But from his first reading, Professor Avogadro was bothered by a nagging contradiction.

Both Dalton and Gay-Lussac started with exactly *two* liters of hydrogen and *one* liter of oxygen. That's a total of *three* liters of gas. But they both ended with only *two* liters of water vapor gas. If every liter of every gas has to have exactly the same number of atoms, then how could all the atoms from three liters of gas fit into just *two* liters of water vapor gas?

The Turin cathedral bell chimed midnight before the answer struck Avogadro's mind. Dalton and Gay-Lussac had used the wrong word. What if they had each substituted "a group of attached atoms" for *atom*?

Avogadro created the word *molecule* (a Greek word meaning, "to move about freely in a gas") for this "group of attached atoms." Then he scratched out equations on paper until he found a way to account for all of the atoms and molecules in Dalton's and Gay-Lussac's experiments.

If each *molecule* of hydrogen contained two atoms of hydrogen, and each *molecule* of oxygen contained two atoms of oxygen, then—if each *molecule* of water vapor contained two atoms of hydrogen and one atom of oxygen, as both scientists reported—each liter of hydrogen and each liter of oxygen would have exactly the same number of *molecules* as each of the two resulting liters of water vapor (even though they contained a different number of atoms)!

And so it was that, without ever touching a test tube or chemical experiment of any kind, without even a background in chemistry, Amedeo Avogadro discovered the existence of molecules and created the basic gas law—every liter of a gas contains the same number of *molecules* of gas.

 **Fun Facts:** The smallest molecule is the hydrogen molecule—just two protons and two electrons. DNA is the largest known naturally occurring molecule, with over four billion atoms—each containing a number of protons, neutrons, and electrons.

# More to Explore

Adler, Robert. *Science Firsts,* New York: John Wiley & Sons, 2002.

Chang, Laura, ed. *Scientists at Work.* New York: McGraw-Hill, 2000.

Downs, Robert. *Landmarks in Science.* Englewood, CO: Libraries Unlimited, 1996.

Haven, Kendall. *Marvels of Science.* Englewood, CO: Libraries Unlimited, 1994.

Morselli, Mario. *Amedeo Avogadro.* New York: D. Reidel, 1995.

# Electromagnetism

## Year of Discovery: 1820

> **What Is It?** An electric current creates a magnetic field and vice versa.
>
> **Who Discovered It?** Hans Oersted

## Why Is This One of the 100 Greatest?

Before 1820, the only known magnetism was the naturally occurring magnetism of iron magnets and of lodestones—small, weak direction finders. Yet the modern world of electric motors and electric generating power plants is muscled by powerful electromagnets. So is every hair dryer, mixer, and washing machine. Our industry, homes, and lives depend on electric motors—which all depend on electromagnetism.

This 1820 discovery has become one of the most important for defining the shape of modern life. Oersted's discovery opened the door to undreamed of possibilities for research and scientific advancement. It made possible the work of electromagnetic giants such as Andre Ampere and Michael Faraday.

## How Was It Discovered?

Hans Oersted was born in 1777 in southern Denmark. He studied science at the university, but leaned far more toward philosophy. Oersted adopted the philosophy teachings of John Ritter, who advocated a natural science belief that there was unity in all natural forces. Oersted believed that he could trace all natural forces back to the *Urkraft*, or primary force. When he was finally given a science teaching position (in 1813), he focused his research efforts on finding a way to trace all chemical reactions back to *Urkraft* in order to create a natural unity in all of chemistry.

Research and interest in electricity mushroomed after Benjamin Franklin's experiments with static electricity and sparks of energy created with Leyden jars. Then, in 1800, Volta invented the battery and the world's first continuous flow of electric current. Electricity became the scientific wonder of the world. Sixty-eight books on electricity were published between 1800 and 1820.

Only a few scientists suspected that there might be a connection between electricity and magnetism. In 1776 and 1777 the Bavarian Academy of Sciences offered a prize to anyone who could answer the question: Is there a physical analogy between electrical and magnetic force? They found no winner. In 1808, the London Scientific Society made the same offer. Again there was no winner.

In the spring of 1820, Hans Oersted was giving a lecture to one of his classes when an amazing thing happened. He made a grand discovery—the only major scientific discovery made in front of a class of students. It was a simple demonstration for graduate-level students of how electric current heats a platinum wire. Oersted had not focused his research on either electricity or magnetism. Neither was of particular interest to him. Still, he happened to have a needle magnet (a compass needle) nearby on the table when he conducted his demonstration.

As soon as Oersted connected battery power to his wire, the compass needle twitched and twisted to point perpendicular to the platinum wire. When he disconnected the battery, the needle drifted back to its original position.

Each time he ran an electric current through that platinum wire, the needle snapped back to its perpendicular position. Oersted's students were fascinated. Oersted seemed flustered and shifted the talk to another topic.

Oersted did not return to this amazing occurrence for three months—until the summer of 1820. He then began a series of experiments to discover if his electric current created a force that *attracted* the compass needle, or *repelled* it. He also wanted to try to relate this strange force to *Urkraft*.

He moved the wire above, beside, and below the compass needle. He reversed the current through his platinum wire. He tried two wires instead of one. With every change in the wire and current, he watched for the effect these changes would produce on the compass needle.

Oersted finally realized his electric current created *both* an attractive and a repulsive force at the same time. After months of study, he concluded that an electric current created a magnetic force and that this force was a whole new type of force—radically different than any of the forces Newton had described. This force acted not along straight lines, but in a circle *around* the wire carrying an electric current. Clearly, he wrote, wires carrying an electric current showed magnetic properties. The concept of electromagnetism had been discovered.

 **Fun Facts:** The aurora borealis, or "northern lights," are an electromagnetic phenomenon, caused when electrically charged solar particles collide with Earth's magnetic field. In the Southern hemisphere these waving curtains of light form around the south pole and are called the aurora australis, or "southern lights."

# More to Explore

Beaumont, LeIonce. *Memoir of Oersted.* Washington, DC: Smithsonian Institution, 1997.

Brain, R. M., ed. *Hans Christian Oersted and the Romantic Quest for Unity.* New York: Springer, 2006.

Cohen, Bernard. *Revolutions in Science.* Cambridge, MA: Harvard University Press, 1995.

Dibner, Bern. *Oersted and the Discovery of Electromagnetism.* Cambridge, MA: Burndy Library, 1995.

Oersted, Hans. *The Discovery of Electromagnetism Made in the Year 1820.* London: H. H. Theiles, 1994.

# First Dinosaur Fossil

## Year of Discovery: 1824

**What Is It?** The first proof that giant dinosaurs once walked the earth.

**Who Discovered It?** Gideon Mantell and William Buckland

## Why Is This One of the 100 Greatest?

Most people (and scientists) assumed that the world and its mix of plants and animals had always been as it was when these scientists lived. The discovery of dinosaur fossils destroyed that belief. This discovery represented the first proof that entire groups of ancient—and now extinct—animals once roamed Earth. It was the first proof that massive beasts (dinosaurs) much larger than anything that exists today once existed.

This discovery was a great leap forward for the fields of archeology and paleontology —both in their knowledge as well as in their field techniques. Dinosaurs have proved to be the most dramatic of all relics from the past and have done more to acquaint the ordinary person with the fact of biological evolution than anything else.

## How Was It Discovered?

People had always found fossil bones, but none had correctly identified them as extinct species. In 1677 Englishman Robert Plot found what 220 years later was identified as the end of the thighbone of a giant biped carnivorous dinosaur. Plot gained great fame when he claimed it was the fossilized testicles of a giant and said it proved that story giants were real.

Science was clearly still in the dark ages until two Englishmen, working independently, both wrote articles on their discovery of dinosaurs in 1824. They share the credit for discovering dinosaurs.

In 1809 (50 years before Darwin's discovery of evolution) English country doctor Gideon Mantell lived in Lewes in the Sussex district of England. While visiting a patient one day, Mantell's wife, Mary Ann, took a short stroll and then presented him with several puzzling teeth she had found. These massive teeth were obviously from an herbivore but were far too large for any known animal. Mantell, an amateur geologist, had been collecting fossil relics of ancient land animals for several years but could not identify these teeth. He returned to the site and correctly identified the rock strata as from the Mesozoic era. Thus, the teeth had to be many millions of years old.

These teeth were not the first large bones Mantell had found, but they were the most puzzling. Mantell took them to famed French naturalist, Charles Cuvier, who thought they came from an ordinary rhinoceros-like animal. Mantell set the teeth aside.

In 1822 Mantell came across the teeth of an iguana and realized that these teeth were exact miniatures of the ones he had found 13 years earlier. Combined with other large bones he had recovered from the site, Mantell claimed that he had discovered an ancient, giant reptile that he named *iguanodon* ("iguana-toothed"). He eagerly published his discovery in 1824.

During this same period William Buckland, a professor at Oxford University, had been collecting fossils in the Stonesfield region of England. During an 1822 outing he discovered the jaw and several thighbones of an ancient and giant creature. (It turned out to be the same species discovered—but not identified—by Robert Plot 150 years before.)

Buckland determined from these bones that this monster had been a biped (two-legged) carnivore. From the bone structure, Buckland claimed that it belonged to the reptile family. Thus he named it *megalosaurus* (giant lizard) and published a paper on it in 1824. With these two publications the era of dinosaurs had been discovered.

 **Fun Facts:** The word *dinosaur* comes from the Greek words meaning "terrible lizard." Lots of dinosaurs were named after Greek words that suited their personality or appearance. Velociraptor means "speedy robber" and triceratops means "three-horned head."

## More to Explore

Cadbury, Deborah. *Terrible Lizard: The First Dinosaur Hunters and the Birth of a New Science.* New York: Henry Holt, 1995.

Dean, Dennis. *Gideon Mantell and the Discovery of Dinosaurs.* New York: Cambridge University Press, 1999.

Debus, Allen. *Paleoimagery: The Evolution of Dinosaurs in Art.* Jefferson, NC: McFarland & Co., 2002.

Hartzog, Brooke. *Iguanodon and Dr. Gideon Mantell.* Cherry Hill, NJ: Rosen Group, 2001.

Klaver, Jan. *Geology and Religious Sentiment: The Effect of Geological Discoveries on English Society between 1829 and 1859.* Amsterdam: Brill Academic Publishers, 1997.

Knight, David, ed. *Geology and Mineralogy Considered with Reference to Natural Theology.* Abingdon, England: Taylor & Francis, 2003.

# Ice Ages

## Year of Discovery: 1837

> **What Is It?** Earth's past includes periods of radically different climate—ice ages—than the mild present.
>
> **Who Discovered It?** Louis Agassiz

## Why Is This One of the 100 Greatest?

It was a revolutionary idea: Earth's climate had not always been the same. Every scientist for thousands of years had assumed that Earth's climate had remained unchanging for all time. Then Louis Agassiz discovered proof that all Europe had once been covered by crushing glaciers. Earth's climate had not always been as it was now. With that discovery, Agassiz established the concept of an ever-changing Earth.

This discovery explained a number of biological puzzles that had confounded scientists for centuries. Agassiz was also the first scientist to record careful and extensive *field data* to support and establish a new theory. Agassiz's work did much to begin the field of geology and our modern view of our planet's history.

## How Was It Discovered?

Louis Agassiz thought of himself as a field geologist more than as a college professor. During weeks of rambling hikes through his native Swiss Alps in the late 1820s he noticed several physical features around the front faces of Swiss valley glaciers. First, glaciers wormed their way down valleys that were "U" shaped—with flat valley bottoms. River valleys were always "V" shaped. At first he thought that glaciers naturally formed *in* such valleys. Soon he realized that the glaciers, themselves, carved valleys in this characteristic "U" shape.

Next he noticed horizontal gouges and scratches in the rock walls of these glacier valleys—often a mile or more in front of the actual glacier. Finally, he became aware that many of these valleys featured large boulders and rock piles resting in the lower end of the valley where no known force or process could have deposited them.

Soon Agassiz realized that the mountain glaciers he studied must have been much bigger and longer in the past and that they, in some distant past, had gouged out the valleys, carried the rocks that scored the valleys' rock walls leaving claw-mark scratches, and deposited giant boulders at their ancient heads.

In the early 1830s Agassiz toured England and the northern European lowlands. Here, too, he found "U"-shaped valleys, horizontal gouges, and scratch marks in valley rock walls, and giant boulders mysteriously perched in the lower valley reaches.

It looked like the signature of glaciers he had come to know from his Swiss studies. But there were no glaciers for hundreds of miles in any direction. By 1835, the awe-inspiring truth hit him. In some past age, all Europe must have been covered by giant glaciers. The past must have been radically different than the present. Climate was not always the same.

In order to claim such a revolutionary idea, he had to prove it. Agassiz and several hired assistants spent two years surveying Alpine glaciers and documenting the presence of the telltale signs of past glaciers.

When Agassiz released his findings in 1837, geologists worldwide were awed. Never before had a researcher gathered such extensive and detailed field data to support a new theory. Because of the quality of his field data, Agassiz's conclusions were immediately accepted—even though they radically changed all existing theories of Earth's past.

Agassiz created a vivid picture of ice ages and proved that they had existed. But it was Yugoslavian physicist Milutin Milankovich, in 1920, who explained *why* they happened. Milankovich showed that Earth's orbit is neither circular, nor does it remain the same year after year and century after century. He proved that Earth's orbit oscillates between being more elongated and being more circular on a 40,000-year cycle. When its orbit pulled the earth a little farther away from the sun in winter, ice ages happened. NASA scientists confirmed this theory with research conducted between 2003 and 2005.

 **Fun Facts:** During the last ice age the North American glacier spread south to where St. Louis now sits and was over a mile thick over Minnesota and the Dakotas. So much ice was locked into these vast glaciers that sea level was almost 500 feet lower than it is today.

## More to Explore

Agassiz, Louis. *Louis Agassiz : His Life and Science*. Whitefish, MT: Kessinger, 2004.

Lee, Jeffery. *Great Geographers: Louis Agassiz*. New York: Focus on Geography, 2003.

Lurie, Edward. *Louis Agassiz: Life in Science*. Baltimore, MD: John Hopkins University Press, 1998.

Tallcott. Emogene. *Glacier Tracks*. New York: Lothrop, Lee & Shepard, 2000.

Teller, James. *Louis Agassiz: Scientist and Teacher*. Columbus: Ohio State University Press, 1997.

Tharp, Louis. *Louis Agassiz : Adventurous Scientist*. New York: Little, Brown, 1995.

# Calories (Units of Energy)

## Year of Discovery: 1843

> **What Is It?** All forms of energy and mechanical work are equivalent and can be converted from one form to another.
>
> **Who Discovered It?** James Joule

## Why Is This One of the 100 Greatest?

We now know that mechanical work, electricity, momentum, heat, magnetic force, etc., can be converted from one to another. There is always a loss in the process, but it can be done. That knowledge has been a tremendous help for the development of our industries and technologies. Only 200 years ago, the thought had not occurred to anyone.

James Joule discovered that every form of energy could be converted into an equivalent amount of heat. In so doing, he was the first scientist to come to grips with the general concept of energy and of how different forms of energy are equivalent to each other. Joule's discovery was an essential foundation for the discovery (40 years later) of the law of conservation of energy and for the development of the field of thermodynamics.

## How Was It Discovered?

Born on Christmas eve, 1818, James Joule grew up in a wealthy brewing family in Lancashire, England. He studied science with private tutors and, at the age of 20, started to work in the family brewery.

Joule's first self-appointed job was to see if he could convert the brewery from steam power to new, "modern" electric power. He studied engines and energy supplies. He studied electrical energy circuits and was fascinated to find that the electrical wires grew hot when current ran through them. He realized that some of the electrical energy was being converted into heat.

He felt it was important for him to quantify that electrical energy loss and began experiments on how energy was converted from electricity to heat. Often he experimented with little regard for safety—his or others. More than once, a servant girl collapsed unconscious from electrical shocks during these experiments. While he never converted the brewery to electrical power, these experiments turned his focus to the process of converting energy from one form to another.

Joule was deeply religious, and it seemed right to him that there should be a unity for all the forces of nature. He suspected that heat was somehow the ultimate and natural form for calculating the equivalence of different forms of energy.

Joule turned his attention to the conversion of mechanical energy into heat. In real life a moving body (with the mechanical energy of momentum) eventually stopped. What happened to its energy? He designed a series of experiments using water to measure the conversion of mechanical motion into heat.

Two of Joule's experiments became famous. First, he submerged an air-filled copper cylinder in a tub of water and measured the water temperature. He then pumped air into the cylinder until it reached 22 atmospheres of pressure. The gas law said that the mechanical work to create this increased air pressure should create heat. But would it? Joule measured a 0.285°F rise in water temperature. Yes, mechanical energy had been converted to heat.

Next, Joule attached paddles onto a vertical shaft that he lowered into a tub of water. Falling weights (like on a grandfather clock) spun the paddles through the tub's water. This mechanical effort *should* be partially converted to heat. But was it?

His results were inconclusive until Joule switched from water to liquid mercury. With this denser fluid, he easily proved that the mechanical effort was converted to heat at a fixed rate. Liquid was *heated* by merely *stirring* it.

Joule realized that all forms of energy could be converted into equivalent amounts of heat. He published these results in 1843 and introduced standard heat energy units to use for calculating these equivalences. Since then, physicists and chemists typically use these units and have named them *joules*. Biologists prefer to use an alternate unit called the *calorie* (4.18 joules = 1 calorie). With this discovery that any form of energy could be converted into an equivalent amount of heat energy, Joule provided a way to advance the study of energy, mechanics, and technologies.

 **Fun Facts:** The calories on a food package are actually kilocalories, or units of 1,000 calories. A kilocalorie is 1,000 times larger than the calorie used in chemistry and physics. A calorie is the amount of energy needed to raise the temperature of 1 gram of water 1 degree Celsius. If you burn up 3,500 calories during exercise, you will have burned up and lost one pound. However, even vigorous exercise rarely burns more than 1,000 calories per hour.

## More to Explore

Cardwell, Donald, ed. *The Development of Science and Technology in Nineteenth-Century Britain.* London: Ashgate Publishing, 2003.

———. *James Joule: A Biography.* New York: St. Martin's Press, 1997.

Joule, James. *The Scientific Papers of James Prescott Joule.* Washington, DC: Scholarly Press, 1996.

Smith, Crosbie. *Science of Energy.* Chicago: University of Chicago Press, 1999.

Steffens, Henry. *James Prescott Joule and the Concept of Energy.* Sagamore Beach, MA: Watson Publishing, 1999.

# Conservation of Energy

## Year of Discovery: 1847

> **What Is It?** Energy can neither be created nor lost. It may be converted from one form to another, but the total energy always remains constant within a closed system.
>
> **Who Discovered It?** Hermann von Helmholtz

## Why Is This One of the 100 Greatest?

Energy is never lost. It can change from one form to another, but the total amount of energy never changes. That principle has allowed scientists and engineers to create the power systems that run your lights and house and fuel your car. It's called conservation of energy and is one of the most important discoveries in all science. It has been called the most fundamental concept of all nature. It forms the first law of thermodynamics. It is the key to understanding energy conversion and the interchangeability of different forms of energy. When Hermann von Hemholtz assembled all of the studies and individual pieces of information to discover this principle, he changed science and engineering forever.

## How Was It Discovered?

Born in 1821 in Potsdam, Germany, Hermann von Hemholtz grew up in a family of gold merchants. At the age of 16, he took a government scholarship to study medicine in exchange for 10 years of service in the Prussian Army. Officially he studied to be a doctor at the Berlin Medical Institute. However, he often slipped over to Berlin University to attend classes on chemistry and physiology.

While serving in the army, he developed a research specialty: proving that the work muscles did was derived from chemical and physical principles and not from some "unspecified vital force." Many researchers used "vital forces" as a way to explain anything they couldn't really explain. It was as if these "vital forces" could perpetually create energy out of nothing.

Helmholtz wanted to prove that all muscle-driven motion could be accounted for by studying physical (mechanical) and chemical reactions within the muscles. He wanted to discredit the "vital force" theory. During this effort, he developed a deep belief in the concept of conservation of effort and energy. (No work could be created without coming from *somewhere* or lost without going *somewhere*.)

He studied mathematics in order to better describe the conversion of chemical energy into kinetic energy (motion and work) and the conversion of physical muscle changes into work in order to prove that all work could be accounted for by these natural, physical processes.

Helmholtz was able to prove that work could not be continually produced from "nothing." That discovery led him to form the principle of conservation of kinetic energy.

He decided to apply this principle of conservation to a variety of different situations. To do that, he studied the many pieces that had been discovered by other scientists—James Joule, Julius Mayer, Pierre Laplace, Antoine Lavoisier, and others who had studied either the conversion of one form of energy into another or the conservation of specific kinds of energy (momentum, for example).

Helmholtz augmented existing studies with his own experiments to show that, time and time again, energy was never lost. It might be converted into heat, sound, or light, but it could always be found and accounted for.

In 1847 Helmholtz realized that his work proved the *general theory* of conservation of energy: The amount of energy in the universe (or in any closed system) always remained constant. It could change between forms (electricity, magnetism, chemical energy, kinetic energy, light, heat, sound, potential energy, or momentum), but could neither be lost nor created.

The greatest challenge to Helmholtz's theory came from astronomers who studied the sun. If the sun didn't *create* light and heat energy, where did the vast amounts of energy it radiated come from? It couldn't be burning it own matter as would a normal fire. Scientists had already shown that the sun would consume itself within 20 million years if it actually burned its mass to create light and heat.

It took Helmholtz five years to realize that the answer was gravity. Slowly the sun was collapsing in on itself, and that gravitational force was being converted into light and heat. His answer was accepted (for 80 years—until nuclear energy was discovered). More important, the critical concept of conservation of energy had been discovered and accepted.

 **Fun Facts:** Conservation of energy plus the Big Bang tell us that all of the energy that ever was or ever will be anywhere in the universe was present at the moment of the Big Bang. All of the fire and heat burning in ever star, all of the fire and energy in every volcano, all of the energy in the motion of every planet, comet, and star—all of it was released at the moment of the Big Bang. Now *that* must have been one BIG explosion!

# More to Explore

Cahan, David. *Hermann von Helmholtz and the Foundations of Nineteenth-Century Science.* Berkeley: University of California Press, 1996.

———, ed. *Science and Culture : Popular and Philosophical Essays.* Chicago: University of Chicago Press, 1995.

Hyder, David. *Kant and Helmholtz on the Physical Meaning of Geometry.* Berlin: Walter De Gruyter, 2006.

McKendrick, John. *Hermann Ludwig Ferdinand von Helmholtz.* London: Longmans, Green & Co., 1995.

Warren, R. M. *Helmholtz on Perception.* New York: John Wiley & Sons, 1998.

# Doppler Effect

## Year of Discovery: 1848

> **What Is It?** Sound- and light-wave frequencies shift higher or lower depending on whether the source is moving toward or away from the observer.
>
> **Who Discovered It?** Christian Doppler

## Why Is This One of the 100 Greatest?

The Doppler Effect is one of the most powerful and important concepts ever discovered for astronomy. This discovery allowed scientists to measure the speed and direction of stars and galaxies many millions of light years away. It unlocked mysteries of distant galaxies and stars and led to the discovery of dark matter and of the actual age and motion of the universe. Doppler's discovery has been used in research efforts of a dozen scientific fields. Few single concepts have ever proved more useful. Doppler's discovery is considered to be so fundamental to science that it is included in virtually all middle and high school basic science courses.

## How Was It Discovered?

Austrian-born Christian Doppler was a struggling mathematics teacher—struggling both because he was too hard on his students and earned the wrath of parents and administrators and because he wanted to fully understand the geometry and mathematical concepts he taught. He drifted in and out of teaching positions through the 1820s and 1830s as he passed through his twenties and thirties. Doppler was lucky to land a math teaching slot at Vienna Polytechnic Institute in 1838.

By the late 1830s, trains capable of speeds in excess of 30 mph were dashing across the countryside. These trains made a sound phenomenon noticeable for the first time. Never before had humans traveled faster than the slow trot of a horse. Trains allowed people to notice the effect of an object's movement on the sounds that object produced.

Doppler intently watched trains pass and began to theorize about what caused the sound shifts he observed. By 1843 Doppler had expanded his ideas to include light waves and developed a general theory that claimed that an object's movement either increased or decreased the frequency of sound and light it produced as measured by a stationary observer. Doppler claimed that this shift could explain the red and blue tinge to the light of distant twin stars. (The twin circling toward Earth would have its light shifted to a higher frequency—toward blue. The other, circling away, would shift lower, toward red.)

In a paper he presented to the Bohemian Scientific Society in 1844, Doppler presented his theory that the motion of objects moving toward an observer compresses sound and light waves so that they appear to shift to a higher tone and to a higher frequency color (blue). The reverse happened if the object was moving away (a shift toward red). He claimed that this explained the often observed red and blue tinge of many distant stars' light. Actually, he was wrong. While *technically* correct, this shift would be too small for the instruments of his day to detect.

Doppler was challenged to prove his theory. He couldn't with light because telescopes and measuring equipment were not sophisticated enough. He decided to demonstrate his principle with sound.

In his famed 1845 experiment, he placed musicians on a railway train playing a single note on their trumpets. Other musicians, chosen for their perfect pitch, stood on the station platform and wrote down what note they heard as the train approached and then receded. What the listeners wrote down was consistently first slightly higher and then slightly lower than what the moving musicians actually played.

Doppler repeated the experiment with a second group of trumpet players on the station platform. They and the moving musicians played the same note as the train passed. Listeners could clearly hear that the notes sounded different. The moving and stationary notes seemed to interfere with each other, setting up a pulsing beat.

Having proved the existence of his effect, Doppler named it the Doppler Shift. However, he never enjoyed the fame he sought. He died in 1853 just as the scientific community was beginning to accept, and to see the value of, his discovery.

 **Fun Facts:** Doppler shifts have been used to prove that the universe is expanding. A convenient analogy for the expansion of the universe is a loaf of unbaked raisin bread. The raisins are at rest relative to one another in the dough before it is placed in the oven. As the bread rises, it also expands, making the space between the raisins increase. If the raisins could see, they would observe that all the other raisins were moving away from them although they themselves seemed to be stationary within the loaf. Only the dough—their "universe"—is expanding.

# More to Explore

Diagram Group. *Facts on File Physics Handbook.* New York: Facts on File, 2006.

Eden, Alec. *Search for Christian Doppler.* New York: Springer-Verlag, 1997.

Gill, T. P. *Doppler Effect: An Introduction to the Theory of the Effect.* Chevy Chase, MD: Elsevier Science Publishing, 1995.

Haerten, Rainer, et al. *Principles of Doppler and Color Doppler Imaging.* New York: John Wiley & Sons, 1997.

Kinsella, John. *Doppler Effect.* Cambridge, England: Salt Publishing, 2004.

# Germ Theory

## Year of Discovery: 1856

> **What Is It?** Microorganisms too small to be seen or felt exist everywhere in the air and cause disease and food spoilage.
>
> **Who Discovered It?** Louis Pasteur

## Why Is This One of the 100 Greatest?

Yogurt and other dairy products soured and curdled in just a few days. Meat rotted after a short time. Cow's and goat's milk had always been drunk as fresh milk. The consumer had to be near the animal since milk soured and spoiled in a day or two.

Then Louis Pasteur discovered that microscopic organisms floated everywhere in the air, unseen. It was these microorganisms that turned food into deadly, disease-ridden garbage. It was these same microscopic organisms that entered human flesh during operations and through cuts to cause infection and disease. Pasteur discovered the world of microbiology and developed the theory that germs cause disease. He also invented pasteurization, a simple method for removing these organisms from liquid foods.

## How Was It Discovered?

In the fall of 1856, 38-year-old Louis Pasteur was in his fourth year as Director of Scientific Affairs at the famed Ecole Normale in Paris. It was an honored administrative position. But Pasteur's heart was in pure research chemistry and he was angry.

Many scientists believed that microorganisms had no parent organism. Instead, they spontaneously generated from the decaying molecules of organic matter to spoil milk and rot meat. Felix Pouchet, the leading spokesman for this group, and had just published a paper claiming to prove this thesis.

Pasteur thought Pouchet's theory was rubbish. Pasteur's earlier discovery that microscopic live organisms (bacteria called yeasts) were always present during, and seemed to cause, the fermentation of beer and wine, made Pasteur suspect that microorganisms lived in the air and simply fell by chance onto food and all living matter, rapidly multiplying only when they found a decaying substance to use as nutrient.

Two questions were at the center of the argument. First, did living microbes *really* float in the air? Second, was it possible for microbes to grow spontaneously (in a sterile environment where no microbes already existed)?

Pasteur heated a glass tube to sterilize both the tube and the air inside. He plugged the open end with guncotton and used a vacuum pump to draw air through the cotton filter and into this sterile glass tube.

Pasteur reasoned that any microbes floating in the air should be concentrated on the outside of the cotton filter as air was sucked through. Bacterial growth on the filter indicated microbes floating freely in the air. Bacterial growth in the sterile interior of the tube meant spontaneous generation.

After 24 hours the outside of his cotton wad turned dingy gray with bacterial growth while the inside of the tube remained clear. Question number 1 was answered. Yes, microscopic organisms did exist, floating, in the air. Any time they concentrated (as on a cotton wad) they began to multiply.

Now for question number 2. Pasteur had to prove that microscopic bacteria could not spontaneously generate.

Pasteur mixed a nutrient-rich bullion (a favorite food of hungry bacteria) in a large beaker with a long, curving glass neck. He heated the beaker so that the bullion boiled and the glass glowed. This killed any bacteria already in the bullion or in the air inside the beaker. Then he quickly stoppered this sterile beaker. Any growth in the beaker now had to come from spontaneous generation.

He slid the beaker into a small warming oven, used to speed the growth of bacterial cultures.

Twenty-four hours later, Pasture checked the beaker. All was crystal clear. He checked every day for eight weeks. Nothing grew at all in the beaker. Bacteria did not spontaneously generate.

Pasteur broke the beaker's neck and let normal, unsterilized air flow into the beaker. Seven hours later he saw the first faint tufts of bacterial growth. Within 24 hours, the surface of the bullion was covered.

Pouchet was wrong. Without the original airborne microbes floating into contact with a nutrient, there was no bacterial growth. They did not spontaneously generate.

Pasteur triumphantly published his discoveries. More important, his discovery gave birth to a brand new field of study, microbiology.

 **Fun Facts:** The typical household sponge holds as many as 320 million disease-causing germs.

# More to Explore

Clark, Donald. *Encyclopedia of Great Inventors and Discoveries*. London: Marshall Cavendish Books, 1991.

Dubos, Rene. *Pasteur and Modern Science*. Madison, WI: Science Tech Publishers, 1998.

Dyson, James. *A History of Great Inventions*. New York: Carroll & Graf Publishers, 2001.

Fullick, Ann. *Louis Pasteur*. Portsmouth, NH: Heinemann Library, 2000.

Gogerly, Liz. *Louis Pasteur*. New York: Raintree, 2002.

Silverthorne, Elizabeth. *Louis Pasteur*. New York: Thomson Gale, 2004.

Smith, Linda. *Louis Pasteur: Disease Fighter*. Berkeley Heights, NJ: Enslow Publishers, 2001.

Yount, Lisa. *Louis Pasteur*. New York: Thomson Gale, 1995.

# The Theory of Evolution

## Year of Discovery: 1858

> **What Is It?** Species evolve over time to best take advantage of their surrounding environment, and those species most fit for their environment survive best.
>
> **Who Discovered It?** Charles Darwin

## Why Is This One of the 100 Greatest?

Darwin's theory of evolution and its concept of survival of the fittest is the most fundamental and important discovery of modern biology and ecology. Darwin's discoveries are 150 years old and are still the foundation of our understanding of the history and evolution of plant and animal life.

Darwin's discovery answered countless mysteries for anthropology and paleontology. It made sense out of the wide distribution and special design of species and subspecies on Earth. While it has always stirred controversy and opposition, Darwin's theory has been verified and supported by mountains of careful scientific data over the past 150 years. His books were best sellers in his day and they are still widely read today.

## How Was It Discovered?

Charles Darwin entered Cambridge University in 1827 to become a priest, but switched to geology and botany. He graduated in 1831 and, at age 22, took a position as naturalist aboard the HMS *Beagle* bound from England for South America and the Pacific.

The *Beagle's* three-year voyage stretched into five. Darwin forever marveled at the unending variety of species in each place the ship visited. But it was their extended stop at the Pacific Ocean Galapagos Islands that focused Darwin's wonder into a new discovery.

On the first island in the chain he visited (Chatham Island), Darwin found two distinct species of tortoise—one with long necks that ate leaves from trees, and one with short necks that ate ground plants. He also found four new species of finches (small, yellow birds common across much of Europe). But these had differently shaped beaks from their European cousins.

The *Beagle* reached the third Galapagos Island (James Island) in October 1835. Here, right on the equator, no day or season seemed any different than any other.

As he did every day on shore, Darwin hoisted his backpack with jars and bags for collecting samples, a notebook for recording and sketching, and his nets and traps and set off across the frightful landscape through twisted fields of crunchy black lava thrown up into giant, ragged waves. Gaping fissures from which dense steam and noxious yellow vapors hissed from deep in the rock blocked his path. The broken lava was covered by stunted, sun-burned brushwood that looked far more dead than alive.

In a grove of trees filled with chirping birds, Darwin found his thirteenth and fourteenth new species of finches. Their beaks were larger and rounder than any he'd seen on other islands. More important, these finches ate small red berries.

Everywhere else on Earth finches ate seeds. In these islands some finches ate seeds, some insects, and some berries! More amazingly, each species of finch had a beak perfectly shaped to gather the specific type of food that species preferred to eat.

Darwin began to doubt the Christian teaching that God created each species just as it was and that species were unchanging. He deduced that, long ago, *one* variety of finch arrived in the Galapagos from South America, spread out to the individual islands, and then adapted (evolved) to best survive in its particular environment and with its particular sources of food. These findings he reported in his book, *A Naturalist's Voyage on the Beagle*.

After his return to England, Darwin read the collected essays of economist Thomas Malthus, who claimed that, when human populations could not produce enough food, the weakest people starved, died of disease, or were killed in fighting. Only the strong survived. Darwin realized that this concept should apply to the animal world as well.

He blended this idea with his experiences and observations on the *Beagle* to conclude that all species evolved to better ensure species survival. He called it natural selection.

A shy and private man, Darwin agonized for years about revealing his theories to the public. Other naturalists finally convinced him to produce and publish *Origin of Species*. With that book, Darwin's discoveries and theory of evolution became the guiding light of biological sciences.

 **Fun Facts:** Bats, with their ultrasonic echolocation, have evolved the most acute hearing of any terrestrial animal. With it, bats can detect insects the size of gnats and objects as fine as a human hair.

# More to Explore

Aydon, Cyril. *Charles Darwin: The Naturalist Who Started a Scientific Revolution.* New York: Carroll & Graf, 2003.

Bowlby, John. *Charles Darwin: A New Life.* New York: W. W. Norton, 1998.

Bowler, Peter. *Charles Darwin: The Man and His Influence.* New York: Cambridge University Press, 1998.

Browne, Janet. *Charles Darwin: Voyaging.* London: Jonathan Cape, 1998.

Dennet, Daniel. *Darwin's Dangerous Idea: Evolution and the Meanings of Life.* New York: Simon & Schuster, 1996.

Jenkins, Steve. *Life on Earth: The Story of Evolution.* New York: Houghton Mifflin, 2002.

Mayr, Ernst. *One Long Argument: Charles Darwin and the Genesis of Modern Evolutionary Thought.* Cambridge, MA: Harvard University Press, 1997.

Woram, John. *Charles Darwin Slept Here.* Rockville Center, NY: Rockville Press, 2005.

# Atomic Light Signatures

## Year of Discovery: 1859

**What Is It?** When heated, every element radiates light at very specific and characteristic frequencies.

**Who Discovered It?** Gustav Kirchhoff and Robert Bunsen

## Why Is This One of the 100 Greatest?

Twenty new elements (beginning with the discovery of cesium in 1860) were discovered using one chemical analysis technique. That same technique allows astronomers to determine the chemical composition of stars millions of light years away. It also allowed physicists to understand our sun's atomic fires that produce heat and light. That same technique allows other astronomers to calculate the exact speed and motion of distant stars and galaxies.

That one technique is spectrographic analysis, the discovery of Kirchhoff and Bunsen, which analyzes the light emitted from burning chemicals or from a distant star. They discovered that each element emits light only at its own specific frequencies. Spectrography provided the first proof that the elements of Earth are also found in other heavenly bodies—that Earth was not chemically unique in the universe. Their techniques are routinely used by scientists in virtually every field of science in the biological, physical, and earth sciences.

## How Was It Discovered?

In 1814, German astronomer Joseph Fraunhofer discovered that the sun's energy was not radiated evenly in all frequencies of the light spectrum, but rather was concentrated in spikes of energy at certain specific frequencies. Some thought it interesting, none thought it important. The idea lay dormant for 40 years.

Gustav Kirchhoff (born in 1824) was an energetic Polish physicist who barely stood five feet in height. Through the mid-1850s he focused his research on electrical currents at the University of Breslau. In 1858, while helping another professor with a side project, Kirchhoff noted bright lines in the light spectrum produced by flames and recalled having read about a similar occurrence in Fraunhofer's articles. Upon investigation, Kirchhoff found that the bright spots (or spikes) in the light from his flame studies were at the exact same frequency and wave lengths that Fraunhofer had detected in solar radiation.

Kirchhoff pondered what this could mean and was struck by what turned out to be a brilliant insight: use a prism to separate any light beam he wanted to study into its constituent parts (instead of peering at it through a sequence of colored glass filters as was the custom of the day). Kirchhoff believed that this would let him find spikes in the radiation coming from any burning gas.

However, the scheme did not work well. The flame he used to heat his gasses was too bright and interfered with his observations.

Enter Robert Bunsen, the German-born chemist. In 1858, 47-year-old Bunsen had been developing photochemistry—the study of light given off by burning elements. During this work, Bunsen had invented a new kind of burner in which air and gas were mixed prior to burning. This burner (which we still use and call a Bunsen burner) produced an extremely hot (over 2700°F) flame that produced very little light.

Kirchhoff and Bunsen connected at the University of Heidelberg in 1859. Standing together, Kirchhoff barely reached Bunsen's shoulder. The pair combined Kirchhoff's prism idea with Bunsen's burner and spent six months to design and build the first spectrograph (a device to burn chemical samples and use a prism to separate the light they produced into a spectrum of individual frequencies).

They began to catalog the spectral lines (specific frequencies where each element radiated its light energy) of each known element and discovered that each and every element always produced the same "signature" set of spectral lines that uniquely identified the presence of that element.

Armed with this discovery and their catalog of each element's characteristic spectral lines, Kirchhoff and Bunsen made the first complete chemical analysis of seawater and of the sun—proving that hydrogen, helium, sodium, and half-a-dozen other trace elements common on Earth existed in the sun's atmosphere. This proved for the first time that Earth was not chemically unique in the universe.

Kirchhoff and Bunsen had given science one of its most versatile and flexible analytical tools and had discovered a way to determine the composition of any star with the same accuracy as we determine sulfuric acid, chlorine, or any other compound.

 **Fun Facts:** Kirchhoff and Bunsen used their spectrograph to discover two new elements: cesium in 1860 (they chose that name because cesium means "sky blue," the color of its spectrograph flame) and rubidium in 1861. This element has a bright red line in its spectrograph. *Rubidium* comes from the Latin word for red.

# More to Explore

Clark, Donald. *Encyclopedia of Great Inventors and Discoveries*. London: Marshall Cavendish Books, 1991.

Diagram Group. *Facts on File Chemistry Handbook*. New York: Facts on File, 2000.

Laidler, Keith. *World of Physical Chemistry*. New York: Oxford University Press, 1995.

Lomask, Milton. *Invention and Technology Great Lives*. New York: Charles Scribner's Sons, 1994.

Philbin, Tom. *The 100 Greatest Inventions of All Time*. New York: Citadel Press, 2003.

Schwacz, Joe. *The Man Behind the Burner: Robert Bunsen's Discoveries Changed the World of Chemistry in More Ways Than One*. Chicago: Thomas Gale, 2005.

Tuniz, R. J. *Accelerator Mass Spectrometry*. New York: CRC Press, 1998.

# Electromagnetic Radiation/ Radio Waves

## Year of Discovery: 1864

**What Is It?** All electric and magnetic energy waves are part of the one electromagnetic spectrum and follow simple mathematical rules.

**Who Discovered It?** James Clerk Maxwell

## Why Is This One of the 100 Greatest?

Throughout most of the nineteenth century, people thought that electricity, magnetism, and light were three separate, unrelated things. Research proceeded from that assumption. Then Maxwell discovered that they are all the same—forms of electromagnetic radiation. It was a startlingly grand discovery, often called the greatest discovery in physics in the nineteenth century. Maxwell did for electromagnetic radiation what Newton did for gravity—gave science mathematical tools to understand and use that natural force.

Maxwell unified magnetic and electrical energy, created the term *electromagnetic* radiation, and discovered the four simple equations that govern the behavior of electrical and magnetic fields. While developing these equations, Maxwell discovered that light was part of the electromagnetic spectrum and predicted the existence of radio waves, X-rays, and gamma rays.

## How Was It Discovered?

James Clerk was born in 1831 in Edinburgh, Scotland. The family later added the name Maxwell. James sailed easily through his university schooling to earn top honors and a degree in mathematics. He held various professorships in math and physics thereafter.

As a mathematician, Maxwell explored the world—and the universe—through mathematic equations. His chose the rings of Saturn as the subject of his first major study. Maxwell used mathematics to prove that these rings couldn't be solid disks, nor could they consist of gas. His equations showed that they must consist of countless small, solid particles. A century later, astronomers proved him to be correct.

Maxwell turned his attention to gasses and studied the mathematical relationships that governed the motion of rapidly moving gas particles. His results in this study completely revised science's approach to studying the relationship between heat (temperature) and gas motion.

**83**

In 1860 he turned his attention to early electrical work by Michael Faraday. Faraday invented the electric motor by discovering that a spinning metal disk in a magnetic field created an electric current and that a changing electric current also changed a magnetic field and could create physical motion.

Maxwell decided to mathematically explore the relationship between electricity and magnetism and the "electrical and magnetic lines of force" that Faraday had discovered.

As Maxwell searched for mathematical relationships between various aspects of electricity and magnetism, he devised experiments to test and confirm each of his results. By 1864 he had derived four simple equations that described the behavior of electrical and magnetic fields and their interrelated nature. Oscillating (changing) electrical fields (ones whose electrical current rapidly shifted back and forth) produced magnetic fields and vice versa.

The two types of energy were integrally connected. Maxwell realized that electricity and magnetism were simply two expressions of a single energy stream and named it *electromagnetic* energy. When he first published these equations and his discoveries in an 1864 article, physicists instantly recognized the incredible value and meaning of Maxwell's four equations.

Maxwell continued to work with his set of equations and realized that—as long as the electrical source oscillated at a high enough frequency—the electromagnetic energy waves it created could and would fly through the open air—without conducting wires to travel along. This was the first prediction of radio waves.

He calculated the speed at which these electromagnetic waves would travel and found that it matched the best calculations (at that time) of the speed of light. From this, Maxwell realized that light itself was just another form of electromagnetic radiation. Because electrically charged currents can oscillate at any frequency, Maxwell realized that light was only a tiny part of a vast and continuous spectrum of electromagnetic radiation.

Maxwell predicted that other forms of electromagnetic radiation along other parts of this spectrum would be found. As he predicted, X-rays were discovered in 1896 by Wilhelm Roentgen. Eight years before that discovery, Heinrich Hertz conducted experiments following Maxwell's equations to see if he could cause electromagnetic radiation to fly through the air (transmit through space in the form of waves of energy). He easily created and detected the world's first radio waves, confirming Maxwell's equations and predictions.

 **Fun Facts:** Astronomers have concluded that the most efficient way of making contact with an intelligent civilization orbiting another star is to use radio waves. However, there are many natural processes in the universe that produce radio waves. If we could translate those naturally produced radio waves into sound, they would sound like static we hear on a radio. In the search for intelligent life, astronomers use modern computers to distinguish between a "signal" (possible message) and the "noise" (static).

# More to Explore

Campbell, Lewis. *The Life of James Clerk Maxwell.* Dover, DE: Adamant Media, 2001.

Francis, C. W. *James Clerk Maxwell: Physicist and Natural Philosopher.* New York: Scribner's, 1994.

Harmon, Peter. *The Natural Philosophy of James Clerk Maxwell.* New York: Cambridge University Press, 2001.

Mahon, Basil. *The Man Who Changed Everything : The Life of James Clerk Maxwell.* New York: John Wiley & Sons, 2004.

Maxwell, James. *Matter and Motion.* Amherst, NY: Prometheus Books, 2002.

# Heredity

Year of Discovery: 1865

> **What Is It?** The natural system that passes traits and characteristics from one generation to the next.
>
> **Who Discovered It?** Gregor Mendel

## Why Is This One of the 100 Greatest?

Gregor Mendel conducted the first serious study of heredity. His findings, his methods, and his discoveries laid the foundation for the field of genetics and the study of genes and heredity. The discoveries of genes, chromosomes, DNA, and the decoding of the human genome (completed in 2003) are all direct descendents of Mendel's work. The medical breakthroughs in the fights to cure dozens of diseases are offshoots of the work begun by Gregor Mendel.

Finally, Mendel's discovery, itself, provided great insights into the role of inherited traits and into the ways those traits are passed form generation to generation.

## How Was It Discovered?

The wide fields and gardens of the Austrian Monastery of Bruun stretched up gently sloping hills surrounding the monastery complex. Tucked into one corner of the monastery's garden complex stood a small 120-foot-by-20-foot plot. This small garden laboratory was used by one of the monks, Father Gregor Mendel, for his experiments on heredity; that is, on how individual traits are blended from an individual through successive generations into a population. In May 1865, he planted his sixth year of experimental pea plants.

English scientist Charles Darwin explained evolution but hadn't successfully addressed *how* characteristics are passed down through the generations, some to dominate (appear) in every generation—some to randomly pop up only every now and then. That was what Mendel wanted to study.

Mendel crossed a strain of tall pea plants with one of short pea plants. He produced a row of all tall plants. And when he planted the seeds of those tall plants he got *mostly* tall with a few short plants. The short trait returned in the second generation.

Similarly, he crossbred yellow peas with green peas and got a generation of all yellow peas. But in the next generation he produced *mostly* yellow with a few green peas. But never a yellow-green. The green color trait returned but the traits never mixed. The same happened when he crossbred smooth-skinned with wrinkled-skinned peas.

Over six years of work, Mendel found the same pattern in every crossbreeding experiment he tried. In the second generation, one plant in four switched and showed the recessive trait (the trait that hadn't showed up at all in the first generation). Always three to one.

He knew that a plant inherited one version of each trait (or gene) from father and mother plants. But what if, in each pairing of traits, one trait were always stronger (dominant), and one always weaker (recessive)? Then, when the traits mixed, a first-generation plant would always show the dominant one (all yellow, or all tall).

But three to one . . . . That happened in the second generation. Mendel realized simple mathematical probability said there could be four possible combinations of traits in a second-generation plant (either dominant or recessive trait from either father or mother plant). In *three* of those combinations at least one dominant trait would be present, and that would dictate what the plant became. In only *one* combination (recessive trait from both parents) would there be nothing but recessive traits present. Three to one.

Traits did not mix. They were inherited from generation to generation and appear only when they are dominant in an individual plant. Traits from countless ancestors flow into each of us, in separate packages called "genes," unblended for us to pass on even if a trait doesn't "show" in our generation.

It was not until 1900 that another scientist—Dutchman Hugo de Vries—realized the scientific value of Mendel's great gift to the world with his insights on heredity.

 **Fun Facts:** Gregor Mendel's concept of heredity required two parents. Dolly the sheep made scientific history in 1997 when she was created from the cells of a single adult sheep in a Scottish lab. She was *cloned,* an exact genetic duplicate of her mother, with no contributing gene cells from a father.

# More to Explore

Bankston, John. *Gregor Mendel and the Discovery of the Gene.* Hockessin, DE: Mitchell Lane, 2004.

Bardoe, Cheryl. *Gregor Mendel: The Friar Who Grew Peas.* New York: Abrams Books for Young Readers, 2006.

George, Wilma. *Gregor Mendel and Heredity.* Wayland, England: Howe Publishers, 1995.

Gribben, John. *Mendel in 90 Minutes.* London: Constable Press, 1997.

Haven, Kendall. *Marvels of Science.* Englewood, CO: Libraries Unlimited, 1995.

Henig, Robin. *The Monk in the Garden: The Lost and Found Genius of Gregor Mendel.* New York: Houghton Mifflin, 2000.

Yannuzzi, Della. *Gregor Mendel: Genetics Pioneer.* New York: Franklin Watts, 2004.

# Deep-Sea Life

## Year of Discovery: 1870

**What Is It?** Eternally black, deep ocean waters are not lifeless deserts, but support abundant life.

**Who Discovered It?** Charles Thomson

## Why Is This One of the 100 Greatest?

Charles Thomson radically changed science's view of deep oceans and of the requirements for life in the oceans. There existed no light in the ocean depths, yet he discovered abundant and varied life. He proved that life can exist without light. He even proved that *plants* can thrive in the lightless depths (though it took another century before scientists figured out *how* plants live without photosynthesis).

Thomson's discovery extended known ocean life from the thin top layer of the oceans into the vast depths and provided the first scientific study of the deep oceans. For his discoveries, Thomson was knighted by Queen Victoria in 1877.

## How Was It Discovered?

Charles Thomson was born in 1830 in the salt air of the Scottish coast. After college, he worked at various university research and teaching positions until, in 1867, he was appointed professor of botany at the Royal College of Science in Dublin, Ireland.

Common wisdom at the time said that, since light only penetrated the top 250 to 300 feet of the oceans, life only existed in that same narrow top layer where light could support the growth of ocean plants. The deep oceans were lifeless, lightless deserts. No one bothered to question the logic of this belief. Then, in early 1866, Michael Sars conducted some deep dredging operations off the coast of Norway as part of a cable-laying project. He claimed that his dredge snared fish at depths of over 1,000 feet.

Scientists scoffed and said that his dredge must have caught the fish either on the way down or on the way back up. He *couldn't* have caught them at a depth that far below the ocean's "life zone" because nothing could live down there.

However, the report caught Thomson's imagination. He began to wonder: What if living creatures *did* lurk in the vast, dark depths of the ocean? Were ocean depths the lifeless desert everyone imagined? Without actually going there, how could anyone really know?

Convinced that this question was worthy of serious scientific investigation, Thomson persuaded the Royal Navy to grant him use of the HMS *Lightning* and HMS *Porcupine* for summer dredging expeditions for three consecutive summers: 1868, 1869, and 1870. During these voyages off the English and Scottish coasts, Thomson used deep sea nets and dredges to see what life he could find in waters over 2,000 feet deep. Most scientists thought that he was wasting his time and the navy's money and would make a fool of himself.

Over those three brief summers, Thomson made over 370 deep-sea soundings. He dragged his nets and dredges through the oceans at depths of up to 4,000 feet (1,250 meters) and consistently found the presence of life at all surveyed depths. His nets always snared a variety of invertebrates and fish.

Thomson had discovered that whole populations of fish lived and thrived in the ocean depths where no light ever penetrated to spoil the total blackness.

He also collected water samples from the deep, inky-black waters and found the constant presence of detritus—dead plant life that fell through the water column to reach the depths without being eaten. Marine animals also died and added to this rain of food to support creatures that lived in the depths.

Thomson found all known marine invertebrate species living at these depths as well as many unknown fish species. He also dredged up bottom-dwelling plants, proving that plants grew and thrived without sunlight. He reported his startling discoveries in his 1873 book *The Depths of the Sea*—published just after Thomson set sail on the *Challenger* for an extended, five-year voyage to complete his 70,000 nautical miles of deep-sea research data collection that proved that deep-sea life existed in all of the world's oceans.

 **Fun Facts:** The largest giant squid ever studied was 36 feet long when it washed up dead on a South American beach. The circular suckers on its two long arms measured 2.2 inches across. Sperm whales have been caught with fresh scars from giant squid suckers measuring over 22 inches across. That translates to a monster squid over 220 feet long! They're out there, but no human has seen one since sailors talked of meeting giant sea monsters hundreds of years ago.

# More to Explore

Collard, Sneed. *The Deep-Sea Floor*. Watertown, MA: Charlesbridge Publishing, 2003.

Gibbons, Gail. *Exploring the Deep Dark Sea*. New York: Little, Brown, 1999.

Hall, Michele. *Secrets of the Ocean Realm*. New York: Carroll &d Graf, 1997.

Herring, Peter. *The Biology of the Deep Ocean*. New York: Oxford University Press, 2002.

Tyler, P. A. *Ecosystems of the Deep Ocean*. Chevy Chase, MD: Elsevier Science Publishing, 2003.

Van Dover, Cindy. *Deep-Ocean Journeys: Discovering New Life at the Bottom of the Sea*. New York: Addison Wesley, 1997.

# Periodic Chart of Elements

## Year of Discovery: 1880

> **What Is It?** The first successful organizing system for the chemical elements that compose Earth.
>
> **Who Discovered It?** Dmitri Mendeleyev

## Why Is This One of the 100 Greatest?

When most people think of the chemical elements, they picture Mendeleyev's Periodic Chart of the Elements. This organizational table has served as the one accepted organizing system for the elements that make up our planet for 125 years. It is so important that it is taught to every student in beginning chemistry classes. It led to the discovery of new elements and has been a cornerstone of chemists' understanding of the properties and relationships of Earth's elements. It has also helped in the design and conduct of chemical experiments and greatly sped the development of science's understanding of the basic elements in the early twentieth century.

## How Was It Discovered?

By 1867, 33-year-old Dmitri Mendeleyev had landed a position as chemistry professor at St. Petersburg University—a remarkable accomplishment for the youngest of 14 children of a Russian peasant. With an untamed thicket of hair, a wild, trailing beard, and dark, penetrating eyes, Mendeleyev was called "that wild Russian" by other chemists in Europe. In 1868 he began work on a chemistry textbook for his students.

The question he faced in beginning the book was how to arrange and organize the growing list of 62 known elements so that his students could understand their characteristics. By this time, Mendeleyev had collected a hoard of data from his own work and—mostly—from the work of others, especially from the English chemists Newland and Meyers and Frenchman de Chancourtois.

Mendeleyev sorted the elements by atomic weight; by family resemblance; by the way they did—or did not—combine with hydrogen, carbon, and oxygen; by the kind of salts they formed; by whether an element existed as a gas, liquid, or solid; by whether an element is hard or soft; by whether an element melts at a high or low temperature; and by the shape of the element's crystals. Nothing allowed him to make sense of all 62 known elements.

Then Mendeleyev, a skilled piano player, realized that the notes on a piano repeated at regular intervals. Every eighth key was a "C." He realized that in seasons, in waves at the beach, even in trees, characteristics repeat over and over after a set period of time or distance. Why shouldn't the same thing happen with the elements?

He wrote each element and its various characteristics on cards and spread them across a table, arranging and rearranging the cards, searching for repeating patterns. He quickly found that every eighth element shared many family traits, or characteristics. That is, *most* of the time, every eighth element shared characteristics with the others in this family. But not always.

Mendeleyev was again stuck. One day that summer, it struck him that it was possible that not all of Earth's elements had been discovered. His chart of the elements had to allow for missing elements.

He returned to his stack of cards and arranged them into rows and columns so that the way that the elements in each column bonded with other elements was the same, and so that the physical characteristics of the elements in each row were the same.

All of the known elements fit perfectly into this two-dimensional chart. However, he had to leave three holes in the chart that he claimed would be filled by three as-yet-undiscovered elements. Mendeleyev even described what these "missing" elements would look like and act like based on the common traits of other elements in their row and column. All Europe laughed and said his predictions were the crazy ramblings of a wild fortuneteller.

Three years later the first of Mendeleyev's "missing" elements was discovered in Germany. The scientific community thought it an interesting coincidence. Within eight years the other two had also been found. All three looked and behaved just as Mendeleyev had predicted.

Scientists around the world were amazed and called Mendeleev a genius who had unlocked the mysteries of the world of chemical elements. His discovery has guided chemical research ever since.

 **Fun Facts:** Mendeleyev's periodic chart helped dispel the ancient alchemist's myth of turning lead into gold. In 1980, American scientist Glenn Seaborg used a powerful cyclotron to remove protons and neutrons from several thousand atoms of lead (atomic number 82), changing it into gold (atomic number 79). No, he didn't create instant wealth. The process is so expensive that each atom of gold he created cost as much as several ounces of gold on the open market.

# More to Explore

Atkins, P. *The Periodic Kingdom.* New York: Weidenfeld and Nicolson, 1999.

———. *Periodic Kingdom: A Journey into the Land of the Chemical Element.* New York: Basic Books, 1997.

Gordon, Michael. *A Well-Ordered Thing: Dmitri Mendeleev and the Shadow of the Periodic Table.* Jackson, TN: Basic Books, 2004.

Jensen, William, ed. *Mendeleev on the Periodic Law.* New York: Dover, 2005.

Strathern, Paul. *Mendeleyev's Dream: The Quest for the Elements.* New York: St. Martin's Press, 2001.

Zannos, Susan. *Dmitri Mendeleev and the Periodic Table.* Hockessin, DE: Mitchell Lane, 2004.

# Cell Division

## Year of Discovery: 1882

> **What Is It?** The process by which chromosomes split so that cells can divide to produce new cells.
>
> **Who Discovered It?** Walther Flemming

## Why Is This One of the 100 Greatest?

Chromosomes carry genes that hold the blueprints for building, operating, and maintaining the cells of your body. Genetics and heredity research could not advance until these physical structures inside the nucleus of each cell had been discovered and studied. Our basic understanding of biology also depends, in part, on our knowledge of how cells divide, replicating themselves countless times over the course of an organism's life.

Both of these key concepts were discovered during one experiment carried out by Walther Flemming. His discoveries form part of the basic foundation of modern biological sciences. Much of what we know today about cell division (called *mitosis*) originated with Flemming's discoveries.

## How Was It Discovered?

For most of the nineteenth century, studies of cells, cell functions, and cell structure through the microscope were hampered because cell walls and all of their internal parts were translucent to transparent. No matter how good the microscope was, these inner structures were seen only as vague grey-on-grey shapes. It was difficult—if not impossible—to make out any detail.

So scientists stained the cells with dyes, hoping to make the cell parts more visible. However, all dyes killed the cells. But there was no other way and, hopefully, the dye would combine with *some* intracellular structures and not with others so that a few would stand out and be easily studied through the microscope. Most dyes, however, didn't work. They smeared the whole cell with dark color and masked the very structures they were supposed to reveal.

Walther Flemming was born in 1843 in Sachsenberg, Germany. He trained as a doctor and taught at universities from 1873 (at the age of 30) until 1905 (age 62). He called himself an anatomist and specialized in the microscopic study of cells.

In 1879 Flemming found a new dye (a by-product of coal tar) that combined well with particular, stringlike materials inside the cell nucleus and did not stain most other cell parts. Finally, a dye existed that allowed him to focus his observations on one particular structure within the cell's nucleus.

He named the material stained by this dye *chromatin* (from the Greek word for color) and began a series of experiments using salamander embryos. Flemming cut tissue-paper thin slices of embryonic cells from fertilized salamander eggs and stained them with this dye.

The dye, of course, killed the cells. This stopped all cell activity and cell division. But it was a price Flemming had to pay in order to study these *chromatin* structures within the cell nucleus. Since the cells were dead before he could observe them, what Flemming saw through his microscope was a series of "still" images of cells frozen in various stages of division. Over time, and with enough samples to study, he was able to arrange these images in order to show the steps of the cell division process.

As the process began, the *chromatin* collected into short, threadlike objects (whose name Flemming changed from *chromatin* to *chromosomes* from the Greek words meaning "colored bodies"). It was soon clear to Flemming that these threadlike chromosomes were a key feature of cell division. Therefore, Flemming named the process *mitosis,* from the Greek word for thread. The words *chromosomes* and *mitosis* are still used today.

Flemming saw that the next step was for each individual *chromosome* thread to break into two identical threads, doubling the number of *chromosomes*. These two identical sets of *chromosomes* then pulled apart, half going to one end of the cell, half going to the other. The cell itself then divided. Each of the two offspring cells was thus stocked with a complete set of *chromosomes* that was identical to the original parent.

Flemming had discovered the process of cell division and published his results in 1882. The real value of Flemming's discovery lay hidden for 18 years. Then, in 1900, Hugo deVries put Flemming's discovery together with Gregor Mendel's discoveries on heredity and realized that Flemming had discovered how hereditary traits were passed from parent to child and from cell to cell.

 **Fun Facts:** Like all living species, humans grow from a single egg cell into complex organisms with trillions of cells. Louise Brown, born July 25, 1978, in Oldham, England, was the first human test-tube baby. Her first cell divisions took place not in her mother's womb, but in a laboratory test tube.

## More to Explore

Adler, Robert. *Medical Firsts.* New York: John Wiley & Sons, 2004.

Alberts, Bruce. *Molecular Biology of the Cell.* Abingdon, England: Taylor & Francis, 1999.

Boorstin, Daniel. *The Discoverers: A History of Man's Search to Know His World and Himself.* New York: Random House, 1997.

Enslow, Sharyn, ed. *Dynamics of Cell Division.* New York: Oxford University Press, 1998.

Larison, L. L. *The Center of Life: A Natural History of the Cell.* New York: New York Times Book Co., 1997.

Snedden, Robert. *Cell Division and Genetics.* Portsmouth, NH: Heinemann, 2002.

# X-Rays

## Year of Discovery: 1895

**What Is It?** High-frequency radiation that can penetrate through human flesh.

**Who Discovered It?** Wilhelm Roentgen

## Why Is This One of the 100 Greatest?

If you have ever had an X-ray as part of a medical checkup, you owe thanks to Wilhelm Roentgen. Medical X-rays have been one of the most powerful, useful, and life-saving diagnostic tools ever developed. X-rays were the first noninvasive technique developed to allow doctors to see inside the body. X-rays led to the more modern MRI and CT technologies.

Chemists have used X-rays to understand and decipher the structure of complex molecules (such as penicillin) and to better understand the electromagnetic spectrum. The discovery of X-rays earned Roentgen the 1901 Nobel Prize in physics.

## How Was It Discovered?

In 1895 Wilhelm Roentgen was just a 40-something academic professor at the University of Wurzburg, Germany, doing ho-hum research into the effects of passing electricity through gas-filled bottles. In November of that year he began experiments in his home basement lab with a Crookes' tube (a device that amplified an electrical signal by passing it through a vacuum).

On November 8, he happened to notice that a photographic plate that had been wrapped in black paper and tucked inside a leather case in the bottom drawer of his desk had mysteriously been exposed and imprinted with the image of a key. The only key in the room was an oversized key for a garden gate he had tossed into the desk's center drawer over a year ago. The image on his photographic plate was of that key.

Even more strange, he found that the key in the center drawer lay along a straight line from his glass Crookes' tube mounted on the wall to the photographic plate deep in the bottom drawer. But no visible rays emitted from the Crookes' tube and surely no light could have penetrated through the desk and leather case to the photographic plate. What could have mysteriously flown across the room and passed through wood, leather, and paper to expose the photographic plate? Whatever it was, it could not pass through the metal key—which was why a dark gray image of the key was outlined on his photograph.

Other scientists theorized that rays would be emitted from a Crookes' tube and had named them cathode rays after the name of one of the metal plates inside the tube. Crookes thought these rays might come from another world. But no one had detected, measured, or studied these unknown rays.

Roentgen suspected that cathode rays had somehow exposed his film. Two weeks later he was able to prove the existence of these mysterious rays, which he named "X-rays" since "X" was used to represent the unknown. By this time, he had seen that X-rays could pass through wood, paper, cardboard, cement, cloth, and even most metals—but not lead.

For this experiment, Roentgen coated a sheet of paper with barium platino-cyanide (a kind of fluorescent salt) and hung it on the far wall of his lab. When he connected power to his Crookes' tube, the fluorescent sheet glowed a faint green. When he held an iron disk in front of the paper, the paper turned back to black where the iron disk blocked the X-rays.

Roentgen was shocked to also see the outline of every bone in his hand and arm in faint green outlines on the fluorescent paper. When he moved a finger, the bones outlined in glowing green also moved.

On seeing these first X-ray images, Roentgen's wife shrieked in terror and thought that the rays were evil harbingers of death. Roentgen, however, began six weeks of intensive study before releasing his results on the nature and potential of X-rays.

Within a month Wilhelm Roentgen's X-rays were the talk of the world. Skeptics called them death rays that would destroy the human race. Eager dreamers called them miracle rays that could make the blind see again and could beam complex charts and diagrams straight into a student's brain.

Doctors called X-rays the answer to a prayer.

 **Fun Facts:** The Z Machine at the Sandia National Laboratories, New Mexico, can, very briefly, produce X-rays with a power output roughly equivalent to 80 times that of *all* of the world's electrical generators.

# More to Explore

Aaseng, Nathan. *The Inventors.* Minneapolis, MN: Lerner Publications, 1998.

Claxton, Keith. *Wilhelm Roentgen.* London: Heron Books, 1994.

Dibner, Bern. *Wilhelm Conrad Röntgen and the Discovery of X-Rays.* New York: Franklin Watts, 1998.

Esterer, Arnulf. *Discoverer of X-Rays: Wilhelm Roentgen.* New York: J. Messner, 1997.

Garcia, Kimberly. *Wilhelm Roentgen and the Discovery of X-Rays.* Hockessin, DE: Mitchell Lane, 2002.

Nitske, Robert. *The Life of Wilhelm Conrad Röntgen, Discoverer of the X-Ray.* Tucson: University of Arizona Press, 1996.

# Blood Types

## Year of Discovery: 1897

**What Is It?** Humans have different types of blood that are not all compatible.

**Who Discovered It?** Karl Landsteiner

## Why Is This One of the 100 Greatest?

Blood was blood—or so the world thought. Then Austrian physician Karl Landsteiner discovered that there were four types of blood. Some could be safely mixed and some could not. That discovery has saved millions of lives. The day that Karl Landsteiner's results were published, blood transfusions became a safe and risk-free part of surgery. A patient's chances of surviving surgical procedures greatly increased. By making surgery safer, he made many new surgical procedures possible and practical.

Landsteiner's discovery also greatly advanced human understanding of blood structure and blood chemistry and paved the way for a number of key medical discoveries in the early twentieth century.

## How Was It Discovered?

Vienna, Austria, was a glamorous city in 1897—as modern as any in the world. Dr. Karl Landsteiner worked in the University of Vienna hospital, where he conducted cause-of-death (post mortem) medical examinations.

One April day that year, Landsteiner examined four patients who had died during surgery. All died for the same reason: blood agglutination (clotting). Each patient had received blood transfusions and died when his or her own red blood cells clumped together with red blood cells in the blood they were given into thick clots.

Landsteiner had seen this often during his thousands of post mortem examinations and wondered why it only happened with *some* patients.

That evening, Landsteiner played piano for his wife and several friends. It was the one thing Karl felt he did well. Most who heard him thought he should give up medicine for a brilliant career as a pianist.

In the middle of a familiar piece, it suddenly occurred to Landsteiner that the answer had to be something in the patients' *blood*. What if all blood was not the same, as everyone supposed?

The next morning Landsteiner collected blood from 20 patients, wanting to see if he could predict which samples were safe to mix with each other.

In long rows of test tubes, he mixed a few drops of each patient's blood with a few drops of blood from every other patient.

In his microscope, he checked to see which red blood cells clumped together, and which did not. Before he had checked half the test tubes under a microscope, Karl was stunned to find that he could easily divide the blood samples into two distinct groups. Red blood cells from any member of one group agglutinated (stuck to) red blood cells from *every* member of the other group. But the cells *never* stuck to blood cells of other members from the same group.

He named these groups "A" and "B." Not all blood was compatible. Different people's blood *was* different!

He continued testing and found blood samples that didn't agglutinate with *either* type "A" or "B" red blood cells. Landsteiner realized that there must be a *third* group. People in this group could safely donate blood to anyone. He named this third blood group type "O."

Then he found one blood sample that agglutinated with *both* type A and type B blood. There existed a *fourth* type of blood that reacted to *both* A and B blood, just as type O blood reacted to *neither*.

Karl named this fourth group type "AB."

Blood was not all the same. There were four distinct types. Safe transfusions required a doctor to determine the blood types of both patient and donor. It seemed like such a simple, obvious idea, and yet is one that has saved millions of lives.

 **Fun Facts:** Humans have four blood types (A, B, AB, and O). Cats have the same number of possible blood types. Cows, however, have over 800!

# More to Explore

Adler, Robert. *Medical Firsts.* New York: John Wiley & Sons, 2004.

Eibl, M., ed. *Episode Recognition Since Landsteiner's Discovery.* New York: Springer, 2002.

Haven, Kendall. *Marvels of Science.* Englewood, CO: Libraries Unlimited, 1995.

Heidelberger, Michael. *Karl Landsteiner: June 14, 1868–June 26, 1943.* New York: Columbia University Press, 1995.

Showers, Paul. *A Drop of Blood.* New York: Crowell Publishers, 1999.

Speiser, Paul. *Karl Landsteiner, the Discoverer of the Blood-Groups and a Pioneer in the Field of Immunology.* Frankfurt, Germany: Hollineck, 1994.

# Electron

## Year of Discovery: 1897

**What Is It?** The first subatomic particle ever discovered.

**Who Discovered It?** J. J. Thomson

## Why Is This One of the 100 Greatest?

Atoms had never been seen. Defined as the smallest particles possible and the basic building blocks of all matter, they were invisibly small—in the late nineteenth century still more theoretical than real. How could someone claim to have found something *smaller*? How could particles *get* any smaller?

Thomson discovered the electron and proved that it existed—without ever being able to see or isolate one. Electrons were the first subatomic particles to be discovered, the first particle of matter identified that was smaller than an atom. This discovery also finally provided some physical proof of, and description of, the basic unit that carried electricity. Thomson's experiments and discovery began a new field of science—particle physics.

## How Was It Discovered?

He was born Joseph John Thomson in December, 1856, in Manchester, England. By age 11 he had dropped his first names and used only his initials, J. J. Thomson began engineering studies at age 14 at Owens College and later brought a math and engineering background to the study of physics. In 1884 he was appointed to chair Cambridge's famed Cavendish physics lab. Thirteen years later and still at Cavendish, Thomson conducted the experiment that discovered the electron.

Cathode rays were discovered by German Julius Plucker in 1856. However, scientists couldn't agree on what cathode rays were. A great controversy boiled: were they waves or were they particles? Science's greatest minds argued back and forth.

In 1896 Thomson decided to design experiments that would settle this dispute. He built a cathode ray tube and fired its mysterious rays at a metal plate. The plate picked up a negative charge. This proved that cathode rays had to carry a negative charge. Next, he confirmed with a fluorescent-coated ruler that a magnetic field would deflect cathode rays. (Others had conducted this experiment.)

Thomson attached thin metal plates inside his cathode ray tube to a battery and showed that an electrical field could also deflect cathode rays. (The spot that lit up on his fluorescent ruler shifted when he connected the battery.)

99

Finally, Thomson built a new cathode ray tube with a thin slit through a metal plate. Cathode rays were channeled through this narrow slit. Beyond that metal plate he added a magnetic field to deflect cathode rays in one direction, followed by an electric field that would deflect them back in the other direction.

Thomson knew the force these two fields created. Once he measured the amount of deflection (change of direction) each force created in the stream of cathode rays, he could calculate the mass of the particles in this cathode ray stream. That would finally solve the mystery by identifying the specific particles.

He ran his experiment and didn't believe his results. The ratio of electric charge to particle mass was way too big, and that meant that the mass of these particles had to be *much* smaller than any known particle.

He repeated the experiment a hundred times. He ripped apart and rebuilt each piece of equipment. The results were always the same. The mass of this particle had to be less than 1/1000 of the mass of a proton (a hydrogen atom)—one thousand times smaller than the smallest atom—supposedly the smallest possible particle.

Thomson had discovered a new particle—the first subatomic particle. It took hundreds of demonstrations and several detailed articles before anyone believed that his new particles existed.

In 1891 Irish physicist George Stoney had named the fundamental unit (particle) of electricity the "electron" without having any idea what that particle was like. Thomson decided to use Stoney's name (*electron*) for his new particle since it carried electrical current. In 1898 a Frenchman named Bequerel found photographic proof of the existence of subatomic particles to confirm Thomson's discovery.

 **Fun Facts:** If an electron weighed the same as a dime, a proton would weigh the same as a gallon of milk

# More to Explore

Dahl, Per. *Flash of the Cathode Rays: A History of J J Thomson's Electron.* Abingdon, England: Taylor & Francis, 1997.

Davis, E. *J.J. Thomson and the Discovery of the Electron.* London: CRC, 1997.

Rayleigh, D. *The Life of Sir J.J. Thomson: Sometime Master of Trinity College, Cambridge.* New Castle, DE: Dawsons of Pall Mall, 1996.

Sherman, Josepha. *J. J. Thomson & the Discovery of Electrons.* Hockessin, DE: Mitchell Lane, 2005.

Thompson, George. *J. J. Thomson: Discoverer of the Electron.* New York: Anchor Books, 1998.

———. *J.J. Thomson and the Cavendish Laboratory in His Day.* New York: Doubleday, 1996.

# Virus

## Year of Discovery: 1898

> **What Is It?** The smallest, simplest living organism and causative agent for many human diseases, from simple colds to deadly yellow fever.
>
> **Who Discovered It?** Dmitri Ivanovsky and Martinus Beijerinick

## Why Is This One of the 100 Greatest?

Far smaller than cells and bacteria, viruses are the smallest life forms on Earth—so small they can only reproduce inside some host cell and do it by taking over control of that cell. Viruses are so small they easily slip through virtually any filter or trap. Their discovery answered many medical questions at the beginning of the twentieth century and completed Pasteur's germ theory.

Viruses cause many of the most dangerous human diseases. Until they were discovered, medical science had ground to a halt in its advance on curing these human illnesses. When Beijerinick discovered viruses, he actually discovered a new life form, one too small to be seen with any microscope other than a mighty electron microscope.

## How Was It Discovered?

French scientist Louis Pasteur discovered germs (microscopic bacteria) and claimed that germs caused disease and rot. However, he was never able to find a microorganism (germs) that caused rabies, though he tried for over a decade before giving up in 1885. It left a shadow of doubt over his germ theory.

Another disease for which no one could find an identifiable causative agent was tobacco mosaic disease (so called because a mosaic pattern forms on the leaves of infected plants). In 1892 Russian botanist Dmitri Ivanovsky decided to search for this mysterious agent. (It was safer to work with tobacco mosaic disease than with deadly rabies.) Ivanovsky mashed up infected leaves and passed the fluid through various paper and ceramic filters. These filters were supposed to trap all organisms—even the tiniest bacteria.

However, the fluid that strained through these sets of filters could still infect healthy tobacco plants with mosaic disease. That meant that Ivanovsky hadn't trapped the causative agent in his filters. He tried different filter materials, different treatments, and baths for the leaves and mashed juice. His results were always the same. Whatever caused this disease, Ivanovsky couldn't trap it in a filter.

Ivanovsky refused to believe that any living organism existed that was smaller than bacteria and so concluded that his filters were defective and would not, in fact, catch small bacteria. In disgust, he abandoned his project.

In 1898 Dutch botanist Martinus Beijerinick decided to try his luck at solving the mystery of tobacco mosaic disease. He repeated Ivanovsky's experiment and got the same result. However, Beijerinick was quite willing to conclude that this experiment proved that the causative agent was something new and unknown—something much smaller than bacteria. That was why it hadn't been trapped in his filters. Beijerinick admitted that he did not know what it was, but he claimed that his experiment proved that it existed and that it was super-tiny. He named it a "*virus*," the Latin word for poison.

While this discovery was intellectually interesting to some scientists, few cared about a disease unique to tobacco plants. The notion of viruses received little attention from the medical and scientific communities.

In 1899 German scientist Friedrich Loeffler conducted a similar test and concluded that the agent responsible for foot-and-mouth disease was too tiny to be bacteria and so must be another virus. Two years later, in 1901, American army surgeon Walter Reed exhausted his attempts to discover the cause for yellow fever that had killed so many American soldiers. Then he tested this mosquito-borne disease to see if whatever caused it was small enough to be a virus. It was.

This discovery convinced the scientific world that viruses—1/1000 the size of even a small bacterium—were the cause of many human ailments and had to be studied and treated separately from bacteria. Ivanovsky and Beijerinick discovered viruses, but it took Walter Reed to make the medical and scientific community pay attention.

 **Fun Facts:** What's the most common disease-causing virus? The common group of rhinoviruses, of which there are at least 180 types. Rhinoviruses cause colds and are almost universal, affecting everyone except for those living in the frozen wastes of Antarctica.

## More to Explore

Fuffle, Cady. *Viruses*. New York: Gareth Stevens, 2003.

Gallo, Robert. *Virus Hunting: Aids, Cancer, and the Human Retrovirus: A Story of Scientific Discovery*. New York: Basic Books, 1997.

Kanaly, Michael. *Virus Clans: A Story of Evolution*. New York: Penguin Books, 1999.

Mahy, Brian, ed. *Concepts in Virology: From Ivanovsky to the Present*. Abingdon, England: Taylor & Francis, 1996.

van Iterson, G. *Martinus Willem Beijerinck: His Life and Work*. Washington, DC: Science Tech Publishers, 1995.

# Mitochondria

## Year of Discovery: 1898

> **What Is It?** All-important parts of every cell that provide cell energy and also have their own separate DNA.
>
> **Who Discovered It?** Carl Benda

## Why Is This One of the 100 Greatest?

Mitochondria are tiny energy producers in every cell. One of many tiny structures floating in the cell's cytoplasm (fluid) that are collectively called organelles, mitochondria are considered the most important of all cell parts—besides the nucleus.

Amazingly, mitochondria have their own separate DNA. You depend on them. They depend on you. And yet they are separate living organisms that have proved invaluable in tracking human history and evolution as well as for understanding cell operation. Their discovery in 1898 marked a great turning point for microbiology.

## How Was It Discovered?

Englishman Robert Hooke discovered cells in 1665 when he turned his microscope onto a thin sliver of cork. As microscopes improved and grew in magnification power, scientists struggled to identify cells in other plant and animal tissue.

However, technical problems slowed their progress. More powerful microscopes were increasingly hard to focus and provided sharp focus on smaller and smaller areas. This was called "chromatic aberration." In 1841 the achromatic microscope was invented and eased this problem.

Tissue samples had to be dye-stained so that individual cells (and parts of cells) would show up under the microscope. However, staining often damaged cells and masked the very cell parts it was intended to reveal. In 1871 Camino Gogli developed a staining process he called "black reaction." This process finally offered scientists a chance to see the cell interior that lay beyond cell walls.

In 1781 abbot Felice Fontant glimpsed the nucleus of a skin cell. Scotsman Robert Brown named it the "nucleus" and, while studying orchids, was the one who discovered that the nucleus was an essential part of living cells. In 1891 Wilhelm Waldeyer discovered nerve cells.

By 1895 several researchers had actually watched cells divide through their microscopes and saw that a number of tiny structures (which they called organelles) existed inside each cell.

One of these researchers was Carl Benda, born in 1857 in southern Germany. Even as a youth, Benda had been fascinated by the microscopic world and was one of the first to call himself a *microbiologist* and to make a career out of studying the microscopic world. Benda had been swept up in the excitement of the effort to peer inside a living cell.

By 1898 it was clear that the cell cytoplasm (the internal fluid part of a cell) was not a simple, homogeneous fluid. Tiny structures floated in there doing no-one-knew-what.

During an experiment in 1898, Benda was able to make out hundreds of tiny bodies in the cytoplasm through the membrane of a cell. Benda thought they must be tiny pillars that helped hold the shape of the cell. So he named them *mitochondria,* from the Greek words meaning "threads of cartilage." Neither he nor other scientists at the time gave mitochondria any significance other than that they existed and were part of the internal structure of a cell.

By 1910 scientists were better able to glimpse through cell walls and watch living cells function. Many scientists suspected that mitochondria provided energy to the cell. By 1920, scientists had determined that mitochondria were the power plants that supplied over 90 percent of all cell energy needs.

In 1963 it was discovered that mitochondria had their own DNA (called *mDNA*). This was a shattering discovery and made mitochondria one of the most important parts of a living cell. It meant that we are really cooperating colonies of microscopic bugs. In some far-distant past, tiny mitochondria organisms made a deal with bigger cells. They traded energy for protection. The mitochondria moved inside, but kept their separate DNA. That made these tiny substructures unique among all elements of a living body and an important subject for ongoing research.

But it all started with Benda's discovery—even though he had no idea of the ultimate importance of what he discovered.

 **Fun Facts:** Mitochondria are called the "powerhouse of the cells," where all cell energy is produced. That includes the energy for you to blink your eyes, for your heart to beat, or for you to perform amazing tasks like completing the annual race up the 1,576 steps of the Empire State Building. The current record holder is Belinda Soszyn (Australia) in 1996, with a time of 12 minutes, 19 seconds. Imagine how much energy her mitochondria had to produce!

## More to Explore

Chance, Britton. *Energy-linked Functions of Mitochondria.* Washington, DC: Academic Press, 1994.

Daniell, Henry, ed. *Molecular Biology and Biotechnology of Plant Organelles: Chloroplasts and Mitochondria.* New York: Springer-Verlag, 2005.

Levings, Charles. *Molecular Biology of Plant Mitochondria.* London: Kulwar Academic Publishers, 1995.

Osawa, Syozo. *Evolution of the Genetic Code.* New York: Oxford University Press, 1995.

Scheffler, Immo. *Mitochondria.* Dover, DE: Wiley-Liss, 1999.

# Radioactivity

## Year of Discovery: 1901

> **What Is It?** Atoms are not solid balls and the smallest possible particles of matter, but contain a number of smaller particles within them.
>
> **Who Discovered It?** Marie Curie

## Why Is This One of the 100 Greatest?

Marie Curie's discovery of two naturally radioactive elements, polonium and radium, made headline news, but her real discovery was that atoms were not small solid balls and that there must be even smaller particles inside them. This discovery opened the door to all atomic and subatomic research and even to the splitting of the atom.

Curie carried out her research with radioactive elements before the dangers of radioactivity were understood. She suffered from ill health (radiation sickness) for most of her adult life. Indeed, for many years after her death, her notebooks were still highly radioactive.

Marie Curie's studies rank as one of the great turning points of science. Physics after Curie was completely different than before and focused on the undiscovered subatomic world. She cracked open a door that penetrated inside the atom and has led to most of the greatest advances of twentieth-century physics.

## How Was It Discovered?

In 1896 Marie Curie decided to complete her doctoral dissertation in a totally new field: radiation. It was exciting. It was something no one had ever seen or studied before. Scientists knew that electrically charged radiation flooded the air around uranium, but not much else was known. Marie used a device her husband, professor Pierre Curie, invented to detect electric charges around mineral samples. She named this process radioactivity and concluded that radioactivity was emitted from *inside* a uranium atom.

Since the Curies had had no money of their own to pay for her research, and since the university refused to fund a woman's graduate-level physics research, Marie scrounged for free lab space. She found an abandoned shed that had been used by the Biology Department to hold cadavers. It was unbearably hot in the summer and freezing cold in the winter, with a few wooden tables and chairs and a rusty old stove.

In 1898 Marie was given a puzzling uranium mineral ore called pitchblende, which her tests showed gave off more radioactive emissions than expected from the amount of uranium it contained. She concluded that there must be another substance inside pitchblende that gave off the extra radiation.

She began each test with 3.5 ounces of pitchblende. She planned to remove all of the known metals so that ultimately all that would be left would be this new, highly active element. She ground the ore with mortar and pestle, passed it through a sieve, dissolved it in acid, boiled off the liquid, filtered it, distilled it, then electrolyzed it.

Over the next six months Marie and her husband, Pierre, chemically isolated and tested each of the 78 known chemical elements to see if these mysterious radioactive rays flowed from any other substance besides uranium. Most of their time was spent begging for tiny samples of the many elements they could not afford to buy. Oddly, each time Marie removed more of the known elements, what was left of her pitchblende was always *more* radioactive than before.

What should have taken weeks, dragged into long months because of their dismal working conditions. In March 1901, the pitchblende finally gave up its secrets. Marie had found not one, but *two* new radioactive elements: polonium (named after Marie's native Poland) and radium (so named because it was by far the most radioactive element yet discovered). Marie produced a tiny sample of pure radium salt. It weighed .0035 ounces—less than the weight of a potato chip—but it was a million times more radioactive than uranium!

Because the dangers of radiation were not yet understood, Marie and Pierre were plagued with health troubles. Aches and pains. Ulcer-covered hands. Continuous bouts of serious illnesses like pneumonia. Never-ending exhaustion. Finally, the radiation Marie had studied all her life killed her in 1934.

 **Fun Facts:** Female Nobel Prize laureates accounted for only 34 out of a total of 723 prizes awarded as of 2005. Marie Curie is not only the first woman to be awarded a Nobel Prize, but also one of four persons to have been awarded the Nobel Prize twice.

# More to Explore

Boorse, Henry, and Lloyd Motz. *The Atomic Scientist: A Biographical History.* New York: John Wiley & Sons, 1989.

Born, Max. *Atomic Physics.* New York: Dover Publications, 1979.

Dunn, Andrew. *Pioneers of Science, Marie Curie.* New York: The Bookwright Press, 1991.

Keller, Mollie. *Marie Curie: An Impact Biography.* New York: Franklin Watts, 1982.

McGrayne, Sharon Bertsch. *Nobel Prize Women in Science: Their Lives, Struggles, and Momentous Discoveries.* New York: Carol Publishing Group, A Birch Lane Press Book, 1993.

McKown, Robin. *Marie Curie.* New York: G.P. Putnam's Sons, 1971.

Parker, Steve. *Science Discoveries: Marie Curie and Radium.* New York: HarperCollins, 1992.

Quinn, Susan. *Marie Curie: A Life.* New York: Simon & Schuster, 1996.

Reid, Robert. *Marie Curie.* New York: Dutton, 1998.

# Atmospheric Layers

## Year of Discovery: 1902

**What Is It?** Earth's atmosphere has distinct layers of air, each with unique temperatures, densities, humidities, and other properties.

**Who Discovered It?** Leon Philippe Teisserenc de Bort

## Why Is This One of the 100 Greatest?

What could be more basic to understanding planet Earth than to know what lies between the surface and Earth's center, *or* between the surface and outer space? Yet the twentieth century dawned with science having virtually no concept of what the atmosphere was like more than two miles above the earth's surface.

Teisserenc de Bort was the first to expand science's knowledge into the upper reaches of Earth's atmosphere. His discovery provided the first accurate image of our atmosphere and formed the basis for our understanding of meteorological phenomena (storms, winds, clouds, etc.). Teisserenc de Bort was also the first to take scientific instruments into the upper atmosphere.

## How Was It Discovered?

Born in Paris in 1855, Leon Philippe Teisserenc de Bort was appointed the chief of the Administrative Center of National Meteorology in Paris at the age of 30. There he was frustrated because he believed that science's inability to understand and predict weather stemmed from lack of knowledge about the atmosphere more than three or four kilometers above the surface.

Certainly, manned balloon flights (both hot air and gas filled) had carried instruments into the atmosphere. But these flights never ventured above four or five kilometers in altitude. There wasn't enough oxygen up there for people to breathe.

In 1895 Teisserenc de Bort quit his job to devote full time to developing unmanned, high-altitude gas balloons at his Versailles villa (outside of Paris). Over the next five years, Teisserenc de Bort designed an instrument package in a wicker basket that his balloons would carry aloft. Basic thermometers and barometers were connected to recording devices so that he would have written records of upper atmospheric conditions once the balloon returned to Earth.

He also designed a release system and parachute to deploy after the basket released from the rising balloon to bring his instrument package gently back down.

Teisserenc de Bort found that tracking the basket and parachute were more difficult than he first thought, even when he used a telescope. Each launch involved a mad scramble across the countryside to keep the descending package in sight. Even so, a few were never found, some sunk in rivers or lakes, and some were smashed when the parachutes failed.

Still, Teisserenc de Bort persisted—and was amazed at what he discovered. Atmospheric temperature decreased steadily at a constant rate of 6.5°C per kilometer of altitude (19°F per mile). This decrease was expected.

However, at an altitude of around 11 km (7 miles, or about 37,000 feet) the temperature stopped decreasing at all. It remained level at around -53°C up to over 48,000 feet (as high as Teisserenc de Bort's balloons would fly).

At first Teisserenc de Bort didn't believe that the temperature could possibly stop decreasing. He suspected that the instruments rose to a height where solar heating warmed the thermometer and compensated for continued atmospheric temperature decrease.

He began to launch at night. It was harder to track the parachute's descent, but it prevented any possibility of solar heating. Even at night, his results were the same. The temperature above 11 km remained constant.

After 234 tests, Teisserenc de Bort finally concluded that his measurements were accurate and that there were two, separate layers to the atmosphere. Near the surface lay an 11-km-thick lower layer where temperature changes created currents, winds, clouds, and weather. Above that was a region where constant temperature allowed air to settle into quiet, undisturbed layers

He named the lower layer the *troposphere,* from the Greek words meaning "sphere of change," and the upper layer the *stratosphere,* from the Greek words meaning "sphere of layers."

Teisserenc de Bort's discovery is still the basis of our understanding of the atmosphere.

 **Fun Facts:** Scientists now know that the atmosphere has many layers, but the troposphere is the layer where *all* of Earth's weather occurs.

# More to Explore

Emanuel, Kerry. *Atmospheric Convection.* New York: Oxford University Press, 1997.

Hewitt, C. N., ed. *Handbook of Atmospheric Science: Principles and Applications.* Boston: Blackwell Publishers, 2003.

Jones, Phil. *History and Climate.* London: Kluwer Academic Press, 2001.

Parker, Sybil, ed. *McGraw-Hill Encyclopedia of Ocean and Atmospheric Sciences.* New York: McGraw-Hill, 1997.

Stull, Ronald. *Introduction to Boundary Layer Meteorology.* London: Kluwer Academic Press, 1998.

Wallace, John. *Atmospheric Science, First Edition: An Introductory Survey.* New York: Academic Press, 1997.

# Hormones

## Year of Discovery: 1902

> **What Is It?** Chemical messengers that trigger action in various organs within the body.
>
> **Who Discovered It?** William Bayliss and Ernst Starling

## Why Is This One of the 100 Greatest?

At the dawn of the twentieth century, scientists thought that all control signals in the human body were sent electrically along nerve fibers. Then Bayliss and Starling discovery that *chemical* messengers (called hormones) as well as electric signals trigger body organs to function. This startling discovery started a whole new field of medical science: endocrinology. It revolutionized physiology and has been called one of the greatest discoveries of all time related to the human body.

Once discovered and commercially produced, these hormones were hailed as miracle drugs when made available in the marketplace. Adrenalin (the first hormone to be discovered) was the first "blockbuster" drug of the twentieth century. Other hormones followed close behind.

## How Was It Discovered?

Bayliss and Starling get credit for discovering hormones. However, we must give some credit to those who, several years before, actually discovered the first hormone—even though they did not realize the true significance of their discovery.

During a long series of animal experiments in 1894, British physiologist Edward Albert Sharpey-Schafer showed that fluid extracted from the adrenal gland would raise blood pressure if injected into an animal's blood stream. He thought it interesting, but did not see any practical value to his find. In 1898 American pharmacologist John Abel recognized the medical value of this substance and studied its origin and chemistry. He isolated the key chemical in this fluid and named it *epinephrine* (from the Greek words meaning "above the kidney," since that's where the adrenal gland is housed).

Two years later, Japanese entrepreneur and chemist Jokichi Takamine set up a lab in New York to create a synthetic version of epinephrine in pure crystalline form that could be commercially produced. In 1901 he succeeded, and called it *adrenaline* because the natural chemical came from the adrenal gland. While Takamine realized the commercial value of his creation (and quickly patented the name and manufacturing process), he did not take note of the biological significance of finding a chemical substance that traveled through the bloodstream to deliver an activation message to an organ.

In 1902 two professors and medical researches at University College of London began a study of digestive juices. One was 40-year-old William Bayliss. His partner was his 34-year-old brother-in-law, Ernst Starling.

Medical scientists knew that the pancreas began to secrete digestive juice as soon as the food content in the stomach first entered the small intestine. But how did the pancreas know that it should begin to produce juice at that moment? All assumed an electric signal was somehow sent through nerve cells. Bayliss and Starling decided to test this theory.

They cut the nerves leading to the pancreas of a laboratory dog. Yet the pancreas still performed on cue. Upon close examination, they found that the lining of the dog's small intestine secreted a liquid substance as soon as stomach acid reached it. This fluid (which they named *secretin*) traveled through the bloodstream to the pancreas and signaled the pancreas to leap into action.

Unlike Takamine, Bayliss and Starling instantly realized that this was the first documented case of a signal being sent *chemically* through the body instead of *electrically* along nerve fibers. They announced their findings, to the delight and wonder of the scientific community.

Bayliss suspected that many more such chemical messengers existed and would be found. As soon as he read a report on Takamine's work, Bayliss realized that Takamine had discovered another in this group of chemical messengers when he isolated adrenalin.

In 1905 Starling coined the name *hormones* for this growing group of chemical messengers, from the Greek words meaning "to arouse to activity." The third hormone to be discovered was *cortisone,* in 1935, by American biochemist Edward Calvin. Now, almost 30 hormones have been discovered that speed signals through your body, and their importance can hardly be overstated.

 **Fun Facts:** Robert Earl Hughes, the world's largest man, weighed 484 kg (1,067 lb.) at his death in 1958. Years after his death, scientists discovered that he had too little of the hormone thyroxin in his system. Without this vital hormone, his body couldn't burn the food he ate, and so his body continually stored it as fat.

# More to Explore

Bliss, Michael. *Discovery of Insulin.* Chicago: University of Chicago Press, 1994.

Fox, Ruth. *Milestones in Medicine.* New York: Random House, 1995.

Frayn, Keith. *Metabolic Regulation: A Human Perspective.* Boston: Blackwell Publishers, 2003.

Henderson, John. *A Life of Ernest Starling.* New York: Oxford University Press, 2004.

Maleskey, Gale. *Hormone Connection.* New York: Rodale Press, 2001.

# $E = mc^2$

## Year of Discovery: 1905

> **What Is It?** The first established relationship between matter and energy.
>
> **Who Discovered It?** Albert Einstein

## Why Is This One of the 100 Greatest?

For all of history, matter was matter and energy was energy. The two were separate, unrelated concepts. Then Einstein established the relationship between matter and energy by creating the most famous equation in the history of humankind, $E = mc^2$. (The second most famous is the Pythagorean Theorem for a right triangle, $A^2 = B^2 + C^2$.)

Einstein's equation for the first time defined a quantified relationship between matter and energy. It meant that these two aspects of the universe that had always been thought of as separate were really interchangeable.

This one equation altered the direction of physics research, made Michelson's calculation of the speed of light (1928) critical, and led directly to the nuclear bomb and nuclear energy development.

## How Was It Discovered?

In 1903, 24-year-old Albert Einstein landed a job as a patent clerk for the Swiss patent office. His whole job was to check the technical correctness of patent submissions. Though he had always dreamed of, and aimed for, a career in science, he had utterly failed to gain an entry into that world. He had failed high school and was barred from teaching.

He had married his high school girlfriend. He was a low-level bureaucrat scraping by in Berne, Switzerland, and it seemed that that was all he would ever be.

Though he had been shunned in his formal education, Einstein was still a passionate amateur mathematician and physicist. He spent virtually all of his free time mulling over the great mysteries and problems facing physicists of the day.

Einstein worked best through what he called mind experiments. He searched for vivid mental images that would shed new light on, and provide a new perspective on, complex physics problems. Then he applied the mathematics he knew so well to explain the images and to understand their physics implications.

By 1904 Einstein was attempting to extend the existing physics of the day by focusing on the relationships between light, space, and time. He was able to show that light exists as both waves and as particles. (A particle, or quanta, of light we call a photon.)

This work led to Einstein's revolutionary concept of relativity. From the mathematics that described this concept, he came to several startling conclusions. Time was as rubbery as space. It slowed down as an object sped up. Objects increase in mass as they approach nearer to light speed. Einstein's theory of relativity established a direct link between space and time and showed that they both warp around heavy objects (like stars). Their measurement is only possible in a relative, not an absolute, sense.

From this theoretical foundation, Einstein continued his mathematical development and showed that, as an object approaches the speed of light, its length decreases, its mass increases, and time slows down. (This concept was later confirmed with precision clocks carried on high-speed jet airplanes.)

If matter changed as it sped up, then matter and energy had to be somehow related to each other. Einstein realized that his theory of relativity showed that matter has to be a highly concentrated form of energy. He suspected that he could deduce a mathematical relationship between the two.

Einstein realized that this revolutionary concept contradicted the famed and completely accepted concepts of conservation of mass (Lavoisier, 1789) and conservation of energy (Hemholtz, 1847). Einstein was saying that these two giants of science were both wrong and that neither energy nor matter were independently conserved. However, combined, the total energy in this energy-matter system had to still be conserved.

Einstein viewed the energy-matter equation he derived ($E = mc^2$) like frosting on the cake of his relativity theory. He submitted an article on it almost as an afterthought to his theory of relativity, as a sequel to it. To Einstein, this equation was only of interest as a physics and science concern, as a way to view the theoretical interchange between mass and energy. He did not think it was particularly important.

Others, however, quickly realized the implications of Einstein's equation for weapons design and for nuclear energy production. "The world," said Aldous Huxley after reviewing Einstein's physics, "is not only queerer than we imagine, it is queerer than we *can* imagine."

 **Fun Facts:** Einstein's famous equation tells us exactly how much energy exists in any given object (or mass). However, only one reaction releases all of this energy: a matter–antimatter collision, the only perfect conversion of matter into energy in our universe.

## More to Explore

Bartusiak, Marcia. *Einstein's Unfinished Symphony: Listening to the Sounds of Space-Time.* Washington, DC: Joseph Henry Press, 2000.

Bernstein, Jeremy. *Einstein.* New York: Penguin, 1995.

Brian, Denis. *Einstein: A Life.* New York: John Wiley & Sons, 1996.

Calaprice, Alice. *The Quotable Einstein.* Princeton, NJ: Princeton University Press, 1996.

Folsing, Albrecht. *Albert Einstein: A Biography.* New York: Viking, 1997.

Goldsmith, Donald. *The Ultimate Einstein.* New York: Byron Press, 1997.

Goldsmith, Maurice, ed. *Einstein: the First Hundred Years.* New York: Pergamon Press, 1996.

Overbye, Dennis. *Einstein in Love: A Scientific Romance.* New York: Viking, 2000.

Parker, Barry. *Einstein's Dream: The Search for a Unified Theory of the Universe.* New York: Plenum, 2000.

Whitrow, G., ed. *Einstein: The Man and His Achievements.* New York: Dover Publications, 1997.

# Relativity

## Year of Discovery: 1905

> **What Is It?** Einstein's theory that space and time merge to form the fabric of the universe that is warped and molded by gravity.
>
> **Who Discovered It?** Albert Einstein

## Why Is This One of the 100 Greatest?

Albert Einstein is one of only three or four scientists in history who have changed the fundamental ways in which humans view the universe. Einstein's theory of relativity changed humankind's core assumptions concerning the nature of the universe and of Earth's and of humans' place in it.

The twentieth century's developments in technology, science, and math owe their foundation to this unassuming scientist in a deep and fundamental way. He has touched our lives probably more than any other scientist in history. But for the first 26 years of his life, no one thought he had any chance of entering the world of science at all.

## How Was It Discovered?

Raised in Munich, Germany, Albert Einstein showed no early signs of genius. He was described as a dull child who didn't play well with other children. Grammar school teachers called him irksome and disruptive. At 16 he was expelled from school. Albert's father encouraged him to apply to the Polytechnic Institute in Zurich, Switzerland, and learn a trade to help support the family.

But Albert failed the entrance exam. A school administrator was, however, impressed with Albert's math abilities and arranged for him to complete high school in nearby Aarua, Switzerland. At 17, Albert transferred to Zurich.

There he showed promise in math and science, but piled up far too many discipline reports. He was free with his opinions whether they were offensive or not. His teachers gave him bad reports. One called him "a lazy dog."

Einstein hoped to teach after graduation but his grades weren't good enough. He dropped out of science in disgust and supported himself with odd jobs. In 1902 he landed a job as a clerk in the Swiss Patent Office, assigned to check the technical correctness of patent applications. It appeared that all doors leading to a science career had been firmly closed.

It was while riding on a Berne, Switzerland, trolley car in the spring of 1904 that the image first flashed across Albert Einstein's mind. It was an image of a man in an elevator that was falling from a great height. Einstein realized immediately that the image of this "thought experiment" could bring focus to a problem that had been plaguing him (and all of science) for years.

Einstein realized that the man in the elevator would not know he was falling because, relative to his surroundings (the elevator), he wasn't falling. The man—like us—would not be able to detect that he (and his elevator) were caught in, and being pulled by, a gravitational field. If a horizontal light beam entered the side of the elevator, it would strike the far wall higher up because the elevator would have dropped while the light beam crossed. To the man, it would appear that the light beam bent upwards. From our perspective (*relative* to us), gravitational fields bend light. Light not only could be, but routinely was, bent by the gravitational fields of stars and planets.

It was a revolutionary concept, worthy of one of the world's greatest scientific minds. Einstein regularly used these imaginative "thought experiments" to shed light on complex questions of general principles. It was a new and unique way to approach the study of physics and led Einstein to write a series of four papers, which he submitted to a science journal in 1905. One of those four papers presented the special theory of relativity (relativity principles applied to bodies either moving at a steady velocity or at rest). Impressed, the journal published all four papers in a single issue. Another presented Einstein's relation between matter and energy.

The papers from this "amateur" mathematician had a deep, instant, and profound effect in the scientific community. One was accepted as a doctoral thesis by Zurich University, which granted Einstein a Ph.D.

Virtually all physicists shifted their studies to focus on Einstein's theories.

In 1916, with war raging across Europe, Einstein published his general theory of relativity, which described relativity theory applied to objects moving in more complex ways with nonlinear acceleration. The world applauded.

 **Fun Facts:** We know that the look and sound of moving objects appear and sound different depending on whether the receiver is stationary or moving. Special relativity is based on the mind-boggling concept that, no matter how fast you travel, the speed of light appears to remain the same!

# More to Explore

Bartusiak, Marcia. *Einstein's Unfinished Symphony: Listening to the Sounds of Space-Time.* Washington, DC: Joseph Henry Press, 2000.

Bernstein, Jeremy. *Einstein*. New York,:Penguin, 1995.

Brian, Denis. *Einstein: A Life.* New York: John Wiley & Sons, 1996.

Calaprice, Alice. *The Quotable Einstein.* Princeton, NJ: Princeton University Press, 1996.

Folsing, Albrecht. *Albert Einstein: A Biography.* New York: Viking, 1997.

Goldsmith, Donald. *The Ultimate Einstein.* New York: Byron Press, 1997.

Goldsmith, Maurice, ed. *Einstein: The First Hundred Years.* New York: Pergamon Press, 1996.

Overbye, Dennis. *Einstein in Love: A Scientific Romance.* New York: Viking, 2000.

Parker, Barry. *Einstein's Dream: The Search for a Unified Theory of the Universe.* New York: Plenum, 2000.

Whitrow, G., ed. *Einstein: The Man and His Achievements.* New York: Dover Publications, 1997.

# Vitamins

## Year of Discovery: 1906

> **What Is It?** Trace dietary chemical compounds that are essential to life and health.
>
> **Who Discovered It?** Christiaan Eijkman and Fredrick Hopkins

## Why Is This One of the 100 Greatest?

We label foods by their vitamin content. We spend billions of dollars every year buying vitamin supplements. Vitamins are essential to life and health. Yet any awareness of vitamins—even the very notion of vitamins—is only 100 years old. It had not occurred to anyone to search for trace elements in food that human bodies needed. They had only considered measuring the amount of food and the calories in it.

The discovery of vitamins revolutionized nutritional science and the public's awareness of health, diet, and nutrition. It radically changed biological science and the study of how the human body functions.

## How Was It Discovered?

During the early 1890s, the disease beriberi wreaked havoc on the Dutch East India Company's operations in India. Since Pasteur had discovered germs, scientists assumed that all diseases were caused by germs. Yet Company doctors could find no germ for beriberi.

In 1896, 35-year-old Dutch physician Christiaan Eijkman traveled to India to try his luck at the investigation. Shortly after he arrived, a massive outbreak of beriberi swept through the flock of chickens at the research facility used for bacteriological research.

Eijkman began frantic research on the diseased flock when, just as suddenly, the disease vanished. Eijkman was baffled until he interviewed the cook who fed the chickens and found that, just before and during the outbreak, he had switched the chickens' feed to white rice intended for human consumption. When company officials had yelled at him for feeding expensive polished (white) rice to chickens, the cook had switched back to normal chicken feed using brown rice.

He found that he could cause beriberi at will by switching chicken feed to white (polished) rice and cure it by switching back. He examined local jail diets and found that where prisoners were fed a diet of brown rice, no beriberi occurred. In jails that used white rice, beriberi outbreaks were common.

Eijkman believed that something in brown rice *cured* beriberi and wrote a report claiming victory over the disease. He never considered looked at it the other way: that beriberi was caused by the *absence* of something that was present in brown rice.

Frederick Hopkins was an American medical researcher who was born as the Civil War broke out in 1861. In 1900 he isolated an amino acid. (Other researchers had discovered two others before him but had not investigated their importance.) Hopkins called his amino acid *tryptophan*. From a review of other research, he found that farm animals could not be kept alive if their only sources of protein were things that included no tryptophan. No matter how much protein they got, animals seemed to require trace amounts of tryptophan to survive.

By 1906 chemists had isolated at least 13 amino acids. Each was an essential building block of protein molecules. It occurred to Hopkins that these particular amino acids (which were commonly found in foods) were essential to life. Not for the protein and calories they provided; those could come from anywhere. There was something else these amino acids provided that was essential to life—even if only supplied in trace amounts.

Hopkins reviewed Eijkman's work and discovered that it was an amino acid in brown rice feed that prevented beriberi. He found that it was not just fruit that prevented scurvy (as first discovered by Lind in 1747). It was a particular amino acid in fruit.

Hopkins decided that diseases such as beriberi, scurvy, pellagra, and rickets were not caused by a *thing* (a germ) but by the *absence* (or deficiency) of something. Hopkins believed that these diseases were caused by a dietary deficiency of *amine* groups of molecules (combinations of nitrogen and hydrogen atoms found in amino acids). He named this group of acids by combining the Latin word for life with "amines" and got *vitamines*.

A few years later, researchers discovered that not all essential vitamins contained amines. They dropped the "e" to form the word *vitamin*—which we still use today. However, research in nutrition has ever since been shaped by Hopkins's discovery of vitamins.

 **Fun Facts:** Think all sweets are bad for you? Hershey's Sugar Free Chocolate Syrup has 10 percent vitamin E per serving.

# More to Explore

Apple, Rima. *Vitamania: Vitamins in American Culture*. New Brunswick, NJ: Rutgers University Press, 1996.

Becker, Stanley. *Butter Makes Them Grow: An Episode in the Discovery of Vitamins*. Hartford: Connecticut Agricultural Experiment Station, 1997.

Carpenter, Kenneth. *Forgotten Mysteries in the Early History of Vitamin D*. Washington, DC: American Institute of Nutrition, 2005.

Rucker, Robert. *Handbook of Vitamins*. New York: CRC Publishers, 2001.

Yan, Kun. *Stories of the Discovery of Vitamins: The Young Doctors Collection*. Bloomington, IN: Authorhouse, 2005.

# Radioactive Dating

## Year of Discovery: 1907

---

**What Is It?** The use of radioactive decaying elements to calculate the age of rocks.

**Who Discovered It?** Bertram Boltwood

---

## Why Is This One of the 100 Greatest?

Nothing is more basic than knowing your age—or the age of your house, or of a tree in your yard. For science, the same is true for Earth and for the rocks that make up Earth's crust.

Scientists had been estimating Earth's age for thousands of years. However, these were little more than guesses. Boltwood discovered the first reliable way to calculate the age of a rock. Since some rocks are nearly as old as the earth, dating these rocks provided the first reasonable estimate of Earth's age.

Boltwood's discovery also allowed scientists to date individual rock layers and strata and to study the history of Earth's crust. It led to aging techniques developed for plants, documents, societies, and ancient buildings. Boltwood gave back to geology a sense of time that the misestimates of previous researchers had taken away.

## How Was It Discovered?

Radioactivity was discovered by Marie Curie at the end of the nineteenth century. In 1902 Frederick Soddy (who later discovered isotopes) and Ernst Rutherford jointly discovered that uranium and thorium radioactively decayed at a constant rate. (It always takes exactly the same amount of time for exactly half of the radioactive atoms in a sample to decay. It's called a *half-life*.) They also discovered that these two radioactive elements fissioned (radioactively decayed) into other elements in a fixed sequence—they always fissiioned in the same way into the same elements. The stage was set for someone to figure out how to use this new information.

Bertram Boltwood was born in 1870 in Amherst, Massachusetts. He studied physics (and later taught physics) at Yale University. While doing research in 1905, Boltwood noticed that when he analyzed the composition of minerals containing uranium or thorium, he always found lead.

Thinking that this find might be significant, he studied 43 mineral samples and ranked them by their estimated age. The amount of lead in these samples always increased as the samples grew older, just as the amount of uranium in them decreased. Boltwood concluded

**119**

that the radioactive decay series starting with uranium ended by creating lead—which was not radioactive. (Uranium eventually decayed into lead.) He studied the same process with thorium minerals and found the same result.

Boltwood surmised that, if uranium and thorium decayed at fixed, known rates, then he should be able to use the amount of lead and the amount of either of these radioactive materials in a rock sample to determine how old the rock is—that is, how long it had been since the radioactive decay process in that rock began. In his test samples, he used a Geiger counter to estimate how many atoms of uranium decayed per minute and an early mass spectrometer to determine how much of each trace element existed in the rock sample.

Knowing how much lead and uranium currently existed in the sample, knowing how fast the uranium decayed, and knowing the half-life of that particular uranium isotope, Boltwood could then calculate how long radioactive decay had been occurring in that rock. This would tell him how old the rock was.

In 1907 Boltwood published his calculations for the ages of 10 mineral samples. In every case they were startlingly old, showing that these rock samples (and the earth) were tens—and even hundreds—of times older than previously thought. Boltwood estimated the age of Earth at over 2.2 billion years (low based on present knowledge, but well over 10 times older than any previous estimate).

In 1947 American chemist Willard Libby realized that the recently discovered carbon isotope, carbon-14, could be used to date plant and animal remains in the same way that uranium was used to date rocks. Libby's carbon-14 dating accurately dated plant tissue back to 45,000 years and has been used to date paper samples as well as plant tissue.

 **Fun Facts:** Radiometric dating can be performed on samples as small as a billionth of a gram. The uranium-lead radiometric dating scheme is one of the oldest available, as well as one of the most highly respected. It has been refined to the point that any error in dates of rocks about three billion years old is no more than two million years. The measurement is 99.9 percent accurate.

# More to Explore

Badash, Lawrence, ed. *Rutherford and Boltwood: Letters on Radioactivity.* New Haven, CT: Yale University Press, 1999.

Dickin, Alan. *Radiogenic Isotope Geology.* New York: Cambridge University Press, 2005.

Glut, Donald. *Carbon Dates.* Jefferson, NC: McFarland & Co., 1999.

Liptak, Karen. *Dating Dinosaurs and Other Old Things.* New York: Lerner Publishing Group, 1998.

Roth, Etinne. *Nuclear Methods of Dating.* New York: Springer-Verlag, 1997.

# Function of Chromosomes

## Year of Discovery: 1909

> **What Is It?** Genes are grouped (linked) in groups that are strung along chromosomes.
>
> **Who Discovered It?** T. H. Morgan

## Why Is This One of the 100 Greatest?

Morgan's discovery that genes were linked into groups and strung along chromosomes was the second major step in peeling back the mystery of heredity and evolution. Morgan's discovery formed much of the foundation for later discoveries of how genes and chromosomes do their work as well as the structure of the DNA molecule.

Mendel established *that* traits (called "genes") are passed from parents into the next generation. Darwin established the concepts that dictated evolution of species. Still, science had no idea *how* species evolved or *how* individual genes were passed to new generations.

Studying a species of fruit flies, Professor T. H. Morgan at Columbia University both proved that Mendel's theory was correct and established the existence of chromosomes as the carriers for genes.

## How Was It Discovered?

By 1910, 44-year-old professor T. H. Morgan was the head of the biology department at New York's Columbia University. All his energy, however, he saved for his research. Morgan refused to accept Mendel's theories on heredity. Morgan didn't believe in the existence of genes since no one had physically seen a gene.

Neither did he accept Darwin's concept of survival of the fittest as the driving force of evolution. Morgan believed that evolution came from random mutations that slowly worked their way into and through a population. Morgan created "The Fly Room" to prove his ideas.

Morgan's Fly Room laboratory was a small, messy room with the overpowering reek of rotting bananas. Two walls were lined floor to ceiling with rows of corked glass bottles containing tens of thousands of tiny fruit flies. Their constant buzz was difficult to talk over.

He chose to study fruit flies for four reasons. First, they were small (only ¼-inch long). Second, they lived their entire lives on nothing but mashed banana. Third, they created a new generation in less than two weeks. Morgan could study almost 30 generations a year. Finally, they had few genes and so were much easier to study than more complex species.

Morgan searched and waited for a random physical mutation (like eye color) to appear in one of the thousands of fruit flies born each month. He would then carefully track that mutation through subsequent generations to see if spread across the population and proved his theory. It was a mind-numbing effort for Morgan and his assistants. Each month, many thousands of new fruit flies had to be carefully examined under the microscope for mutations.

In September 1910 Morgan found a mutation—a male fruit fly with clear white eyes instead of the normal deep red. The white-eyed male was carefully segregated in his own bottle and mated with a normal red-eyed female.

If the eyes of these hatchlings were white, off-white, or even rose colored (as Morgan believed they would be), this random mutation—that provided no real Darwinian survival benefit or advantage—would have evolved (permanently changed) the species and Morgan's theory of evolution by mutation would have been confirmed.

It took three days to examine the 1,237 new flies. Every one had normal red eyes. Morgan was crushed. The mutation had disappeared. It hadn't changed the species at all. Morgan was wrong.

By October 20 the grandchildren of the original white-eyed male were hatched. One-quarter of this generation had white eyes; three-quarters had normal red eyes. 3 to 1: That was Mendel's ratio for the interaction of a dominant and a recessive characteristic. T. H. Morgan's own experiment had just proved himself wrong and Mendel's gene theory right!

Additional mutations occurred frequently over the next two years. By studying these mutations and their effect on many generations of descendents, Morgan and his assistants realized that many of the inherited genes were always grouped together. (They called it "linked.")

By 1912 the team was able to establish that fruit fly genes were linked into four groups. Knowing that fruit flies had four chromosomes, Morgan suspected that genes must be strung along, and carried by, chromosomes. After 18 months of additional research, Morgan was able to prove this new theory. Chromosomes carried genes, and genes were strung in fixed-order lines (like beads) along chromosomes.

While attempting to disprove Mendel's work, Morgan both confirmed that Mendel was right and discovered the function of chromosomes and the relationship between chromosomes and genes.

 **Fun Facts:** Fruit flies can lay up to 500 eggs at a time, and their entire lifecycle is complete in about a week.

## More to Explore

Aaseng, Nathan. *Genetics: Unlocking the Secrets of Life.* Minneapolis, MN: Oliver Press, 1996.

Allen, Garland. *Thomas Hunt Morgan: The Man and His Science.* Princeton, NJ: Princeton University Press, 1996.

Edey, Maitland, and Donald Johanson. *BLUEPRINTS: Solving the Mystery of Evolution.* New York: Penguin Books, 1994.

Riley, Herbert. *Thomas Hunt Morgan.* Frankfurt: Kentucky Academy of Sciences, 1994.

Sherrow, Victoria. *Great Scientists.* New York: Facts on File, 1998.

Shine, Ian. *Thomas Hunt Morgan, Pioneer of Genetics.* Frankfurt: University Press of Kentucky, 1996.

Sturtevant, A. H. *A History of Genetics.* Cold Spring Harbor, NY: Cold Spring Harbor Laboratory Press, 2001.

# Antibiotics

## Year of Discovery: 1910

> **What Is It?** Chemical substances that kill infectious microscopic organisms without harming the human host.
>
> **Who Discovered It?** Paul Ehrlich

## Why Is This One of the 100 Greatest?

The word "antibiotic" comes from the Greek words meaning "against life." Early folk medicine relied on some natural compounds that cured certain diseases—the ground bark of a tree, certain cheese molds, certain fungi. Doctors knew *that* these natural compounds worked, but had no idea of *how* or *why* they worked.

Paul Ehrlich conducted the first modern chemical investigation of antibiotics and discovered the first antibiotic chemical compounds. His work opened a new era for medical and pharmacological research and founded the field of chemotherapy. Antibiotics (penicillin, discovered in 1928, is the most famous) have saved many millions of lives and trace their modern origin to Paul Ehrlich's work.

## How Was It Discovered?

Paul Ehrlich was born in Germany in 1854. A gifted student, he entered graduate school to study for a medical degree. There he became deeply involved in the process of staining microscopic tissue samples so that they would show up better under the microscope. The problem was that most dyes destroyed the tissue samples before they could be viewed. Ehrlich struggled to find new dyes that wouldn't harm or kill delicate microscopic organisms. This work showed Ehrlich that *some* chemical compounds killed *some* types of tissue and made him wonder if the process could be controlled.

By 1885 it had become clear that the causative agent for many illnesses was microorganisms. Many scientists made a great effort to study these bacteria under the microscope. Again Ehrlich found that many of the available dyes and stains killed the organisms before they could be studied. This finding inspired Ehrlich to propose that chemical compounds may exist that could kill these organisms without harming the human patient, thus curing an illness by killing only its causative agent.

In the mid-1890s, Ehrlich shifted his focus to studies of the immune system and how to control the reaction between chemical toxins and antitoxins. Again it occurred to Ehrlich that, just as antitoxins specifically sought a toxin molecule to which they were related and destroyed it, so, too, he might be able to create a chemical substance that would go straight to some disease-causing organism and destroy it. Ehrlich called such a chemical substance a "magic bullet." It seemed that 25 years of work had led him directly to this idea.

During this same period, many specific disease-causing bacteria were being identified and studied. This gave Ehrlich well-understood targets to attack as he sought ways to create magic bullets. He chose to start with *spirochaete*, the microorganism that caused syphilis. Ehrlich began testing different chemicals using an arsenic base for his compounds. Arsenic had been effective in destroying a number of other microorganisms.

By 1907, Ehrlich had reached the 606th compound to be tested. He tested this compound on rabbits infected with syphilis. It cured the rabbits. Ehrlich named it *salvarsan* and conducted over 100 additional tests to be sure it worked and that it wouldn't harm human patients. He then worked for two more years to develop a form of this drug that was easier to manufacture and that was easier to administer. Of the thousand variations he tried, version number 914 was the best. He named it *neosalvarsan*.

Ehrlich's final test of neosalvarsan was to give it to terminal patients suffering from the dementia that was the final stage of syphilis. While neosalvarsan helped all of these patients, remarkably, several completely recovered.

Neosalvarsan was the first man-made chemical that would specifically destroy a target organism and not affect the human patient. This discovery founded the field of chemotherapy.

 **Fun Facts:** Resistance to antibiotics works by the ordinary rules of natural selection: that segment of the bacteria population that has a natural ability to counter the drug's effect will survive, so that their genes eventually are shared by the entire population. Many disease-causing viruses and bacteria have developed virtual immunity to many antibiotics, making medical planners fear massive disease outbreaks in the near future.

# More to Explore

Asimov, Isaac. *Asimov's Chronology of Science and Discovery.* New York: Harper & Row, 1989.

Baumier, Ernest. *Paul Ehrlich: Scientist for Life.* Teaneck, NJ: Holmes & Meier, 1994.

Dyson, James. *A History of Great Inventions.* New York: Carroll & Graf Publishers, 2001.

Ehrlich, Paul. *Studies in Immunity.* New York: John Wiley & Sons, 1990.

Pickstone, John, ed. *Medical Innovations in Historical Perspective.* New York: Palgrave Macmillan, 1993.

Zannos, Susan. *Paul Ehrlich and Modern Drug Development* . Hockessin, DE: Mitchell Lane, 2002.

# Fault Lines

## Year of Discovery: 1911

**What Is It?** Earthquakes happen both along, and because of, fault lines in the earth's crust.

**Who Discovered It?** Harry Reid

## Why Is This One of the 100 Greatest?

Scientists now know that they can predict the locations of future earthquakes by mapping the locations of fault lines. However, just a century ago this simple truth was not known.

Harry Reid's discovery that earthquakes happen along existing fault lines provided the first understanding of the source and process of earthquakes. This discovery laid the foundation for the discovery of Earth's crustal plates and plate tectonics in the late 1950s.

Reid's discovery was called a major breakthrough in earth science and provided the first basic understanding of Earth's internal processes and of how rocks behave under stress.

## How Was It Discovered?

By 1750, scientists knew that there were fault lines (like long cracks) snaking through Earth's upper crust where two dissimilar kinds of rocks came together. By 1900, scientists knew that these fault lines were associated with earthquakes.

The mistake scientists made, however, was to agree that earthquakes caused the fault lines. It was as though the crust had been a smooth block of rock that had been cracked by an earthquake, with one side sliding past the other to create the rock mismatch. Earthquakes happened, and fault lines were the telltale residues of past earthquakes.

Harry Fielding Reid was born in Baltimore in 1859. When he received his early schooling in Switzerland, these ideas were what were taught in geology classes. They were what Reid learned. However, earthquakes and fault lines were of little interest to Reid. Living in Switzerland focused his primary interest on mountains and glaciers.

Reid returned to Baltimore to attend college at Johns Hopkins University in 1865 (at the age of 16). He stayed long enough to receive a doctorate in geology in 1885. Beginning in 1889, Reid took positions as a university professor with a research emphasis on glaciers.

Reid traveled extensively through Alaska and the Swiss Alps mapping and studying glaciers, their movement, their formation, and their effects on the landscape. He wrote articles and papers on glacial structure and movement.

In April 1906 the great San Francisco earthquake struck and most of the city either toppled or was burned. In late 1906 the state of California formed the California State Earthquake Investigation Commission to study the San Francisco earthquake and to determine the risk to the state of possible future earthquakes. Reid was asked to serve as a member of this nine-member commission.

This commission study turned Reid's interest toward earthquakes and fault lines. He mapped and studied the San Andreas fault line and roamed the central California coastal region mapping other fault lines. Always he searched for an answer to the question: What caused earthquakes?

Reid carefully studied the rocks along California fault lines and concluded that they suffered from long-term physical stress, not just from the jolt of a sudden earthquake. Reid saw that great stresses must have existed in the rocks along the San Andreas fault line for centuries—even for millennia—before the earthquake happened.

That meant that the fault lines had to have existed *first* and stress along them caused the earthquake. Stress built up and built up in the rocks until they snapped. That "snap" was an earthquake.

Reid developed the image of the rock layers along fault lines acting like rubber bands. Stresses deep in the earth along these fault lines pulled the rocks in different directions, causing these rocks to stretch—like elastic. Once the stress reached the breaking point, the rocks elastically snapped back—causing an earthquake.

Fault lines caused earthquakes, not the other way around. That meant that studying fault lines was a way to *predict* earthquakes, not merely study their aftermath. Reid had discovered the significance of the earth's spider web maze of fault lines.

 **Fun Facts:** The destructive San Francisco earthquake of 1906 horizontally shifted land surfaces on either side of the San Andreas fault up to 21 ft (6.4 m).

# More to Explore

Branley, Franklyn. *Earthquakes*. New York: HarperTrophy, 1998.

Harrison, James. *Discover Amazing Earth*. New York: Sterling Publishing Co., 2005.

Sherrow, Victoria. *Great Scientists*. New York: Facts on File, 1998.

Thomas, Gordon. *The San Francisco Earthquake*. New York: Day Books, 1996.

Ulin, David. *The Myth of Solid Ground*. New York: Penguin, 2005.

# Superconductivity

> **What Is It?** Some materials lose all resistance to electrical current at super-low temperatures.
>
> **Who Discovered It?** Heike Kamerlingh Onnes

## Why Is This One of the 100 Greatest?

Superconductivity is the flow of electrical current without any resistance to that flow. Even the best conductors have some resistance to electrical current. But superconductors do not. Unfortunately, superconductors only exist in the extreme cold of near absolute zero.

Even though the practical application of this discovery has not yet been realized, superconductivity holds the promise of super-efficient electrical and magnetic motors, of electrical current flowing thousands of miles with no loss of power, and of meeting the dream of cheap and efficient electricity for everyone. Superconductivity will likely spawn whole new industries and ways of generating, processing, and moving electrical energy. But that potential still lies in the future.

## How Was It Discovered?

Heike Onnes was born in 1853 in Groningen, the Netherlands, into a wealthy family that owned a brick making factory. As he went through college and graduate school, he drew considerable attention for his talent at solving scientific problems. By the time he was 18, Onnes had become a firm believer in the value of physical experimentations and tended to discount theories that could not be demonstrated by physical experiment.

At the age of 25, Onnes focused his university research on the properties of materials at temperatures approaching the coldest possible temperature (-456°F or -269°C). The existence of that temperature, the temperature at which all heat energy is gone and all motion —even inside an atom—ceases, was discovered by Lord Kelvin, and is called 0° Kelvin (0°K) or *absolute zero.*

Several theories existed about what happened near 0°K. Lord Kelvin believed that absolute zero would stop the motion of electrons. Electrical current would cease and resistance to that current would be infinitely large. Others believed the opposite—that resistance would fall to zero and electrical currents would flow forever.

Everyone had a theory. Onnes decided to find out, to test the theories.

However, there was a problem. No method existed to cool anything anywhere near -269°C. Luckily, Onnes was the physics department chair at the University of Leyden, and that department came equipped with a well-funded physics lab that Onnes could use.

In 1907 Onnes invented thermometers that could measure temperatures as extreme as absolute zero. In 1908 he discovered a way to cool the gas helium so cold that it turned into a liquid. He was able to continue to chill the super-cold liquid until, late that year, he chilled liquid helium to 0.9°K—less than one degree above absolute zero! Onnes realized that he could use this liquid helium to chill other materials to near 0°K to measure their electrical resistance.

By 1911 Onnes had developed canisters capable of holding and storing his super-cold liquid helium and had set up a small production line. He began his electrical studies by chilling first platinum and then gold to near absolute zero. However, the electrical currents he measured were erratic, his results inconclusive.

Onnes decided to switch to liquid mercury. He filled a U-shaped tube with mercury and attached wires to each end of the U. The wires were attached to a meter to measure electrical resistance. He used liquid helium at 0.9°K to cool the mercury.

As the temperature dipped below 40°K (-229°C) electrical resistance began to drop. It dropped steadily as the temperature dipped below 20°K. And then, at 4.19°K resistance abruptly disappeared. It fell to zero.

Onnes repeated the experiment many times over the next few months and always got the same result. Below 4.19°K, there was no resistance to the flow of electricity. An electric current would flow unimpeded for ever! He called it *superconductivity.*

Onnes had discovered superconductivity, but he could not theoretically explain it. He only suspected that it had something to do with the (then) recently discovered Quantum Theory. It was not until 1951 that John Bardeen developed a mathematical theory to explain superconductivity.

A search began to find ways to create superconductivity at higher (more practically reached) temperatures. The current record (using—unfortunately—toxic ceramic compounds made with mercury and copper) is 138°K (-131°C). Once a way is found to create superconductivity at warmer temperatures, the value of Onnes's discovery will be unlimited.

 **Fun Facts:** AT CERN, the European high-energy physics research lab, scientists used a one-time jolt of electricity to start an electrical current flowing through a superconductor circuit. That electrical current ran—with no additional voltage input—for five years with no loss of power. In common house wires, an electrical current would stop within a few milliseconds once the voltage is removed because of the resistance of electrical wires.

# More to Explore

Ford, P. J. *The Rise of Superconductors.* New York: CRC Press, 2005.

Gale Reference. *Biography: Heike Kamerlingh Onnes.* New York: Gale Research, 2004.

Lampton, Christopher. *Superconductors.* Berkeley Heights, NJ: Enslow, 1997.

Matricon, Jean. *The Cold Wars: A History of Superconductivity.* New Brunswick, NJ: Rutgers University Press, 2003.

Shachtman, T. *Absolute Zero and the Conquest of Cold.* New York: Houghton Mifflin, 1999.

# Atomic Bonding

## Year of Discovery: 1913

---

**What Is It?** The first working theory of how electrons gain, lose, and hold energy and how they orbit the nucleus of an atom.

**Who Discovered It?** Niels Bohr

---

## Why Is This One of the 100 Greatest?

Marie Curie opened the century by proving that there *was* a subatomic world. Einstein, Dirac, Heisenberg, Born, Rutherford, and others provided the new theoretical descriptions of this subatomic world. But *proving* what lurked within an atom's shell, and what governed its behavior, lingered as the great physics challenges of the early twentieth century.

It was Niels Bohr who discovered the first concrete model of the electrons surrounding an atom's nucleus—their placement, motion, radiation patterns, and energy transfers. Bohr's theory solved a number of inconsistencies and flaws that had existed in previous attempts to guess at the structure and activity of electrons. He combined direct experiment with advanced theory to create an understanding of electrons. It was an essential step in science's march into the nuclear age.

## How Was It Discovered?

Niels Bohr was only 26 in 1912—very young to step into the middle of a heated physics controversy. But that spring, as a new physics professor at the University of Copenhagen, Bohr realized atomic theory no longer matched the growing body of experimental atomic data. One of Bohr's experiments showed that classical theories predicted that an orbiting electron would continuously lose energy and slowly spiral into the nucleus. The atom would collapse and implode. But that didn't happen. Atoms were amazingly stable. Something was wrong with the existing theories—and Bohr said so.

There was no way to actually see an atom, no way to peer inside and directly observe what was going on. Scientists had to grope in the dark for their theories, sifting through indirect clues for shreds of insight into the bizarre workings of atoms.

Atomic experimenters were building mountains of data. They recorded the particles created from atomic collisions. They measured the angles at which these new particles raced away from the collision site. They measured electrical energy levels. But few of these data fit with atomic theories.

As Bohr began to organize his teaching in 1913, he read about two new experimental studies. First, Enrico Fermi found that atoms always emitted energy in the same few amounts (or bursts) of energy. He called these bursts discrete quanta (quantities) of energy.

Second, chemists had studied the amount of energy that each element's atoms radiated. They found that if they passed this radiation through a prism, the radiation was not continuous over the whole frequency spectrum, but came in sharp spikes at certain discrete frequencies. Different elements showed different characteristic patterns in these energy spikes. Neither study fit with existing theories.

Bohr studied and compared these different, and apparently unrelated, bits of data, knowing that the new data had to relate somehow—since they dealt with characteristics and emissions from the same source: atoms.

Bohr sifted and resifted the data and the theories over an eight-month period, searching for a way to make the experimental data fit with some atomic theory. By late that year he had discovered a revolutionary idea: Electrons must not be as free to roam as previously thought.

He theorized that the electrons circling an atom's nucleus could only exist in certain, discrete, fixed orbits. In order to jump to a closer orbit, an electron would have to give off a fixed amount of energy (the observed spikes and quanta of radiated energy). If an electron were to jump into a higher orbit, it would have to absorb a fixed quanta of energy. Electrons couldn't go wherever they wanted or carry any amount of energy. Electrons must be in one or another of these few specific orbits. Electrons must gain and lose energy in specific quanta.

Bohr's atomic model was a revolutionary idea and a complete departure from previous ideas. However, it fit well with experimental observations and explained all of the inconsistencies of previous theories. This model also explained how and why chemical elements bonded with each other as they did.

Bohr's discovery received instant acclaim and acceptance. For 50 years it served as the accepted model of an atom and of the motion of electrons within the atom.

 **Fun Facts:** Niels Bohr worked at the secret Los Alamos laboratory in New Mexico, on the Manhattan Project (the code name for the effort to develop atomic bombs for the United States during World War II).

# More to Explore

Aserud, Finn. *Redirecting Science: Niels Bohr and the Rise of Nuclear Physics.* London: Cambridge University Press, 1990.

Blaedel, Niels. *Harmony and Unity: The Life of Niels Bohr.* Chicago: Science Technology Publishing, 1988.

Moore, Ruth. *Niels Bohr: The Man, His Science, and the World They Changed.* Cambridge, MA: MIT Press, 1985.

Murdoch, D. R. *Niels Bohr's Philosophy of Physics.* London: Cambridge University Press, 1999.

Rozental, S. *Niels Bohr: His Life and Work.* New York: John Wiley & Sons, 1997.

# Isotopes

## Year of Discovery: 1913

---

> **What Is It?** Isotopes are different forms of the same chemical element that have identical physical and chemical properties but different atomic weights.
>
> **Who Discovered It?** Frederick Soddy

## Why Is This One of the 100 Greatest?

Isotopes of an element are slightly different forms of that element. Isotopes have the same chemical, physical, and electrical properties as the original element, but have a different number of neutrons in their nucleus. The discovery of isotopes created a new dimension and concept for physics and chemistry.

This discovery answered baffling problems that had stymied physics researchers studying radioactive elements. The study of isotopes became a key foundation for the development of atomic power and weapons. Isotopes are also critical to geology since carbon dating and other rock-dating techniques all depend on the ratios of specific isotopes.

This one discovery removed roadblocks to scientific progress, opened new fields of physics and chemistry research, and provided essential research tools to earth science research.

## How Was It Discovered?

Frederick Soddy was born in 1877 in Sussex, England. In 1910 Soddy accepted a position at the University of Glasgow as a lecturer in radioactivity and chemistry.

The study of radioactive elements was still exciting and new. Radioactive elements were identified by differences in their mass, atomic charge, and radioactive properties, including the kinds and energies of different particles they emitted.

However, using this system, scientists had already identified 40 to 50 radioactive elements. But there existed only 10 to 12 places for all of these radioactive elements on the periodic chart of elements. Either Mendeleyev's periodic chart was wrong or—for some unknown reason—radioactive elements fell outside the logic and order of the periodic chart.

Neither answer made any sense, and radioactive research ground to a halt.

Soddy decided to study the three known subatomic particles emitted by the various radioactive elements (alpha, beta, and gamma particles). Soddy found that alpha particle held a positive charge of two (as would two protons) and a mass equal to four protons. Gamma

**133**

rays had neither charge nor mass, only energy, so they didn't affect the nature of the atom at all.

Beta particles had no measurable mass but held a negative charge of one. They were apparently just electrons.

When an atom emitted a beta particle, it *lost* a negative charge. Soddy realized that was the same as *gaining* a positive charge. Emit an alpha particle and lose two positive charges from the nucleus. Emit a beta particle and gain one.

Because the periodic table was organized by the number of protons in the nucleus of an atom—from the lightest element (hydrogen) up to the heaviest known element (uranium), Soddy realized that the emission of an alpha particle would, in effect, shift the atom two spaces to the left on the periodic chart and the emission of a beta particle shifted it one place to the right.

It must be, he concluded, that atoms of many elements could exist in several different spaces on the periodic chart. Soddy used new spectrographic research techniques (discovered by Gustav Kirchhoff and Robert Bunsen in 1859) to show that—even though they had a different atomic mass and so occupied different spaces on the periodic chart—atoms of uranium and thorium were still the same, original element.

This meant that more than one element could occupy the same spot on the periodic chart and that atoms of one element could occupy more than one spot and still be the same, original element. Soddy named the versions of an element that occupied spots on the periodic chart—other than that element's "normal" spot—*isotopes,* from the Greek words meaning "same place."

Later that same year (1913), American chemist Theodore Richards measured the atomic weights of lead isotopes resulting from the radioactive decay of uranium and of thorium and proved Soddy's theory to be true.

However, Soddy's explanation of his discovery was not completely accurate. Chadwick's discovery of the *neutron* (in 1932) was needed to correct Soddy's errors and to complete the understanding of Soddy's concept of isotopes.

Soddy had tried to explain his isotopes using only protons and electrons. Chadwick discovered that as many neutrally charged neutrons existed in the nucleus as did positively charged protons. Gaining or losing neutrons didn't change the electric charge of or the properties of the element (since elements were defined by the number of protons in the nucleus). It *did*, however, change the atomic mass of the atom and so created an isotope of that element.

Soddy discovered the concept of isotopes. But an understanding of neutrons was needed in order to fully understand them.

 **Fun Facts:** Isotopes are more important than most people think. Every ancient rock, fossil, human remain, or plant ever dated was dated using isotopes of various elements. Natural radioactivity is created by isotopes. The atomic bomb uses an isotope of uranium.

# More to Explore

Clayton, Donald. *Handbook of Isotopes in the Cosmos.* New York: Cambridge University Press, 2003.

James, Richard. *Adventures of the Elements.* Pittsburgh: Three Rivers Council, 1997.

Kauffman, George. *Frederick Soddy: Early Pioneer in Radiochemistry.* New York: Springer, 2002.

Merricks, Linda. *The World Made New: Frederick Soddy, Science, and Environment.* New York: Oxford University Press, 1996.

Rattanski, P. M. *Pioneers of Science and Discovery.* Charleston, WV: Main Line Books, 1997.

# Earth's Core and Mantle

## Year of Discovery: 1914

> **What Is It?** The earth is made up of layers, each of a different density, temperature, and composition.
>
> **Who Discovered It?** Beno Gutenberg

## Why Is This One of the 100 Greatest?

It is impossible to see, to venture, or even to send probes more than a few miles under the surface of Earth. Almost all of the 4,000+ miles from the surface to the center is unreachable to humans. Yet scientists could not begin to understand our planet and its formation without having an accurate knowledge of that interior.

Beno Gutenberg provided the first reasonable accounting of Earth's interior. His discovery proved that Earth wasn't a solid homogeneous planet, but was divided into layers. Gutenberg was the first to correctly estimate the temperature and physical properties of Earth's core. His discoveries have been so important that he is often considered the father of geophysics.

## How Was It Discovered?

Born in 1889 in Darmstadt, Germany, Beno Gutenberg loved science as a boy and always knew he'd be a meteorologist. As he began his second year of university meteorological study in 1907, he saw a notice announcing the formation of a department of the new science of geophysics (Earth physics) at the University of Göttingen.

The idea of a whole new science fascinated Gutenberg. He transferred to Göttingen and, while holding onto a major in meteorology, studied under Emil Wiechert, a pioneer in the emerging science of seismology—the study of seismic waves caused by earthquakes and earth tremors.

By the time of his graduation in 1913, Gutenberg had shifted from meteorology (study of the atmosphere) to geophysics (study of Earth's interior). It was a case of being in the right place at the right time. Gutenberg had access to all of Wiechert's data and studies, the most extensive and comprehensive collection of seismic data in the world. Wiechert had focused on collecting the data. Gutenberg focused on studying the patterns of those data.

Gutenberg found that, typically, seismic waves did not reach all parts of the earth's surface, even when the tremor was strong enough to have been detected everywhere. There always existed a *shadow zone* more or less straight across the globe from an event where no seismic waves were ever detectable.

He also noticed that seismic waves seemed to travel at different speeds on different trajectories through the earth. This all made Gutenberg suspect that the interior of the earth was not a solid, homogeneous mass. It must have several separate layers or regions.

Gutenberg settled on the image of the earth as an egg. The surface of the earth was thin and brittle like an eggshell. He realized that there must be a core to Earth (like an egg yoke) that was more dense than the surrounding mantle (the egg white).

If this image held true, seismic waves approaching the core would change speeds and be diffracted (bent) because of the density difference between layers. One of the kinds of seismic waves that Gutenberg studied was *transverse waves*. These waves would not enter the core at all. Knowing that transverse waves dissipate quickly in the liquid ocean, Gutenberg surmised that Earth's core also had to be liquid.

Gutenberg had enough data from the recorded diffractions of enough seismic waves to calculate how big the core had to be and what its density had to be in order to create the diffraction patterns seismologists recorded. The core of the earth, he said, had a radius of 2,100 miles.

Based on these calculations, on chemical experiments he ran in early 1914, and on the measured chemical composition of meteorites, Gutenberg estimated that the core was a liquid mixture of nickel and iron, while the mantel was made up of rock material.

Gutenberg's model was quickly accepted and was not improved upon until 1938. In that year, Inge Lehman completed a detailed study of "P" waves (another kind of seismic wave) with vastly improved equipment from that used in 1914. Her research showed that Earth's core was divided into a solid inner core and a surrounding liquid outer core. She also broke the mantle into an inner and an outer mantle. This discovery completed our basic image of Earth's interior.

 **Fun Facts:** The crust of the earth is solid. So is the inner core. But in between, the outer core and mantle (90 percent of the mass of the earth) are liquid to molten semi-solid. We do not live on a particularly solid planet.

# More to Explore

Crossley, D. *Earth's Deep Interior.* Abingdon, England: Taylor & Francis, 1997.

Gibbons, Gail. *Planet Earth: Inside Out.* New York: HarperCollins, 1998.

Gutenberg, Beno. *Seismicity of the Earth and Associated Phenomena.* New York: Textbook Publishers, 2003.

Jacobs, John. *Earth's Core.* Chevy Chase, MD: Elsevier Science Books, 1997.

Manzanero, Paula, ed. *Scholastic Atlas of Earth.* New York: Scholastic, 2005.

Vogt, Gregory. *Earth's Core and Asthenosphere.* New York: Lerner Group, 2004.

# Continental Drift

> **What Is It?** Earth's continents drift and move over time.
>
> **Who Discovered It?** Alfred Wegener

## Why Is This One of the 100 Greatest?

Before Wegener's discovery, scientists thought that the earth was a static body—never changing, now as it always has been. Alfred Wegener's discovery that Earth's continents drift across the face of the planet led to modern tectonic plate theories and to a true understanding of how Earth's crust, mantel, and core move, flow, and interact. It created the first sense of Earth's dynamic history.

Wegener's discovery solved nagging mysteries in a dozen fields of study—and stirred up new questions still being debated today. This discovery stands as a cornerstone of our modern understanding of earth sciences.

## How Was It Discovered?

Albert Wegener was born in 1880 in Berlin. Always restless and more of a *doer* than a *thinker*, he switched his college major from astronomy to meteorology because "astronomy offered no opportunity for physical activity." Upon graduation, Wegener signed on for meteorological expeditions to Iceland and Greenland in 1906 and 1908.

While on tour in 1910, Wegener noticed the remarkable fit of the coastlines of South America and Africa. He was not the first scientist to notice this fit, but one of the first to think that it was important.

In 1911, new ocean maps showed the Atlantic Ocean continental shelves. (Continental shelves are shallow, underwater shelves extending out from continents.) Wegener noticed an even better fit between the continental shelves of South America and Africa. They "fit like pieces of a jigsaw puzzle."

Wegener knew that this perfect fit couldn't be just a coincidence and suspected that those two continents were once connected—even though they were now separated by several thousand miles of ocean. This was a radical notion since all scientists assumed that the continents never moved from their fixed positions on Earth.

In that same year, Wegener read studies that noted the same fossil finds in South America and in corresponding parts of coastal Africa. Many scientists proposed that there once existed a land bridge between the two so that plant and animal species could intermix. This bridge, they assumed, long ago sank to the bottom of the sea.

**138**

Wegener believed a land bridge was impossible. It would have left telltale signs on the ocean floor and would create gravitational anomalies that did not exist. In 1912, he decided to build a body of evidence from a variety of fields to prove that the continents had once been joined.

He used the extensive fieldwork of Eduard Suess to provide most of his geological data. Suess discovered that, in place after place, rocks on coasts that faced each other across the oceans often matched exactly.

Wegener poured through the findings of hundreds of geologic surveys to show that the rock formations, mix of rock kinds, and rock stratification on the two continents (South America and Africa) matched up and down the coastline. He found formations known as pipes (associated with diamonds) on both sides of the south Atlantic, exactly opposite each other.

He also collected records of past and present plant communities on both sides of the Atlantic and mapped them to show how they matched up and down the coast.

The only explanation Wegener could offer for these similarities was that South America and Africa used to be joined as a single continent and one or both had since drifted off. He extended his theory to cover all continents (e.g., North America used to be joined with Europe) and arrived at the conclusion that, at one time, all of Earth's land masses had been joined in a single massive continent that he named Pangaea (Greek for "all Earth")

Wegener published his discoveries and his theory in 1915. Scientists around the world were both skeptical of his conclusions and impressed by the amount of, and variety of, data he presented. Wegener had discovered continental drift, but stumbled when he couldn't say *how* the continents drifted (what force drove them through the denser oceanic floor). Forty years later, Harvey Hess discovered sea floor spreading and filled this hole in Wegener's theory.

 **Fun Facts:** The Himalayas, the world's highest mountain system, are the result of the ongoing collision of two huge tectonic plates (the Eurasia plate and the Indian subcontinent), which began about 40 million years ago.

# More to Explore

Cohen, Bernard. *Revolutions in Science.* Cambridge, MA: Harvard University Press, 1995.

Hallam, Anthony. *A Revolution in the Earth Sciences: From Continental Drift to Plate Tectonics.* New York: Clarendon Press, 1993.

LeGrand, H. *Drifting Continents and Shifting Theories.* New York: Cambridge University Press, 1998.

Oreskes, Naomi. *The Rejection of Continental Drift: Theory and Method in American Earth Sciences.* New York: Oxford University Press, 1999.

Wegener, Alfred, and Kurt Wegener. *The Origins of Continents and Oceans.* New York: Dover, 1996.

# Black Holes

## Year of Discovery: 1916

> **What Is It?** A collapsed star that is so dense, and whose gravitational pull is so great, that not even light can escape it. Such stars would look like black holes in a black universe.
>
> **Who Discovered It?** Karl Schwarzschild

## Why Is This One of the 100 Greatest?

Many consider black holes to be the ultimate wonder of the universe, the strangest of all stellar objects. Black holes might be the birthplace of new universes, even new dimensions. Black holes might mark the beginning and end of time. Some consider them to be possible time travel machines as well as a way to travel faster than the speed of light. Many believe that black holes could be the ultimate future energy source, providing power stations throughout the galaxy.

Certainly, black holes were first a theoretical, and then a practical, great mystery of astronomy in the twentieth century. Their discovery led science a giant step closer to understanding the universe around us and provided a solid confirmation of Einstein's theory of relativity.

## How Was It Discovered?

A black hole is not really a hole at all. It is a collapsed star that crushed in on itself. As the star condenses, its gravity increases. If the collapsed star's gravity becomes so strong that not even light (particles traveling at light speed) can escape the gravitational pull, then it will appear like a black hole (in the pitch black background of space).

Two men get the credit for the discovery of these bizarre and unseeable phenomena. The first was German astronomer wonder-boy, Karl Schwarzschild. As a child, Schwarzschild was fascinated by celestial mechanics (the motion of the stars), and he published his first two papers on the theory of how double stars move when he was only 16 (in 1889). In 1900, Schwarzschild presented a lecture to the German astronomical society in which he theorized that space did not act like a regular three-dimensional box. It warped in strange ways, pulled and pushed by gravity. Schwarzschild called it "the curvature of space."

Five years later, Einstein published his energy equation and his theory of relativity, which also talked of the curvature of space. In 1916, while serving in the German army on the Russian front during World War I, Schwarzschild was the first to solve Einstein's equations for general relativity. He found that, as a star collapsed into a single point of unimaginably dense matter, its gravitational pull would increase so that a particle would have to be traveling faster and faster to escape from that gravity (called the escape velocity). Schwarzschild's calculations showed that as a massive star collapsed to a single point of infinitely dense matter, its escape velocity would exceed the speed of light. *Nothing* would escape such a collapsed star. It would be as if the star disappeared and no longer existed in our universe.

With these calculations, Schwarzschild had discovered the concept of a black hole. The terms we now use to describe a black hole (event horizon, escape velocity, etc) were all created by Schwarzschild in 1916. Schwarzschild mathematically "discovered" black holes, but he didn't believe they physically existed. He thought it was only a mathematical exercise.

Fifty years later, astronomers began to seriously search for Schwarzschild's invisible collapsed stars. Astronomers realized that, since a black hole couldn't actually be seen, the only way to detect one was to track unexplained motion of the stars that they *could* see and show that that motion was the result of the gravitational pull of a nearby, unseeable black hole. (Astronomer John Wheeler coined the name "black hole" in 1970.)

In 1971, calculations by Wheeler's team confirmed that the X-ray binary star, Cygnus X-1, was a star circling a black hole. That was the first time a black hole had ever been physically detected.

It wasn't until 2004 that a black hole was identified in the Milky Way galaxy, by Professor Phil Charles of the University of Southampton and Mark Wagner of the University of Arizona, this one located 6,000 light years away from Earth in our galaxy's halo. But it was Karl Schwarzschild in 1916 who discovered what black holes "looked like" and how to locate one.

 **Fun Facts:** Discovered in January 2000, the closest black hole is only 1,600 light years from Earth and is known as V4641 Sgr. Such normal black holes are several times the mass of the sun. But supermassive black holes reside in the hearts of galaxies and can be as massive as several hundred million times the mass of the sun.

# More to Explore

Asimov, Isaac. *Black Holes, Pulsars, and Quasars.* New York: Gareth Stevens, 2003.

Davis, Amanda. *Black Holes.* Minneapolis, MN: Powerkids Press, 2003.

Jefferies, Daivd. *Black Holes.* New York: Crabtree Publishing, 2006.

Nardo, Don. *Black Holes.* New York: Thomson Gale, 2003.

Rau, Dana. *Black Holes.* Mankato, MN: Capstone Press, 2005.

Sipiera, Paul. *Black Holes.* New York: Scholastic Library, 1997.

# Insulin

> **What Is It?** Insulin is a hormone produced by the pancreas that allows the body to pull sugar from blood and burn it to produce energy.
>
> **Who Discovered It?** Frederick Banting

## Why Is This One of the 100 Greatest?

Frederick Banting discovered a way to remove and use the pancreatic "juice" of animals to save the lives of diabetic humans. This hormone is called insulin. Its discovery has saved millions of human lives. Diabetes used to be a death sentence. There was no known way to replace the function of a pancreas that had stopped producing insulin. Banting's discovery changed all that.

Although insulin is not a cure for diabetes, this discovery turned the death sentence of diabetes into a manageable malady with which millions of people live healthy and normal lives.

## How Was It Discovered?

In early 1921, 28-year-old Canadian orthopedic surgeon Frederick Banting developed a theory—actually, it was more of a vague idea—for a way to help people suffering from diabetes.

The outer cells of the pancreas produced strong digestive juices. But the inner cells produced a delicate hormone that flowed straight into the blood. Muscles got their energy from sugars in the bloodstream, which came from food. But the body couldn't pull sugar out of the bloodstream without that hormone from the inner cells of the pancreas.

When the inner cells of a person's pancreas stopped making that hormone, their muscles couldn't draw sugar from the bloodstream, and the bloodstream became overloaded with sugar and struggled to get rid of it through excess urination. The body dehydrated; and the patient became deathly ill. This condition was called diabetes.

In 1920 there was no cure for diabetes. It was always fatal.

Researchers had tried obtaining the pancreatic hormone (which they referred to as "juice") from animals. But when a pancreas was ground up, the digestive juices from the outer cells were so strong that they destroyed the delicate juice from the inner cells before it could be used.

Banting read an article by Dr. Moses Barron that described the fate of several patients in whom a blockage had developed in the ducts carrying pancreatic outer cell digestive juices to the stomach. These strong acids had been trapped in the outer cells of the pancreas and had destroyed those cells. The cells literally shut down and dried up.

Banting wondered if he could intentionally kill the outer pancreatic cells of an animal and then harvest its inner cell juice for use by diabetic humans.

His plan was simple enough. Operate to tie off the ducts from a dog's pancreatic outer cells to the stomach, wait the eight weeks Dr. Barron had mentioned in his article, and hope that the outer cells had dried up and died. Finally, in a second operation, he would harvest the dog's pancreas and see if it still contained life-giving inner cells and their precious juice. He would artificially create diabetes in another dog s and see if the pancreatic fluid from the first dog could keep it alive.

With no funding, Banting talked his way into the use of a lab and six test dogs. The surgery was simple enough. Now he had to wait eight weeks for the outer cells to die.

However, early in week six the diabetic dog slid into a coma. This was the last stage before death. Banting couldn't wait any longer. He operated on one of the other dogs, successfully removing its pancreas. He ground up this tissue and extracted the juice by dissolving it in a chloride solution.

He injected a small amount of this juice into the diabetic dog. Within 30 minutes the dog awakened from its coma. Within two hours it was back on its feet. In five hours it began to slide back down hill. With another injection it perked up, with enough energy to bark and wag its tail.

Banting was ecstatic. His hunch had been right!

Dr. John Marcum named the juice, "insulin" during the two years that he and Dr. Banting searched for a way to create this precious juice without harming lab dogs—a feat they eventually accomplished.

 **Fun Facts:** In 1922 a 14-year-old boy suffering from type I diabetes was the first person to be treated with insulin. He showed rapid improvement.

# More to Explore

Bankston, John. *Frederick Banting and the Discovery of Insulin*. Hockessin, DE: Mitchell Lane, 2001.

Bliss, Michael. *Discovery of Insulin*. Chicago: University of Chicago Press, 1994.

Fox, Ruth. *Milestones in Medicine*. New York: Random House, 1995.

Li, Alison. *J. B. Collip and the Evolution of Medical Research in Canada.* Toronto: McGill-Queens University Press, 2003.

Mayer, Ann. *Sir Frederick Banting.* Monroe, WI: The Creative Co., 1994.

Stottler, J. *Frederick Banting.* New York: Addison-Wesley, 1996.

# Neurotransmitters

## Year of Discovery: 1921

> **What Is It?** Chemical substances that transmit nerve impulses between individual neuron fibers.
>
> **Who Discovered It?** Otto Loewi

## Why Is This One of the 100 Greatest?

Like cracking the genetic code, like the creation of the atomic bomb, the discovery of how the brain's system of neurons communicates is one of the fundamental science developments of the twentieth century.

Nerves signal sensations to the brain; the brain flashes back commands to muscles and organs through nerves. But how? Otto Loewi's discovery of neurotransmitters (the chemicals that make this communication possible) revolutionized the way scientists think about the brain and even what it means to be human. Neurotransmitters control memory, learning, thinking, behavior, sleep, movement, and all sensory functions. This discovery was one of the keys to understanding brain function and brain organization.

## How Was It Discovered?

In 1888 German anatomist Heinrich Walder-Hartz was the first to propose that the nervous system was a separate network of cells. He named these nerve fibers *neurons*. He concluded that the ends of individual nerve cells approached each other closely, but didn't actually touch. In 1893 Italian scientist Camillo Colgi used a new method for staining cells that brought out exceptionally fine detail under a microscope and proved that Walder-Hartz was correct.

Walder-Hartz's discovery, however, created a scientific controversy. If neurons didn't actually touch, how did they communicate? Some scientists argued that signals had to be sent electrically, since electrical currents existed in the brain. Some argued that nerve signals had to be sent chemically since there were no solid electrical connections between individual neurons. Neither side could prove its position.

Otto Loewi was born in Frankfurt, Germany, in 1873. He wanted to become an art historian but buckled under family pressure and agreed to attend medical school. After barely passing his medical examination, Loewi worked in the City Hospital in Frankfurt. However, he became depressed by the countless deaths and great suffering of tuberculosis and pneumonia patients left to die in crowded hospital wards because there was no therapy for them.

Loewi quit medical practice and turned to pharmacological research (the study of drugs and their effects on human organs). Over the next 25 years (1895 to 1920) he studied how different human organs responded to electrical and chemical stimuli. His papers reported on many human organs including the kidney, pancreas, liver, and brain.

By 1920 Loewi was focusing much of his attention on nerves. He was convinced that chemicals carried signals from one nerve fiber to the next. But, like other researchers, he couldn't prove it.

Loewi later said that the answer came to him in a dream. It was the night before Easter Sunday, 1921. Loewi woke up with a start around midnight and scribbled notes about the dream's idea. The next morning he was unable to read his scrawled notes. Nor could he remember what the dream had been about. All he could remember was that the notes and the dream were critical.

The next night he awoke at 3:00 A.M. from the same dream, remembering it clearly. He didn't dare go back to sleep. He rose and drove to his lab, where he performed the simple experiment from his dream—an experiment that has become famous.

Loewi surgically removed the still-beating hearts from two frogs and placed each in its own container of saline (salt) solution. He left the autonomic nerve (the *Vagus* nerve) attached to heart number one, but not to the second heart. When he applied a tiny electrical current to heart number 1's *Vagus* nerve, the heart slowed down. When he then allowed some saline solution from container 1 to flow into container 2, the second heart slowed down to match the slower rate of the first heart.

Electricity could not have affected the second heart. It had to be some chemical released into the saline solution by heart 1's *Vagus* nerve that then communicated with and controlled heart 2. Loewi had proved that nerve cells communicate with chemicals. Loewi called this chemical *vagusstoff*.

A friend of Loewi's, Englishman Henry Dale, was the first to isolate and decode this chemical's structure, which we now call *acetylcholine*. Dale coined the name *neurotransmitters* for this group of chemicals that nerves use for communication.

 **Fun Facts:** The longest nerve cell in your body, the sciatic nerve, runs from your lower spine to your foot, roughly two to three feet in length!

# More to Explore

Adler, Robert. *Medical Firsts*. New York: John Wiley & Sons, 2004.

Lanzoni, Susan. *A Lot of Nerve*. New York: Thomson Gale, 2006.

Masters, Roger, ed. *The Neurotransmitter Revolution*. Cairo: Southern Illinois University Press, 1996.

Valenstein, Elliot. *The War of the Soups and the Sparks: The Discovery of Neurotransmitters and the Dispute Over How Nerves Communicate*. New York: Columbia University Press, 2005.

Webster, Roy. *Neurotransmitters, Drugs and Brain Function*. New York: John Wiley & Sons, 2001.

# Human Evolution

**What Is It?** Humanoids evolved first in Africa and, as Darwin had postulated, developed from the family of apes.

**Who Discovered It?** Raymond Dart

## Why Is This One of the 100 Greatest?

Humans have always wondered how we came to be on this planet. Virtually every culture and religion has created myths to explain the creation of humans. In the early twentieth century, most scientists believed that the first humans appeared in Asia or Eastern Europe. Then Dart discovered the Taung skull and provided the first solid evidence both of an African evolution of the first humanoids and a fossil link between humans and apes, substantiating one part of Darwin's theories. This discovery redirected all of human evolutionary research and theory and has served as a cornerstone of science's modern beliefs about the history and origin of our species.

## How Was It Discovered?

Raymond Dart was born in Queensland, Australia, in 1893 on a bush farm where his family was struggling to raise cattle. He excelled in school and received scholarships to study medicine, specializing in neural anatomy (the anatomy of skull and brain). In 1920 he gained a prestigious position as assistant to Grafton Elliot Smith at the University of Manchester, England. But their relationship soured and, in 1922, shortly after his thirtieth birthday, Dart was sent off to be a professor of anatomy at the newly formed University of Witwatersrand in Johannesburg, South Africa. Dart arrived feeling bitterly betrayed and outcast.

In 1924 Dart learned of several fossil baboon skulls that had been found at a nearby limestone quarry at Taung. Dart asked that they be sent to him along with any other fossils found at the site. He did not anticipate finding anything particularly interesting in these fossils, but the new university's anatomical museum desperately needed anything it could get.

The first two boxes of fossil bones were delivered to Dart's house one Saturday afternoon in early September 1924, just as he was dressing for a wedding reception to be held at his house later that afternoon. He almost set the boxes aside. But curiosity made him open them there in his driveway. The first box contained nothing of particular interest.

However, on top of the heap of rock inside the second box lay what he instantly recognized as undoubtedly a cast or mold of the interior of a skull—a fossilized brain (rare enough in and of itself). Dart knew at first glance that this was no ordinary anthropoid (ape) brain. It was three times the size of a baboon's brain and considerably larger than even an adult chimpanzee's.

The brain's shape was also different from that of any ape Dart had studied. The forebrain had grown large and bulging, completely covering the hindbrain. It was closer to a human brain and yet, certainly, not fully human. It had to be a link between ape and human.

Dart feverishly searched through the box for a skull to match this brain so that he could put a face on this creature. Luckily he found a large stone with a depression into which the brain cast fit perfectly. He stood transfixed in the driveway with the brain cast and skull-containing rock in his hands, so long that he was late for the wedding.

He spent the next three months patiently chipping away the rock matrix that covered the actual skull, using his wife's sharpened knitting needles. Two days before Christmas, a child's face emerged, complete with a full set of milk teeth and permanent molars still in the process of erupting. The Taung skull and brain were that of an early humanlike child.

Dart quickly wrote an article for *Nature* magazine describing his discovery of the early humanoid and showed how the structure of the skull and spinal cord connection clearly showed that the child had walked upright. Dart claimed to have discovered the "missing link" that showed how humans evolved in the African plain from apes.

The scientific community were neither impressed with Dart's description nor convinced. All European scientists remained skeptical until well-respected Scotsman Robert Broom discovered a second African skull in 1938 that supported and substantiated Dart's discovery.

 **Fun Facts:** Darwin believed that humanoids emerged in Africa. No one believed him for 50 years, until Dart uncovered his famed skull in 1924.

# More to Explore

Avi-Yonah, Michael. *Dig This!* Denver, CO: Runestone Press, 1993.

Gundling, Tom. *First in Line: Tracing Our Ape Ancestry.* New Haven, CT: Yale University Press, 2005.

Leakey, Mary. *Disclosing the Past.* New York: McGraw-Hill, 1996.

Leroi-Gourhan, Andre. *The Hunters of Prehistory.* New York: Atheneum, 2000.

McIntosh, Jane. *The Practical Archaeologist.* New York: Facts on File, 1999.

Phillipson, David W. *African Archaeology.* Cambridge: Cambridge University Press, 2001.

Scheller, William. *Amazing Archaeologists and Their Finds.* New York: Atheneum, 1994.

Tanner, Nancy Makepeace. *On Becoming Human.* Cambridge: Cambridge University Press, 2001.

Tattersall, I. *The Fossil Trail: How We Know What We Think We Know About Human Evolution.* New York: Oxford University Press, 1995.

Trinkaus, E. *The Neanderthals: Changing the Image of Mankind.* New York: Alfred A. Knopf, 1992.

Wheelhouse, Frances. *Dart: Scientist and Man of Grit.* Hornsby, Australia: Transpareon Press, 2001.

# Quantum Theory

## Year of Discovery: 1925

> **What Is It?** A mathematical system that accurately describes the behavior of the subatomic world.
>
> **Who Discovered It?** Max Born

## Why Is This One of the 100 Greatest?

In the first 20 years of the twentieth century, physics buzzed with the incredible discovery of the subatomic world. Long before microscopes were powerful enough to allow researchers to see an atom, scientists used mathematics to probe into the subatomic world of electrons, protons, and alpha and beta particles.

Albert Einstein, Werner Heisenberg, Max Planck, Paul Dirac, and other famed researchers posed theories to explain this bizarre new territory. But it was quiet, unassuming Max Born who discovered a unified quantum theory that systematically, mathematically described the subatomic world.

Max Born's gift to the world was a brand-new field of study we call "quantum mechanics" that is the basis of all modern atomic and nuclear physics and solid state mechanics. It is because of Max Born that we are now able to quantitatively describe the world of subatomic particles.

## How Was It Discovered?

Einstein published his general theory of relativity in 1905. So, for the last year and a half of his university study, 25-year-old Göttingen University mathematics student Max Born lived in a world abuzz with the wonder, implications, and potential of Einstein's bold and revolutionary theory.

Bitterly frustrated that he couldn't find a postgraduate position that would allow him to continue his studies of the subatomic world, Born returned home to live in his childhood room. Working alone for two years at the desk he used for homework as a boy, he tried to apply his mathematical teachings to the problems of subatomic relativity as described in Einstein's theory. Through this work, Max Born discovered a simplified and more accurate method of calculating the minuscule mass of an electron.

Born wrote a paper on his findings that generated an offer for a full-time position at Göttingen University. Two weeks after he started, the job evaporated. Born limped back home for another full year of independent study and a second paper, a review of the mathematical implications of Einstein's relativity, before he was offered a lecturing position at Göttingen University.

However, the only available research funding was designated for the study of the vibrational energy in crystals. Deeply disappointed, feeling excluded from the grand hunt for the structure of the atom, Born launched his study of crystals. For five years Born and two assistants collected, grew, sliced into paper-thin wedges, studied, measured, and analyzed crystals.

In 1915 Born shifted to the University of Berlin to work with physics giant Max Planck. Planck and Einstein were at the hub of the race to unravel and understand the subatomic world. Born brought his mathematical superiority and his understanding of crystals to aid their efforts. It was a classic case of finally being in the right place at the right time with the right background.

Theories abounded to explain the peculiar behavior of subatomic particles. But no one was able to write down the mathematics that proved and described those theories. The problem had mystified the greatest minds in the scientific world for almost 20 years.

It occurred to Born that the quantum phenomena physicists found so troubling in electrons looked remarkably similar to the behavior of the crystals he had studied for five years.

In 1916 Born started to apply what he had learned with crystals to the immense and complex numerical problem that surrounded subatomic particles. The work stretched the available mathematical tools to their limits. The effort extended over nine years of work on blackboards, on note pads, and with slide rules.

In 1925 Born completed work on "Zur Quantenmechanik," or "On Quantum Mechanics." The phrase had never been used before. The paper exploded across the scientific world. It clearly, mathematically, laid out the fundamentals that Einstein, Planck, Dirac, Niels Bohr, Hermann Minkowski, Heisenberg, and others had talked about. It concretely explained and described the amazing world of subatomic particles.

"Quantum mechanics" became the name of the new field of study that focused on a quantitative description of subatomic phenomena. Max Born became its founder.

 **Fun Facts:** In the bizarre quantum world, many of our "normal" laws do not apply. There, objects (like electrons) can be (and regularly are) in two different places at once without upsetting any of the laws of quantum existence.

# More to Explore

Baggott, Jim. *The Meaning of Quantum Theory.* New York: Oxford University Press, 1998.

Born, Max. *Physics in My Generation.* London: Cambridge University Press, 1996.

Clive, Barbara. *The Questioners: Physicists and the Quantum Theory.* New York: Thomas Crowell, 1995.

Gribbin, John. *In Search of Schrodinger's Cat: Quantum Physics and Reality.* New York: Bantam Books, 1984.

Keller, Alex. *The Infancy of Atomic Physics.* Oxford: Clarendon Press, 1993.

Tanor, Joseph, ed. *McGraw-Hill Modern Men of Science.* New York: McGraw-Hill, 1986.

Wasson, Tyler, ed. *Nobel Prize Winners.* New York: H. W. Wilson, 1987.

# Expanding Universe

## Year of Discovery: 1926

---

**What Is It?** The universe is expanding. The millions of galaxies move ever outward, away from its center.

**Who Discovered It?** Edwin Hubble

---

## Why Is This One of the 100 Greatest?

Hubble's twin discoveries (that there are many galaxies in the universe—not just the Milky Way—and that all of those galaxies are traveling outward, expanding the universe) rank as the most important astronomical discoveries of the twentieth century. These discoveries radically changed science's view of the cosmos and of our place in it. Hubble's work also represents the first accurate assessment of the movement of stars and galaxies.

The discovery that the universe is expanding and ever changing for the first time allowed scientists to ponder the universe's past. This discovery led directly to the discovery of the Big Bang and the origin of the universe as well as to a new concept of time and of the future of the universe.

## How Was It Discovered?

In 1923 Edwin Hubble was a tall, broad-shouldered, powerful astronomer of 33 who, 10 years earlier, had almost chosen a career as a professional boxer over astronomy. Hubble had been hired in 1920 to complete and operate the Mt. Wilson Observatory's mammoth 100-inch telescope in California—the largest telescope in the world.

In the early twentieth century, the universe was thought to contain one galaxy—the Milky Way—plus scattered stars and nebulae drifting around its edges. Hubble decided to use the giant 100-inch telescope to study several of these nebulae and picked Andromeda as his first target—and he made the two most important astronomical discoveries of the twentieth century.

This giant telescope's power showed Hubble that Andromeda wasn't a cloud of gas (as had been thought). It was a dense cluster of millions of separate stars! It looked more like a separate galaxy.

Then Hubble located several Cepheid stars in Andromeda. Cepheid stars pulse. The beat of their pulse is always a direct measure of the absolute amount of light given off by the star. By measuring their pulse rate and their *apparent* amount of light, scientists can determine the exact distance to the star.

Andromeda lay 900,000 light-years away. That proved that Andromeda was a separate galaxy. It lay too far away to be a fringe part of the Milky Way.

Within six months, Hubble had studied and measured 18 other nebulae. They were *all* separate galaxies, ranging from five to 100 million light-years from Earth. Astronomers were shocked to learn that the universe was so big and that it likely contained thousands of separate galaxies.

But Hubble was just beginning. He had noticed a consistent red shift when studying the light emitted from these distant nebulae.

Scientists had discovered that each element (helium, hydrogen, argon, oxygen, etc.) always emitted energy in a characteristic set of specific frequencies that identified the element's presence. If they made a spectrograph (a chart of the energy radiated at each separate frequency) of the light being emitted from a star, the lines on the spectrograph would tell them which elements were present in the star and in what relative quantities.

Hubble found all the common spectrograph lines for helium, hydrogen, and so forth that were normally found in a star. But all the lines on his graph were at slightly lower frequencies than normal. It was called a red shift because when visible light frequencies are lowered, their color shifts toward red. If their frequency is raised, their color shifts toward blue (a blue shift).

Over the next two years, Edwin Hubble conducted exhaustive tests of the 20 galaxies he had identified. He found that every one (except Andromeda) was moving *away* from Earth. More startling, the galaxies moved away from us *and* away from each other. Every galaxy he studied was speeding straight out into open space at speeds of between 800 and 50,000 kilometers per second!

The universe was expanding, growing larger every second as the galaxies raced outward. It was not a static thing that had remained unchanged since the beginning of time. In each moment the universe is different than it has ever been before.

 **Fun Facts:** Because the universe is expanding, every galaxy in existence is moving away from our own Milky Way—except for one. Andromeda, our nearest neighbor, is moving on a collision course with the Milky Way. Don't worry, though: the collision won't occur for several million years.

## More to Explore

Barrow, John. *The Origin of the Universe.* New York: Basic Books, 1994.

Burns, Ruth Ann. *Stephen Hawking's Universe* (video). New York: WNET, 1997.

Haven, Kendall, and Donna Clark. *100 Most Popular Scientists for Young Adults.* Englewood, CO: Libraries Unlimited, 1999.

Munitz, Milton, ed. *Theories of the Universe: From Babylonian Myths to Modern Science.* New York: Free Press, 2001.

Rees, Martin. "Exploring Our Universe and Others." *Scientific American* 281, no. 6 (December 1999): 78–83.

Sandage, Alan. *The Hubble Atlas of Galaxies.* Washington, DC: Carnegie Institution of Washington, 1994.

Sharov, Alexander S., and Igor D. Novikov. *Edwin Hubble: The Discoverer of the Big Bang Universe.* New York: Cambridge University Press, 1993.

Wilson, Robert. *Astronomy through the Ages.* Princeton, NJ: Princeton University Press, 1998.

# Uncertainty Principle

## Year of Discovery: 1927

> **What Is It?** It is impossible to know the position and motion of an elementary particle (e.g., an electron) at the same time.
>
> **Who Discovered It?** Werner Heisenberg

## Why Is This One of the 100 Greatest?

Werner Heisenberg is famed worldwide for discovering the Uncertainty Principle, which states that it is impossible to determine both the position and momentum (motion) of an elementary particle at the same time since the effort to determine either would change the other in unpredictable ways. This pivotal theorem marked a fundamental turning point in science. For the first time it was no longer possible to precisely and completely measure or observe the world. At a certain point, Heisenberg showed, scientists had to step back and take the mathematical equations describing the world on faith.

The Heisenberg Uncertainty Principle also undermined the position of cause and effect as a most basic and unassailable foundation block of scientific research, a position it had enjoyed for over 2,500 years. Aat an elementary particle level, every cause had only a fixed probability of creating an anticipated effect.

## How Was It Discovered?

Opening the mail in his Helgoland, Germany, home, in the fall of 1926, Werner Heisenberg found a letter from famed physicist Max Planck. The letter glowed with praise for Heisenberg's paper presenting the "matrix mechanics" Heisenberg had developed. It was Heisenberg's fifth congratulatory letter from a famed physicist that week.

Every letter hailed Heisenberg's matrix mechanics and talked about its "vast potential." They called it "new and exciting" and "extremely valuable."

But Werner Heisenberg's deep sense of unease was not relieved by these letters. Buried in his matrix equations, Heisenberg had detected what he thought was a hard limit to science. If true, it would be the first time science had been told it was impossible to be more precise. A deep dread rumbled the foundations of Heisenberg's scientific beliefs. Yet there it was in black and white. If he was right, science had reached an unscalable wall.

The great physics debate at that time centered on the image of an atom. Was it a ball of protons surrounded by shells of particle electrons, as Niels Bohr claimed, or were electrons really waves of energy flowing around the central nucleus, as others proposed? It occurred to Heisenberg to forget speculation and begin with what was known—that when electrons

**153**

(whatever they were) became excited, they released quanta of energy at specific characteristic frequencies. Heisenberg decided to develop equations to describe and predict the end result, the spectral lines of this radiated energy.

He turned to matrix analysis to help him derive equations with terms such as frequency, position, and momentum along with precise ways to mathematically manipulate them. The resulting equations, while yielding good results, seemed strange and unwieldy. Uncertain of their value, Heisenberg almost burned the final paper. Instead he sent a copy to someone he had studied with and trusted, Wolfgang Pauli. Pauli instantly recognized the value of Heisenberg's work and notified other physicists.

Heisenberg's discovery, called matrix mechanics, gained him instant fame. But Heisenberg was deeply bothered by what happened when he completed his matrix calculations. Heisenberg noticed that, because of the matrix nature of the calculations, the value of a particle's position could affect the value he had to use for its momentum (the particle's motion), and vice versa.

While dealing with imprecision was not new, it was new to realize that the better he knew one term, the more it would add imprecision to another. The better he knew position, the less he knew about momentum. The more precisely he could determine momentum, the less he would know about position.

Heisenberg had accidentally discovered the principle of uncertainty. In one sweeping discovery he destroyed the notion of a completely deterministic world. Hard limits suddenly existed on science's ability to measure and observe. For the first time, there were places scientists could not go, events they could never see. Cause and effect became cause and chance-of-effect. At the most fundamental level the very approach to physical science was altered. Research was made instantly more complex, and yet new doors and avenues to understanding and progress were opened. Heisenberg's Uncertainty Principle has been a guiding foundation of particle research ever since.

 **Fun Facts:** Werner's best subjects were mathematics, physics, and religion, but his record throughout his school career was excellent all round. In fact his mathematical abilities were such that in 1917 (when he was 16) he tutored a family friend who was at the university studying calculus.

## More to Explore

Daintith, John, et al., eds. *Biographical Encyclopedia of Scientists, Second Edition, Volume 1*. Philadelphia: Institute of Physics Publishing, 1994.

Eggenberger, David, ed. *The McGraw-Hill Encyclopedia of World Biography, Volume 5*. New York: McGraw-Hill, 1993.

Gillispie, Charles, ed. *Dictionary of Scientific Biography, Volume XV*. New York: Charles Scribner's Sons, 1998.

Hoffman, Banesh. *The Strange Story of the Quantum*. Cambridge, MA: Harvard University Press, 1999.

Rensberger, Boyce. *How the World Works: A Guide to Science's Greatest Discoveries*. New York: William Morrow, 1994.

# Speed of Light

## Year of Discovery: 1928

> **What Is It?** The speed at which light travels—a universal constant.
>
> **Who Discovered It?** Albert Michelson

## Why Is This One of the 100 Greatest?

In the late 1800s discovering the true the speed of light had only minor importance because astronomers were the only ones who used this number. (Distances across space are measured in *light-years*—how far light travels in one year's time.) Since their measurements were only approximations anyway, they could accept a 5 percent (or even 10 percent) error in that value.

Then Albert Einstein created his famed energy-matter equation, $E = mc^2$. Instantly the speed of light, "c," became critical to a great many calculations. Discovering its true value jumped to the highest priority. Light speed became one of the two most important constants in all physics. A 1 percent error, or even a 0.1 percent error, in "c" was suddenly unacceptably large.

But the problems of discovering the true speed of light—a speed faster than any clock could measure or other machines could detect—were enormous. Albert Michelson invented half a dozen new precision devices and, after 50 years of attempts, was the first human to accurately measure light speed. His discovery earned Michelson the first Nobel Prize to be given to an American physicist.

## How Was It Discovered?

This was a discovery that was dependent on the invention of new technology and new equipment—just as Galileo's discovery of moons around other planets was dependent on the invention of the telescope.

In 1928, 74-year-old Albert Michelson struggled to make one last try to accurately measure the speed of light and discover the true value of "c" in Einstein's famed equation. He had designed, financed, and completed a dozen attempts over the previous 50 years. Michelson was determined this time to measure the speed of light with no more than a 0.001 percent error. That value would finally be accurate enough to support essential nuclear physics calculations.

Four years earlier, Michelson had turned to the famed gyroscope manufacturer, Elmer Sperry, to improve upon the equipment available for his measurements. Now in 1928, the third, and latest, round of equipment improvements was represented by a small octagonal

**155**

cylinder that had just been driven in a thickly padded crate up the bumpy dirt road to the top of Mt. Baldy in California—Michelson's test site.

The experiment Michelson designed was simple. He shone a light onto this small mirrored cylinder as it rotated at a high speed, driven by a motor (also invented by Sperry) capable of maintaining an exact speed of rotation. At some point as the mirror turned, it would be perfectly aligned to reflect this light beam toward a stationary, curved mirror at the back of the room. However, the rotating mirror would only reflect light back to that mirror for a very small fraction of a second before it rotated on.

This back wall mirror thus got short pulses of light from each face of the rotating mirror. Each pulse reflected through a focusing lens and out through an opening in the wall 22 miles to Mt. San Antonio. There it bounced off a mirror, through a second focusing lens, and straight back to Mt. Baldy. Here the light pulse once again hit the back wall mirror, and finally reflected back to the rotating cylinder.

Even though each pulse of light would complete this 44-mile journey in less than 1/4000 of a second, the rotating cylinder would have already turned *some* by the time that light pulse got back from Mt. San Antonio. Returning light would reflect off the rotating mirror and hit a spot on the shed wall. The angle from the cylinder to that spot would tell Michelson how far the mirror had rotated while a pulse of light made the 44-mile round-trip. That would tell him how fast the light had traveled.

While it all sounded simple, it meant years of work to improve the necessary equipment. Sperry created a better light so that it would last through 44 miles of travel. He created a more accurate motor drive so that Michelson would always know *exactly* how fast the small cylinder was turning.

Sperry designed smoother focusing lenses and a better mirrored cylinder—one that wouldn't vibrate or distort its mirrored sides under the tremendous forces of high-speed rotation.

Michelson switched on the motor and light. Faster than eyes could see, the light stream shot out to Mt. San Antonio and back. It bounced off the rotating cylinder and onto the far wall.

From the cylinder's rotational speed and the placement of that mark on the wall, Michelson calculated the speed of light to be 186,284 miles per second—less than 2 mph off of the modern estimate—an error of less than 0.001 percent. With this discovery, scientists in the fields of physics, nuclear physics, and high-energy physics were able to proceed with the calculations that led to nuclear energy and nuclear weapons.

 **Fun Facts:** Traveling at light speed, your ship could go from New York to Los Angeles 70 times in less than one second. In that same one second you could make seven and a half trips around the earth at the equator.

# More to Explore

Daintith, John, et al., eds. *Biographical Encyclopedia of Scientists, Second Edition, Volume 1*. Philadelphia: Institute of Physics Publishing, 1994.

Garraty, John, ed. *Encyclopedia of American Biography*. New York: Harper & Row, 2000.

Hughes, Thomas. *Science and the Instrument Maker: Michelson, Sperry, and the Speed of Light.* Washington, DC: Smithsonian Institute Press, 1996.

Jaffe, Bernard. *Michelson and the Speed of Light.* New York: Greenwood, 1999.

Livingston, Dorothy. *The Master of Light: A Biography of Albert Michelson.* Los Angeles: Children's Press, 1989.

Wasson, Tyler, ed. *Nobel Prize Winners.* New York: H. W. Wilson, 1987.

# Penicillin

**What Is It?** The first commercially available antibiotic drug.

**Who Discovered It?** Alexander Fleming

## Why Is This One of the 100 Greatest?

Penicillin has saved millions of lives—tens of thousands during the last years of World War II alone. The first antibiotic to successfully fight bacterial infections and disease, penicillin was called a miracle cure for a dozen killer diseases rampant in the early twentieth century.

Penicillin created a whole new arsenal of drugs in doctors' toolkits to fight disease and infection. It opened the door to entire new families and new generations of antibiotic drugs. Penicillin started the vast industry of antibiotic drugs and ushered in a new era of medicine.

## How Was It Discovered?

In 1928, 47-year-old Scottish born Alexander Fleming was named chief biochemist at St. Mary's Hospital in London and given a basement laboratory tucked in next to the boiler room.

As the staff bacteriologist, he grew (or "cultured") bacteria in small, round, glass plates for hospital study and experiment. Using microscopic amounts of a bacterium (often collected from a sick patient), he grew enough of each to determine why the patient was sick and how best to fight the infection. Small dishes of deadly staphylococci, streptococci, and pneumococci bacteria were lined and labeled across the one lab bench that stretched the length of Fleming's lab.

Molds were the one great hazard to Fleming's lab operation. Fleming's lab alternated between being drafty and stuffy, depending on the weather and how hard the boiler worked next door. His only ventilation was a pair of windows that opened at ground level to the parklike gardens of the hospital. Afternoon breezes blew leaves, dust, and a great variety of airborne molds through those windows. It seemed impossible to keep molds from drifting into, and contaminating, most of the bacteria Fleming tried to grow.

On September 28, 1928, Fleming's heart sank as he realized that a prized dish of pure (and deadly) staphylococci bacteria had been ruined by a strange, green mold. The mold must have floated into the dish sometime early the previous evening and had been multiplying since then. Greenish mold fuzz now covered half the dish.

Fleming grunted and sighed. Then he froze. Where this strange green mold had grown, the staphylococci bacteria had simply disappeared. Even bacteria more than an inch from the mold had turned transparent and sickly.

What kind of mold could destroy one of the most hearty, tenacious, and deadly bacteria on earth? No other substance then known to man could attack staphylococci so successfully.

It took two weeks for Fleming to isolate and culture enough of the tough green mold to complete an identification: *Penicillium notatum*. Within a month he had discovered that the mold secreted a substance that killed bacteria. He began to call this substance "penicillin."

Through culture dish experiments he discovered that penicillin could easily destroy all the common human-killing bacteria—staphylococci, streptococci, pneumococci, even the toughest of all, the bacilli of diphtheria. The only bacterium penicillin fought but did not destroy was the weak, sensitive bacterium that caused influenza (flu).

Fleming spent six months testing penicillin on rabbits to establish that the drug was safe for human use before, in late 1929, announcing the discovery of his miracle mold that had drifted in the window.

However, penicillin was difficult and slow to grow. It worked wonders but was available in such small quantities that it did little practical good. In 1942 Dorothy Hodgkin, a British researcher, developed a new process, called X-ray crystalography, to decipher the structure of a penicillin molecule. It took her 15 months and thousands of X-ray images of the molecules in a penicillin crystal to identify each of the 35 atoms in a penicillin molecule. Dr. Hodgkin was awarded the 1964 Nobel Prize for her work.

American doctors Howard Florey and Ernst Chain were able to use Hodgkin's map to synthetically produce penicillin molecules in mass production beginning in 1943. For their effort, Florey and Chain were awarded the 1945 Nobel Price in Medicine jointly with Alexander Fleming, the discoverer of penicillin.

 **Fun Facts:** American researchers in Peoria, Illinois, were able to develop commercial production of penicillin first, because two of penicillin's favorite foods turned out to be a strain of local Illinois corn and rotting cantaloupes, donated by a Peoria market. Those food bases helped researchers increase their production of penicillin from 400 million to over 650 *billion* units a month

# More to Explore

Bankston, John. *Alexander Fleming and the Story of Penicillin*. Hockessin, DE: Mitchell Lane, 2001.

Birch, Beverly. *Alexander Fleming: Pioneer with Antibiotics*. New York: Thomson Gale, 2002.

Hantula, Richard. *Alexander Fleming*. New York: Gareth Stevens, 2003.

Parker, Steve. *Alexander Fleming*. Portsmouth, NH: Heinemann, 2001.

Snedden, Robert. *Scientists and Discoveries*. Portsmouth, NH: Heinemann, 2001.

Tocci, Salvatori. *Alexander Fleming: The Man Who Discovered Penicillin*. Berkeley Heights, NJ: Enslow, 2002.

# Antimatter

## Year of Discovery: 1929

**What Is It?** Antimatter are particles of the same mass and composition as protons and electrons, but with an opposite electrical charge.

**Who Discovered It?** Paul Dirac

## Why Is This One of the 100 Greatest?

Science fiction space ships are regularly powered by antimatter drives. Futuristic bombs are designed around antimatter. Yet neither you nor anyone you've ever met has even once seen a particle of antimatter. Antimatter does not come in fist-sized chunks, but as stray, individual subatomic particles.

Paul Dirac is considered by many to be the greatest British theoretical physicist since Newton. Dirac was the first to predict the necessary existence of positrons and antiprotons, or antimatter. The concept of antimatter provided a new avenue of research and understanding in physics. Dirac's antimatter discovery has become the theoretical framework for modern particle physics. Modern cosmologists and physicists are able to extend and apply the precepts of quantum physics, quantum electrodynamics, and quantum mechanics in large part because of Dirac's discovery.

## How Was It Discovered?

Shy, retiring, and secretive by nature, 21-year-old Cambridge University physics graduate student Paul Dirac had made few friends, but had gained a reputation for mathematical brilliance.

By 1923, the theories of relativity and quantum mechanics were well-established, but their limits and the exact implications and meaning were not. Quantum mechanics, the study of systems so small that Newtonian physics breaks down, was based on the assumption that subatomic matter acts both like particles and waves. The contradictions and paradoxical implications of this assumption and the mathematics used to try to describe it were drawing physics toward a crisis.

Through a series of cunning research efforts and precise, articulate papers, Dirac began to chip away at these inconsistencies, bringing clarity and reason to what had previously seemed to be chaotic uncertainty. He improved the methods to calculate a particle's speed as defined by "Eddington's equations". He resolved the discrepancies of the covariance of Niels Bohr's frequency condition.

Still as a graduate student, he published five important papers and turned his focus to the more general problem of uniting quantum mechanics (the laws governing the micro-world of elementary particles) and relativity (the laws governing the macro-world of planetary and universal gravitation). To this work Dirac brought his engineer's ability to accept and use approximations when exact calculations were not possible and where exact measurements did not exist. This talent allowed Dirac to venture into new areas of analysis whose lack of exact measurements had stopped previous researchers.

Dirac worked mostly in the world of advanced mathematics for these studies. He used the results of a number of lab studies conducted by other researchers to test and verify his equations and mathematical models.

Through completion of his doctoral work and through the first five years of his work as a researcher at Cambridge, Dirac struggled to resolve the apparent incompatibility of these two major systems of thought and analysis. By 1929 Dirac had realized that his calculations required that several subatomic particles had to exist that had never been detected or thought of before. In order for the equations that he had developed and tested against lab results to work, an entire set of new particles had to exist. These new particles would mimic the mass and composition of the known particles, but would have the opposite electrical charge.

Protons and neutrons were known. Dirac concluded that negatively charged particles of equivalent mass must also exist. The existence of this antiproton, or antimatter, was confirmed 25 years later.

Similarly, Dirac concluded that if an electron existed, positively and neutrally charged particles of similar mass (positron and neutrino respectively) must also exist. The existence of positrons was confirmed two years later, in 1932. Neutrinos were positively identified in the mid-1970s, but their mass was not confirmed until work done by Japanese researchers in 1998.

Dirac thus discovered the existence of antimatter and proved that the particles we can see, touch, and deal with represent only half of the kinds of particles that inhabit our universe. In so doing, Dirac moved science closer to an accurate view of the physical world.

 **Fun Facts:** When matter converts to energy, some residue is always left. Only part of the matter can be converted into energy. Not so with antimatter. When antimatter collides with matter, 100 percent of both matter and antimatter are converted into usable energy. A gram of antimatter would carry as much potential energy as 1,000 space shuttle external tanks carry.

# More to Explore

Daintith, John, et al., eds. *Biographical Encyclopedia of Scientists, Second Edition, Volume 1.* Philadelphia: Institute of Physics Publishing, 1994.

Devine, Elizabeth, ed. *The Annual Obituary, 1983.* Chicago: St. James Press, 1990.

Dirac, Paul. *The General Theory of Relativity.* New York: John Wiley & Sons, 1995.

———. *The Principles of Quantum Mechanics.* London: Cambridge University Press, 1998.

Kragh, Helge. *Dirac: A Scientific Biography.* New York: Cambridge University Press, 1996.

Pais, Abraham. *Paul Dirac: The Man and His Work.* New York: Cambridge University Press, 2005.

Scheller, Bill. *Spaced Out!: An Extreme Reader . . . from Warps and Wormholes to Killer Asteroids.* New York: Penguin, 1999.

Wasson, Tyler, ed. *Nobel Prize Winners.* New York: H. W. Wilson, 1987.

# Neutron

## Year of Discovery: 1932

> **What Is It?** A subatomic particle located in the nucleus of an atom with the mass of a proton but no electrical charge.
>
> **Who Discovered It?** James Chadwick

## Why Is This One of the 100 Greatest?

The discovery of neutrons has been hailed as a major landmark of twentieth-century science. First, this discovery completed our understanding of the structure of atoms. Second, because they have no electrical charge, neutrons have been by far the most useful particles for creating nuclear collisions and reactions and for exploring the structure and reaction of atoms. Neutrons were used by Ernest Lawrence at UC Berkeley to discover a dozen new elements. Neutrons were essential to the creation of nuclear fission and to the atomic bomb.

## How Was It Discovered?

Since the discovery that a subatomic world existed (in 1901), only the two electrically charged particles—proton and electron—had been discovered. Scientists assumed that these two particles made up the whole mass of every atom.

But there was a problem. If atoms were made up of protons and electrons, *spin* didn't add up correctly. The idea that each subatomic particle possessed a "spin" was discovered in 1925 by George Uhlenbeck and Samuel Goudsmit in Germany. For example, a nitrogen atom has an atomic mass of 14 (a proton has a mass of 1) and its nucleus has a positive electrical charge of +7 (each proton has a charge of +1); to balance this positive charge, seven electrons (charge of -1 each) orbit around the nucleus. But somehow, seven additional electrons had to exist inside the nucleus to cancel out the positive electrical charge of the other seven protons.

Thus, 21 particles (14 protons and 7 electrons) should reside in each nitrogen nucleus, each with a *spin* of either +½ or -½. Because 21 is an odd number of particles, no matter how they combined, the total spin of each nitrogen nucleus would *have* to have a ½ in it. But the measured spin of a nitrogen nucleus was always a whole integer. No half. Something was wrong.

Ernest Rutherford proposed that a proton-electron must exist and that a nitrogen nucleus has seven protons and seven proton-electrons (for 14 particles—an even number—and the correct spin total). But it was only theory. He had no idea of how to detect a proton-electron since the only known way to detect a particle was to detect its electrical charge.

**163**

Enter James Chadwick. Born in 1891 in England, Chadwick was another of the crop of physicists who learned their atomic physics under Rutherford. By the mid-1920s Chadwick was obsessed with the search for Rutherford's uncharged proton-electron.

In 1928 Chadwick began to use beryllium for his experiments. Beryllium was a small, simple atom with an atomic mass of *9*. He bombarded beryllium with alpha particles from polonium (a radioactive element) and hoped that some beryllium atoms would be struck by alpha particles and burst apart into two new alpha particles (each with a mass of *4*).

If that happened, these two alpha particles would carry all of the electrical charge of the original beryllium nucleus, but not all of its mass. One atomic unit of mass (the mass of a proton) would be left over from beryllium's original mass of 9. But that last proton-sized particle from the breakup of this beryllium nucleus would have no electrical charge. It would therefore have to be the proton-electron (now called *neutron*) Chadwick sought.

If this experiment worked, Chadwick would create a stream of neutrons along with alpha particles. However, it took three years for Chadwick to find a way to detect the presence of any neutrons he created in this way. He used a strong electrical field to deflect alpha particles (all electrically charged). Only uncharged particles would continue straight along the target path.

Happily, Chadwick found that *something* was still smashing into a block of paraffin wax he placed at the end of the target path. That "*something*" hit the paraffin hard enough to break new alpha particles loose from the wax. That *something* had to have come from the collision of alpha particles with beryllium atoms, had to be at least the size of a proton (to break new alpha particles loose in the paraffin), and couldn't have an electrical charge since it wasn't deflected by the electrical field. It had to be a neutron.

Chadwick had discovered the neutron. He had proved that they existed. But it was Rutherford, not Chadwick, who named it *neutron* for its neutral electrical charge.

 **Fun Facts:** A neutron has nearly 1,840 times the mass of the electron. How does that size compare with a proton?

# More to Explore

Adler, Robert. *Science Firsts,* New York: John Wiley & Sons, 2002.

Bortz, Fred. *Neutron.* Cherry Hill, NJ: Rosen Publishing Group, 2004.

Brown, Andrew. *The Neutron and the Bomb: A Biography of Sir James Chadwick.* New York: Oxford University Press, 1997.

Bunch, Bryan. *The History of Science and Technology.* New York: Houghton Mifflin, 2004.

Garwin, Laura. *A Century of Nature: Twenty-One Discoveries That Changed Science and the World.* Chicago: University of Chicago Press, 2003.

# Cell Structure

## Year of Discovery: 1933

> **What Is It?** The first accurate map of the many internal structures that make up a living cell.
>
> **Who Discovered It?** Albert Claude

## Why Is This One of the 100 Greatest?

Albert Claude was the first scientist to develop procedures for isolating and studying individual structures within a cell. He is the one who mapped the inner organization and activity of a cell and its many components. He is rightly called the founder of modern cell biology.

Although he never graduated from high school, Claude pioneered the use of centrifuge techniques and the electron microscope for the study of living cells. He discovered a dozen key components of cells, identified the function of other cell substructures, and laid the groundwork for a whole new field of cellular biology.

## How Was It Discovered?

Albert Claude received only a third-grade education before he was forced to quit school and get a mill job. After serving in the Belgian army during World War I, Claude was able to study medicine in college when the Belgian government allowed any returning soldier to attend college—even though the University of Liege was less than eager to accept an illiterate country soldier.

During his studies, Claude submitted a lengthy research proposal to the Rockefeller Institute for Medical Research in New York. It was accepted and Claude immigrated to America.

Claude proposed to study live cancer cells and discover how the disease was transmitted. His proposal called for him to separate cells into different components for individual study, something that had never been tried before. There were no established procedures or equipment for such an operation. Claude had to scrounge crude equipment from machine and butcher shops. He used commercial meat grinders to pulverize samples of chicken cancerous tumors that he suspended in a liquid medium. He used a high-speed centrifuge to separate the ground-up cells into their various subparts—heaviest on the bottom, lightest on top. He called the procedure cell *fractionation*.

He now had test tubes filled with layers of goo and mud. Since no one had ever separated cell subparts before, it took Claude several years of study and practice to determine what each isolated layer was and to learn how to successfully isolate the tumor agent from the rest of the cell. Claude's chemical analysis showed this agent to be a ribonucleic acid (RNA), a known constituent of viruses. This was the first evidence that cancer was caused by a virus.

Claude decided to continue using cell fractionation to study healthy cells. Working full-time in his laboratory over the next six years using a centrifuge and a high-powered microscope, Claude was able to isolate and describe the cell nucleus (the structure that houses the chromosomes), organelles (specialized microscopic structures within a cell that act like organs), mitochondria (tiny rod-shaped granules where respiration and energy production actually happen), and ribosomes (the sites within cells where proteins are formed).

Claude was mapping a new world that had only been guessed at before. Still, his view was limited by the power of his microscope. In 1942 the Rockefeller Institute was able to borrow the only electron microscope in New York, used by physicists attempting to probe inside an atom. This scope was capable of magnifying objects one million times their original size.

However, the scope also bombarded a sample with a powerful beam of electrons in order to create an image. Such an electron stream destroyed fragile living tissue. Claude spent 18 months developing successful methods to prepare and protect cell samples to withstand the electron microscope. By mid-1943 Claude had obtained the first actual images of the internal structure of a cell, images previously unthinkable. In 1945 Claude published a catalog of dozens of new cell structures and functions never before identified.

The names of the scientists who broke the barrier of an atom and discovered what lay inside (e.g., Marie Curie, Max Born, Niels Bohr, Enrico Fermi, and Werner Heisenberg) are well known and revered. Albert Claude single-handedly broke through the barrier of a cell wall to discover and document a universe of subparts and activity inside.

 **Fun Facts:** There are more than 250 different types of cells in your body. yet they all started as, and grew out of, one single cell—the fertilized egg cell.

# More to Explore

Daintith, John, ed. *Biographical Encyclopedia of Science.* 2d ed. Philadelphia: Thomson Scientific, 1994.

Devine, Elizabeth, ed. *The Annual Obituary, 1978.* Chicago, St. James Press, 1999.

Kordon, Claude. *The Language of the Cell.* New York: McGraw-Hill, 1992.

Rensberger, Boyce. *Life Itself: Exploring the Realm of the Living Cell.* New York: Oxford University Press, 1997.

Wasson, Tyler, ed. *Nobel Prize Winners.* New York: H. W. Wilson, 1987.

# The Function of Genes

## Year of Discovery: 1934

> **What Is It?** Beadle discovered how genes perform their vital function.
>
> **Who Discovered It?** George Beadle

## Why Is This One of the 100 Greatest?

Genes are strung along chromosomes and contain directions for the operation and growth of individual cells. But how can a molecule of nucleic acid (a gene) direct an entire complex cell to perform in a certain way? George Beadle answered this critical question and vastly improved our understanding of evolutionary genetics.

Beadle discovered that each gene directs the formation of a particular enzyme. Enzymes then swing the cell into action. His discovery filled a huge gap in scientists' understanding of how DNA blueprints are translated into physical cell-building action. Beadle's groundbreaking work shifted the focus of the entire field of genetics research from the qualitative study of outward characteristics (what physical deformities are created by mutated genes) to the quantitative chemical study of genes and their mode of producing enzymes.

## How Was It Discovered?

George Beadle was supposed to be a farmer. He was born on a farm outside Wahoo, Nebraska, in 1903. But a college study of the genetics of hybrid wheat hooked Beadle on the wonder of genetics. Genetics instantly became his lifelong passion.

In 1937, at the age of 34, Beadle landed an appointment with the genetics faculty at Stanford University. Stanford wanted to develop their study of biochemical genetics. The study of genetics was 80 years old. But biochemical genetics, or the molecular study of how genetics signals were created and sent to cells, was still in its infancy. Beadle teamed with microbiologist Edward Tatum to try to determine how genes exercise their controlling influence.

In concept their work was simple. In practice it was painstakingly tedious and demanding. They searched for the simplest life form they could find, choosing the bread mold *Neurospora* because its simple gene structure had been well documented. They grew trays upon trays of colonies of *Neurospora* in a common growth medium. Then Beadle and Tatum bombarded every colony with X-rays, which were known to accelerate genetic mutations. Within 12 hours most colonies continued to grow normally (they were unmutated), a few died (X-rays had destroyed them), and a precious few lived but failed to thrive (gene mutations now made them unable to grow).

The interesting group was this third one because it had undergone some genetic mutation that made it impossible for the mold to grow on its own. If Beadle and Tatum could discover exactly what this mutated mold now needed in order to grow, they would learn what its mutated gene had done on its own before it was damaged.

Beadle and Tatum placed individual spores from one of these colonies into a thousand different test tubes, each containing the same standard growth medium. To each tube they added one possible substance the original mold had been able to synthesize for itself but that the mutated mold might not be producing. Then they waited to see which, if any, would begin to thrive.

Only one tube began to grow normally—tube 299, the one to which they had added vitamin $B_6$. The mutation to the mold's gene must have left the mold unable to synthesize vitamin $B_6$ and thus unable to grow. That meant that the original gene had produced something that made the cells able to synthesize the vitamin on their own. The second step of Beadle and Tatum's experiment was to search for that something.

Beadle found that when he removed, or blocked, certain enzymes the mold stopped growing. He was able to trace these enzymes back to genes and to show that the mutated gene from tube 299 no longer produced that specific enzyme.

Through this experiment Beadle discovered how genes do their job. He proved that genes produce enzymes and that enzymes chemically direct cells to act. It was a discovery worthy of a Nobel Prize.

 **Fun Facts:** Humans have between 25,000 and 28,000 genes. Different genes direct every aspect of your growth and looks. Some do nothing at all. Called recessive genes, they patiently wait to be passed on to the next generation, when they might have the chance to become dominant and control something.

## More to Explore

Beadle, George. *Language of Life: An Introduction to the Science of Genetics.* New York: Doubleday, 1966.

Davern, Cedric. *Genetics: Readings from Scientific American.* San Francisco: W. H. Freeman, 1998.

Maitland Edey, and Donald Johanson. *BLUEPRINTS: Solving the Mystery of Evolution.* New York: Penguin Books, 1996.

Moritz, Charles, ed. *Current Biography Yearbook, 1990.* New York: H.W. Wilson, 1991.

Tanor, Joseph, ed. *McGraw-Hill Modern Men of Science.* New York: McGraw-Hill, 1996.

Wasson, Tyler, ed. *Nobel Prize Winners.* New York: H. W. Wilson, 1987.

# Ecosystem

## Year of Discovery: 1935

> **What Is It?** The plants, animals, and environment in a given place are all inter-dependent.
>
> **Who Discovered It?** Arthur Tansley

## Why Is This One of the 100 Greatest?

Many scientists over the centuries had studied the relationship of various species to their climate and environment. They studied elements of ecology. However, it wasn't until 1935 that Arthur Tansley realized that *all* species in a given environment were interconnected. Grasses affected top carnivores and the bugs that decomposed dead animals, and fallen trees affected grasses and bushes.

Tansley discovered that every organism is part of a closed, interdependent system—an ecosystem. This discovery was an important development in our understanding of biology and launched the modern environmental movement and the science of ecology.

## How Was It Discovered?

Arthur Tansley was the person who saw the big picture and discovered that all elements of a local ecological system were dependent upon each other, like individual threads in a tightly spun web. But he was not the first person to study ecology.

Aristotle and his student, Theophrastus, studied the relationships between animals and their environment in the fourth century B.C. In 1805, German scientist Alexander von Humbolt published his studies of the relationship between plant species and climate. He was the first to describe *vegetation zones*.

Alfred Wallace, a competitor of Darwin's, was the first to propose (in 1870) a "geography" of animal species, relating animals to their climate and geography. In the early nineteenth century, French scientist Antoine Lavoisier discovered the nitrogen cycle. This cycle linked plants, animals, water, and atmosphere into a single interdependent cycle by tracing how nitrogen cycles through the environment. What science needed was for someone to recognize that all of these individual pieces fit together like pieces in a jigsaw puzzle.

Arthur Tansley was born into a wealthy family in London in 1871. He earned a degree in botany and lectured throughout his working career at University College in London and then at Cambridge. Tansley was active in promoting English plant ecology and helped found the British Ecological Society.

In the late 1920s Tansley conducted a massive plant inventory of England for the Ecological Society. During this study, Tansley began to focus not just on the list of plants he set out to create, but on the relationships between this vast list of plants. Which grasses were found with which others? With which bushes and weeds? Which grasses populated lowland meadows? Which were found on craggy mountainsides? And so forth.

By 1930 Tansley had realized that he couldn't fully analyze the relationships between plants without considering the effects of animals. He began to inventory and map the many browsers—animals that ate grasses. Soon he realized that any study of these browser animals was woefully incomplete unless he included an inventory of the carnivores that controlled browser populations.

Then he realized that he had to include recyclers and decomposers (organisms that broke down decaying plant and animal matter into the basic chemical nutrients for plants). Finally he added the physical (inorganic) environment (water, precipitation, climate, etc.).

Tansley had realized by 1935 that each area he studied represented an integrated, enclosed local system that acted as a single unit and included all organisms in that given area and their relationship to the local inorganic environment. It was a breathtakingly grand concept. Each species was linked to all others. What happened to one affected all others.

Water, sunlight, and some inorganic chemicals entered the system from the outside. All living organisms inside the closed ecological system fed off each other, passing food up and then back down the food web.

Tansley shortened the name from ecological system to *ecosystem*. That term and that concept, however, did not gain popularity until 1953 when American scientist Eugene Odum published *Fundamentals of Ecology*, a book that explained the concept of, and used the term, *ecosystem*.

 **Fun Facts:** An important ecosystem service that most people don't think about is pollination. Ninety percent of the world's food crops would not exist without pollinators like bees, bats, and wasps.

## More to Explore

Anker, Peder. *Imperial Ecology: Environmental Order in the British Empire, 1845–1945*. Cambridge, MA: Harvard University Press, 2002.

Ball, Jackie. *Ecology*. New York: Gareth Stevens, 2003.

Dorling Kindersley Staff. *Ecology: Eyewitness*. New York: DK Publishing, 2000.

Lane, Brian. *Ecology*. New York: DK Publishing, 2005.

Stone, Lynn. *Forests*. Vero Beach, FL: Rourke Publishing, 2004.

# Weak and Strong Force

## Years of Discovery: 1937 and 1983

**What Is It?** The last two of the four fundamental physics forces of nature.

**Who Discovered It?** Carlo Rubbia (weak force) and Hideki Yukawa (strong force)

## Why Is This One of the 100 Greatest?

For several centuries scientists thought that gravity and electromagnetic forces governed the universe. Then twentieth-century physicists found atomic nuclei composed of positively charged protons. Why didn't they fly apart since positive electrical forces repel each other? Further, why did *some* atoms naturally radioactively decay while others did not?

Many physicists proposed that two new forces (weak and strong) must exist. In 1935, Hideki Yukawa discovered the strong force. It was not until 1983 that Carlo Rubbia discovered the two particles that defined the weak force.

These discoveries completed our understanding of the four forces that govern the microscopic quantum world and direct whole clusters of galaxies. The weak and strong forces form the foundation of quantum physics.

## How Was It Discovered?

Newton mathematically defined gravity in 1666. Faraday, Oersted, and Maxwell defined electromagnetism in the early nineteenth century. Scientists thought that these two forces ruled the universe.

However, twentieth-century physicists realized that neither of these forces could hold an atom together. Electromagnetic repulsion of like charges (protons) should rip every atomic nucleus apart. Why did nuclei and atoms exist? Other scientists realized that *some* force had to be responsible for the decay of radioactive nuclei.

Scientists theorized that two new forces had to exist: the *strong force* (the force that held atomic nuclei together) and the *weak force* (that created radioactive decay). No evidence existed to prove that either force actually existed. Though many searched, by the late 1930s no one had detected or proved the existence of either force.

In 1936 Hideki Yukawa reasoned that, since neither the weak nor the strong force had ever been detected, they must act over a range that was smaller than the diameter of an atomic nucleus. (Thus, they would be undetectable outside of that tiny space.) He began a series of experiments in which he smashed protons (hydrogen nuclei) with neutrons to see if the collision products would give him a hint about how the strong force worked.

Yukawa noticed the consistent production of large (for subatomic particles), short-lived particles called *pi-mesons* (a kind of *gluon*) from these collisions. That meant that pi-mesons existed inside the nucleus of atoms since that is where they sprang from.

Yukawa proposed that mesons, in general, represented the attractive force called the strong force. Noting that photons (which represented electromagnetic force) and gravitons (which represented gravitational force) were both virtually massless, he proposed that the greater the mass of these tiny particles, the shorter the distance over which they exerted their effects.

He proposed that the short-range strong force came about from the exchange of the massive *meson* particles between protons and neutrons. Yukawa could describe the mesons he believed represented the strong force, but he could not physically produce one.

In 1947 Lattes, Muirhead, Occhialini, and Powell conducted a high-altitude experiment, flying photographic emulsions at 3,000 meters. These emulsions revealed the pion, which met all the requirements of the Yukawa particle.

We now know that the pion is a meson, both types of the tiny particles called gluons, and that the strong interaction is an exchange of mesons between *quarks* (the subatomic particles that make up protons and neutrons).

The weak force proved harder to confirm through actual discovery. It was not until 1983 that Carlo Rubbia, at the European research center, CERN, first discovered evidence to prove the existence of the weak force. After completing initial work in the 1970s that allowed Rubbia to calculate the size and other physical properties of the missing particles responsible for carrying the weak force, Rubbia and a CERN team set out to find these particles.

Rubbia then proposed that the large synchrotron at CERN be modified so that beams of accelerated protons and antiprotons could be made to collide head-on, releasing energies great enough for weak *boson* particles to materialize. In 1983 his experiments with the colliding-beam apparatus isolated two short-lived particles, the W and Z particles. Rubbia was able to show that these particles were the carriers of the so-called weak force involved in the radioactive decay of atomic nuclei.

The four fundamental forces of nature (and the particles that carry and create each of these forces) had finally been discovered, to complete the standard model that has carried physicists into the twenty-first century.

 **Fun Facts:** Hideki Yukawa was the first Japanese to win the Nobel prize.

# More to Explore

Cottingham, W. N. *An Introduction to Nuclear Physics.* New York: Cambridge University Press, 2001.

Gale Reference Team. *Biography: Hideki Yukawa (1907–1981).* New York: Gale Research, 2004.

Galison, Peter. *How Experiments End*. Chicago: University of Chicago Press, 1997.

Lilley, J. S. *Nuclear Physics*. New York: John Wiley & Sons, 2001.

Taubes, Gary. *Nobel Dreams: Power, Deceit, and the Ultimate Experiment*. Seattle, WA: Microsoft Press, 1996.

Watkins, Peter. *Story of the W and Z*. New York: Cambridge University Press, 1996.

Yukawa, Hideki. *Yukawa, 1907–1981*. Berlin, PA: Berlin Publishing, 1997.

# Metabolism

## Year of Discovery: 1938

**What Is It?** Krebs discovered the circular chain of chemical reactions that turns sugars into energy inside a cell and drives metabolism.

**Who Discovered It?** Hans Adolf Krebs

## Why Is This One of the 100 Greatest?

Muscles do the work for your body. You eat food and—somehow—it turns into energy that your muscles burn to move. But how? How does this thing called metabolism work?

The process of metabolism in human bodies is so important to our understanding of human anatomy that three Nobel prizes have been given to people who contributed to our understanding of it. The third was given to Hans Adolf Krebs, who finally solved the mystery and discovered how our bodies metabolize food into energy. It was one of the great medical discoveries of the twentieth century.

## How Was It Discovered?

British physiologist Archibald Hill believed that muscles should produce heat when they contracted. By 1913, he had developed ways to measure changes as small as 3/1000 of a degree. To his surprise he discovered that, during muscle contraction, no heat was produced nor was any oxygen consumed.

Five years later, German Otto Meyerhof discovered that, during muscle contraction, the chemical glycogen disappears and lactic acid appears. He named this process *anaerobic,* from the Greek words meaning "without oxygen." He later discovered that oxygen was used in the muscle cells *later* to break down lactic acid. Other researchers found that when they added any of four different carbon-based acids to muscle tissue slices, it stimulated the tissue to absorb oxygen.

Even though these discoveries seemed important, they created as much confusion about the process of how muscles work as they provided answers. Someone had to make sense of these different, seemingly confusing studies.

Hans Krebs was born in 1900 in Germany, the son of a surgeon. He studied chemistry and medicine and was then hired to conduct research at Cambridge University. He focused this research on the chemical process of muscle metabolism.

Beginning in 1937, Krebs studied pigeon liver and breast muscle tissue. He was able to measure the amounts of certain groups of acids—some that contain four carbon atoms each and other groups of acids that contain six carbon atoms each—that were created when sugars are oxidized (combined with oxygen). He also noted that this process created carbon dioxide, water, and energy.

These results were confusing. What did all these chemicals have to do with simple metabolism of sugars into energy? Krebs saw citric acid being broken down and yet at the same time, citric acid was being produced. The same was true for a number of other acids.

Slowly Krebs realized that the process worked in a circle—a circle with seven separate chemical steps. It started with citric acid. Each step produced the chemicals and acids that were needed for the next step in the cycle. In the last step, citric acid was produced to start the cycle all over again.

The cycle continues endlessly in each of our cells. Along the way, glucose molecules (sugars) supplied by the blood are consumed. Two waste products were produced by this seven-step cycle: carbon dioxide and free hydrogen atoms. These hydrogen atoms then combine with oxygen and a form of high-energy phosphate to create water and ATP, the chemical that stores energy for cells just like a battery.

Sugar molecules enter the cycle, and carbon dioxide, water, and ATP to power the cells exit the cycle. By 1938 Krebs had unraveled this amazingly complex and yet amazingly efficient seven-step chemical cycle—specifically designed to accomplish a seemingly simple task: convert sugars in the blood into energy for muscle cells. Amazingly, each muscle cell in our bodies creates these seven sequential reactions, each sparked by a different enzyme, every minute of every day. And Hans Krebs discovered how it works.

 **Fun Facts:** The average person's body could theoretically generate 100 watts of electricity using a bio-nano generator, a nano-scale electrochemical fuel cell that draws power from blood glucose much the same way the body generates energy using the Krebs Cycle.

## More to Explore

Bailey, Donna. *Energy for Our Bodies*. New York: Steck-Vaughn, 1999.

Curran, Christina. *Metabolic Processes and Energy Transfers: An Anthology of Current Though*. Cherry Hill, NJ: Rosen Central, 2005.

Hewitt, Sally. *Full of Energy*. New York: Scholastic Library Publishing, 1998.

Holmes, Frederick. *Hans Krebs: Architect of Intermediary Metabolism*. New York: Oxford University Press, 1999.

Nichols, Peter. *Biology of Oxygen*. Jefferson, NC: McFarland, 1997.

# Coelacanth

## Year of Discovery: 1938

**What Is It?** A living fish species thought to be extinct for 80 million years.

**Who Discovered It?** J. L. B. Smith

## Why Is This One of the 100 Greatest?

The scientific world was shocked in 1938 when a coelacanth was discovered. All scientists believed that this fish had been extinct for 80 million years. No fossil or trace of it had been found in more recent strata. This discovery shattered the belief that the known fossil record represented a complete and accurate record of the arrival and extinction of species on this planet. It confirmed that the deep oceans hold biological mysteries still untapped and unimagined.

Equally important, the coelacanth is a "living fossil." Unchanged for over 400 million years, this fish is a close relative of the fish that, hundreds of millions of years ago, was the first creature to crawl out of the sea onto land—the first amphibian, the first land creature. Thus, the coelacanth is one of our earliest ancestors. This discovery has been called the most important zoological find of the twentieth century, as amazing as stumbling upon a living dinosaur.

## How Was It Discovered?

In the late 1930s, 32-year-old Margorie Courtenay-Latimer was the curator of a tiny museum in the port town of East London on the Indian Ocean side of South Africa. Local fishing boat captain Hendrick Gossen always called her when he returned to port with unusual or interesting fish that she might want for her collection. Usually these finds turned out to be nothing important.

On December 23, 1938, just before Margorie closed the museum for her Christmas holiday, she got a call from Gossen. She almost didn't go. She wanted to go home to wrap presents.

However, she decided to swing quickly by the piers on her way. She climbed onto Gossen's boat and noticed a blue fin protruding from beneath a pile of rays and sharks heaped upon the deck. She had never seen such an iridescent blue on a fish fin before and she literally gasped.

Pushing the overlaying fish aside revealed what she described as "the most beautiful fish I ever saw." It was five feet long, pale mauve-blue with iridescent markings. She had no idea what the fish was, but knew it was unlike anything previously caught in local waters. Besides the unique coloring, this fish's fins did not attach to a skeleton, but to fleshy lobes on the sides of its body as if they could be used to support the fish and allow it to crawl.

Back in her small museum office with the precious fish, she thumbed through reference books and found a picture that led her to a seemingly impossible conclusion. It looked exactly like a prehistoric fish that had been extinct for 80 million years.

She mailed a detailed description of the fish to professor J. L. B. Smith, a chemistry and biology teacher at Rhodes University, 50 miles south of East London. Unfortunately, Smith had already left for Christmas vacation and did not read her message until January 3, 1939. He immediately wired back, "IMPORTANT! PRESERVE SKELETON, ORGANS, AND GILLS OF FISH DESCRIBED!"

By this time, however, the fish's innards (including gills) had been thrown away and the fish had been mounted for museum display. Smith reached Margorie's museum on February 16 and immediately confirmed Margorie's tentative identification. The fish *was* a coelacanth (SEE-la-kanth), a fish believed to be extinct for over 80 million years.

The find was important not only because coelacanths had been thought extinct for such a long time, but also because this recent specimen showed that they had remained unchanged for over 400 million years!

But Smith needed a second, *complete* specimen to be sure. He posted a £100 (British) reward for a complete specimen. Yet none were found. It was a tortuously long 14 years before, on December 21, 1952, fishing captain Eric Hunt was handed a complete coelacanth by native fishermen on the island of Comoro, between Zanzibar and Africa.

Hunt carried this second complete coelacanth to Smith and the discovery was confirmed. Smith published the discovery in his 1956 book on Indian Ocean marine species and rattled the imagination of the world. If an 80-million-year-old creature could lurk undetected in oceans, what else swam, hidden, through the depths? World interest in marine science skyrocketed.

Since 1956, over 200 coelacanths have been caught in the same general area. But it was the vigilant observation of Margorie Courtenay-Latimer and the knowledge of J. L. B. Smith that kept this monumental discovery from being just another fish dinner.

 **Fun Facts:** The International Union for the Conservation of Nature and Natural Resources recently surveyed 40,177 species. Of that total, 16,119 are now listed as threatened with extinction. This includes one in three amphibians and a quarter of the world's coniferous trees, as well as one in eight birds and one in four mammals.

# More to Explore

Smith, J. L. B. *J. L. B. Smith Institute of Ichthyology: 50 Years of Ichthyology*. London: Cassell, 1994.

Thompson, Keith. *Living Fossil: The Story of the Coelacanth*. New York: W. W. Norton, 2001.

Walker, Sally. *Mystery Fish: Secrets of the Coelacanth*. New York: Lerner Group, 2005.

Weber, Valerie. *Coelacanth*. New York: Gareth Stevens, 2005.

Weinberg, Samantha. *Fish Caught in Time: The Search for the Coelacanth*. New York: HarperCollins, 2001.

# Nuclear Fission

## Year of Discovery: 1939

> **What Is It?** The discovery of how to split uranium atoms apart and produce vast amounts of energy.
>
> **Who Discovered It?** Lise Meitner

## Why Is This One of the 100 Greatest?

Nuclear fission—the splitting of uranium atoms to produce energy—was one of the great physics advances of the twentieth century. It answered one of the great physics puzzles of the age and opened the door to the atomic age. This discovery is the basis for nuclear power and nuclear weapons.

For her discoveries, Lise Meitner has been called "the most significant woman scientist of this century." Enrico Fermi deserves credit for many major discoveries in the field of atomic physics. But Fermi is most famous for creating the world's first self-sustained nuclear reaction. Fermi put Meitner's discovery to practical use and is thus the founding father of nuclear power.

## How Was It Discovered?

Lise Meitner and Otto Hahn were researchers at the Kaiser Wilhelm Institute in Berlin, Germany. As part of their study of radioactive elements, Meitner and Hahn had struggled for years to create atoms heavier than uranium (transuranic elements). They bombarded uranium atoms with free protons. It seemed obvious that some would hit the nucleus and stick, creating an element heavier than uranium. But it never worked.

They had tested their methods with other heavy metals. Each performed exactly as expected. *Everything* worked as Lise's physics equations said it should—until they reached uranium, the heaviest known element. Throughout the 1930s, no one could figure out why the experiment always failed with uranium.

There was no physical reason why heavier atoms couldn't exist. But in over 100 tries, it had never worked. Obviously, something was happening in their experiments that they did not understand. They needed a new kind of experiment to show them what really happened when they bombarded uranium nuclei with free protons.

Finally Otto conceived a plan using nonradioactive barium as a marker to continuously detect and measure the presence of radioactive radium. If uranium decayed into radium, the barium would detect it.

Three more months were consumed with preliminary tests to establish how barium reacted to radioactive radium in the presence of uranium and to remeasure the exact decay rates and decay patterns of radium.

Before they could finish and conduct their actual experiment, Lise had to flee to Sweden to escape the rise of Hitler's Nazi party. Otto Hahn had to conduct their grand experiment alone.

Two weeks after Hahn completed this test, Lise received a lengthy report describing his failure. He bombarded uranium with a concentrated stream of protons. But he didn't even get radium. He detected only more barium—far more barium than he started with. Bewildered, he begged Lise to help him figure out what had happened.

One week later, Lise took a long snowshoe walk through the early winter snows. A flash image appeared in her mind of atoms tearing themselves apart. The picture was so vivid, so startling, and so strong that she could almost feel the pulsing atomic nuclei and smell the sizzle of each atom as it ripped itself apart in her imagination.

Instantly she knew that she had just been given their answer. Adding extra protons must have made the uranium nuclei unstable. They had split apart. One more experiment confirmed that, when radioactive uranium is bombarded with free protons, each uranium atom split in two, creating barium and krypton. In the process immense amounts of energy were released.

Meitner had discovered the process of nuclear fission.

Almost four years later, at 2:20 P.M. on December 2, 1942, Enrico Fermi flipped the switch that raised hundreds of neutron-absorbing cadmium control rods out of stacks of graphite blocks laced with several tons of uranium oxide pellets. Fermi had stacked 42,000 graphite blocks in an underground squash court situated under the west bleachers of Stagg's field, the University of Chicago football field. It was the world's first nuclear reactor—the product of Meitner's discovery. The 1945 creation of the atomic bomb was the second application of Meitner's fission.

 **Fun Facts:** After Lise Meitner's death, the 109th element on the Periodic Chart of Elements was named after her: "meitnerium."

# More to Explore

Barron, Rachel. *Lise Meitner: Discoverer of Nuclear Fission.* New York, Franklin Watts, 2000.

Boorse, Henry, and Lloyd Motz. *The Atomic Scientist: A Biographical History.* New York: John Wiley & Sons, 1989.

Grinstein, Louise S., Rose K. Rose, and Miriam H. Rafailovich. *Women in Chemistry and Physics: A Biobibliographic Sourcebook.* Westport, CT: Greenwood Press, 1993.

Kass-Simon, G., and Patricia Farnes, eds. *Women of Science: Righting the Record.* Bloomington: Indiana University Press, 1990.

McGrayne, Sharon Bertsch. *Nobel Prize Women in Science: Their Lives, Struggles, and Momentous Discoveries.* New York: Carol Publishing Group, A Birch Lane Press Book, 1993.

Sime, Ruth Lewis. *Lise Meitner: A Life in Physics.* Berkeley: University of California Press, 1996.

Stille, Darlene R. *Extraordinary Women Scientists.* Chicago: Children's Press, 1995.

Wasson, Tyler, ed. *Nobel Prize Winners.* New York: H. W. Wilson, 1987.

Yount, Lisa. *Twentieth-Century Women Scientists.* New York: Facts on File, 1996.

# Blood Plasma

## Year of Discovery: 1940

> **What Is It?** Plasma is that portion of human blood that remains after red blood cells have been separated out.
>
> **Who Discovered It?** Charles Drew

## Why Is This One of the 100 Greatest?

Whole blood can be safely stored for only a few days. That had always meant that blood donations had to come from local sources and be given at the time of need. Blood couldn't travel long distances. People with unusual blood types often had to do without during surgery and suffered accordingly.

Drew discovered the process of separating blood into red blood cells and blood plasma. This discovery greatly extended the shelf life of stored blood and has saved thousands —and probably millions—of lives. Drew's discovery made blood banks practicable. His process and discovery are still used by the Red Cross today for its blood donation and storage program.

## How Was It Discovered?

The idea of blood transfusions is thousands of years old and was practiced by Roman doctors. However, there was a problem: many patients died from the transfusion. No one could understand why this happened until Karl Landsteiner discovered the four blood types in 1897 (A, B, O, and AB). By 1930, other researchers had further divided these groups into eight types by identifying the RH factor for each group (e.g.: O+, O-, A+, A-, etc.).

With these discoveries, blood transfusions became virtually 100 percent safe. But now hospitals had to store *eight* kinds of blood in order to have whatever supply was needed for surgeries. However, most donated blood had to be thrown away because it spoiled before being used. Some common blood types ran out and patients faced grave danger when they had to undergo surgery without it. Blood storage became a critical problem for surgeries and hospitals in general.

Charles Drew was born in mid-summer in 1904 in Washington, D.C. An all-American football player at Amherst College, Drew chose to study medicine rather than play sports.

In 1928 Drew was accepted into medical school at McGill University in Canada (one of the few university medical schools to accept blacks in 1928). There Drew studied under Dr. John Beattie, a visiting professor from England. In 1930 Beattie and Drew began a study of ways to extend safe blood storage time from the existing limits of between two and six days. This short shelf life drastically limited available blood supplies.

Drew graduated in 1935 and left the university with little progress having been made. In 1938, he took a research position at Columbia University in New York City and continued his blood research. There, he developed a centrifuge technique that allowed him to separate red blood cells from the rest of blood. This "rest" he called *blood plasma*.

He quickly determined that red blood cells contain the unique substances that divide blood into the eight blood types. Blood plasma, however, was universal. No matching was necessary. Blood plasma from any donor was compatible with any recipient. This made plasma especially attractive for blood supplies.

Drew tested plasma and showed that it lasted far longer than whole blood. Next, he showed that red blood cells, separated from plasma, also could be stored longer than whole blood.

In 1939 Drew discovered that plasma could be dehydrated, shipped long distances, and then safely rehydrated (reconstituted) by adding water just before surgery. Suddenly blood donors could be thousands of miles from recipients.

In 1940 Drew published his doctorial dissertation. In it he presented his statistical and medical evidence that plasma lasted longer than whole blood and detailed the process of separating blood into red blood cells and plasma and the process for dehydrating plasma. It served as a blueprint for managing the national blood supply. In 1941 Drew created the first "bloodmobiles"—trucks equipped with refrigerators—and started the first blood drive (collected for British airmen and soldiers).

Drew had discovered plasma and how to safely store blood for long transport, and had created a practical system of blood banks and bloodmobiles to collect, process, store, and ship blood wherever it was needed. Finally, blood transfusions were both safe and practical.

 **Fun Facts:** Is all blood red? No. Crabs have blue blood. Their blood contains copper instead of iron. Earthworms and leeches have green blood; the green comes from an iron substance called chlorocruorin. Many invertebrates, such as starfish, have clear or yellowish blood.

## More to Explore

Jackson, Garnet. *Charles Drew, Doctor.* New York: Modern Curriculum Press, 1997.

Salas, Laura. *Charles Drew: Pioneer in Medicine.* Mankato, MN: Capstone Press, 2006.

Schraff, Anne. *Charles Drew: Pioneer in Medicine.* Berkeley Heights, NJ: Enslow, 2003.

Shapiro, Miles. *Charles Drew: Founder of the Blood Bank.* New York: Steck-Vaughn, 1997.

Whitehurst, Susan. *Dr. Charles Drew: Medical Pioneer.* Chanhassen, MN: Child's World, 2001.

# Semiconductor Transistor

## Year of Discovery: 1947

**What Is It?** Semiconductor material can be turned, momentarily, into a super-conductor.

**Who Discovered It?** John Bardeen

## Why Is This One of the 100 Greatest?

John Bardeen won his first Nobel Prize for discovering the transistor effect of semiconductor materials. Most materials either conduct electric flow (conductors) or block that flow (insulators). But a few materials *sometimes* permitted *some* electric flow (semiconductors). Though they had been identified by the late 1800s, no one knew the value of semiconductors until Bardeen discovered the transistor effect.

The transistor has been the backbone of every computing, calculating, communicating, and logic electronics chip and circuit built in the last 50 years. The transistor revolutionized the worlds of electronics and made most of the modern pieces of essential electronic and computing hardware possible. There is no area of life or science that has not been deeply affected by this one discovery

## How Was It Discovered?

John Bardeen was a true child prodigy, skipping fourth, fifth, and sixth grades and receiving a master's degree in physics at 21. With a Ph.D. from Harvard, he taught physics at the University of Minnesota until, in 1945, he was hired by Bell Laboratories, a high-tech communications and electronics research plant.

In the fall of 1947 Bardeen joined forces with William Shockley and Walter Brattain, who were already studying the possible use of semiconductor materials in electronics. Shockley shared the "industrial dream" of freeing electronics from the bulkiness, fragility, heat production, and high power consumption of the vacuum tube. To allow semiconductors to replace tubes, Shockley had to make semiconductor material both amplify and rectify electric signals. All of his attempts had failed.

Bardeen first studied and confirmed that Shockley's mathematics were correct and that his approach was consistent with accepted theory. Shockley's experiments should work. But the results they found using germanium, a common semiconductor, didn't match the theory.

Bardeen guessed that unspecified surface interference on the germanium must be blocking the electric current. The three men set about testing the responses of semiconductor surfaces to light, heat, cold, liquids, and the deposit of metallic films. On wide lab benches they tried to force electric current into the germanium through liquid metals and then through soldered wire contact points. Most of November and much of December 1947 were consumed with these tests.

They found that the contact points worked—sort of. A strong current *could* be forced through the germanium to a metal base on the other side. But rather than amplifying a signal (making it stronger), it actually consumed energy (made it weaker).

Then Bardeen noticed something odd and unexpected. He accidentally misconnected his electrical leads, sending a micro-current to the germanium contact point. When a very weak current was trickled through from wire solder point to base, it created a "hole" in the germanium's resistance to current flow. A weak current converted the semiconductor into a superconductor.

Bardeen had to repeatedly demonstrate the phenomenon to convince both himself and his teammates that his amazing results weren't fluke occurrences. Time after time the results were the same with any semiconductor material they tried: high current, high resistance; low current, virtually no resistance.

Bardeen named the phenomenon "transfer resistors," or transistors. It provided engineers with a way to both rectify a weak signal and boost it to many times its original strength. Transistors required only 1/50 the space of a vacuum tube and 1/1,000,000 the power and could outperform vacuum tubes. For this discovery, the three men shared the 1956 Nobel Prize for Physics.

 **Fun Facts:** The first transistor radio, the Regency TR-1, hit the market on October 18, 1954. It cost $49.95 (the equivalent of $361 in 2005 dollars!). It wasn't until the late 1960s that transistor radios became cheap enough for everyone to afford one.

# More to Explore

Aaseng, Nathan. *American Profiles: Twentieth-Century Inventors.* New York: Facts on File, 1991.

———. *The Inventors: Nobel Prizes in Chemistry.* Minneapolis, MN: Lerner, 1988.

Hoddeson, Lillian. *True Genius: The Life and Science of John Bardeen.* Washington, DC: National Academy Press, 2005.

Olney, Ross. *Amazing Transistor: Key to the Computer Age.* New York: Simon & Schuster Children's, 1998.

Phelan, Glen. *Flowing Currents: The Quest to Build Tiny Transistors.* Washington, DC: National Geographic Society, 2006.

Riordan, Michael. *Crystal Fire: The Birth of the Information Age.* New York: W. W. Norton, 1997.

# The Big Bang

> **What Is It?** The universe began with the giant explosion of an infinitely dense, atom-sized point of matter.
>
> **Who Discovered It?** George Gamow

## Why Is This One of the 100 Greatest?

The study of our history and origins is critical to understanding who we are. That includes the history of humans, of life on our planet, of our planet itself, and of the universe as a whole. But how can anyone study a history that came and went unseen billions of years ago?

Gamow's work represents the first serious attempt to create a scientific, rational description of the beginning of our universe. It was Gamow who named that moment of explosive birth the "Big Bang," a name still used today. Gamow was able to mathematically re-create the conditions of the universe billions of years ago and to describe how those initial conditions led to the present universe we can see and measure. His discoveries began scientific study of the ancient past.

## How Was It Discovered?

In 1926 Edwin Hubble discovered that the universe is expanding—growing larger. That discovery made scientists wonder what the universe looked like in the past. Has it always been expanding? How small did it used to be? Was there some moment when the universe began? What did it look like way back then?

Some began to speculate about when and how the universe began. In 1927 Georges Lemaitre proposed that Hubble's discovery meant that at some distant point in the past, the entire universe had been compressed into a single infinitely dense atom of matter. He called it the *cosmic egg*. By 1930 a few scientists had attempted to describe this "cosmic egg" and how it exploded to create our universe's ongoing expansion.

George Gamow was born in 1904 in Odessa, Ukraine. As a young astronomy student, Gamow was known as much for his practical jokes and late-night parties as for his science. Still, by 1934 he had immigrated to America and secured a professorship of theoretical physics at George Washington University in Washington, DC. It was there that Gamow first heard of the cosmic egg concept. The problem with this theory was that there was no science, no data, no numerical studies to back it up.

185

Gamow decided to use available physics, mathematics, and quantum theory tools to prove whether the universe began as a single immeasurably dense atom called the cosmic egg. He started with Einstein's equations on general relativity.

In the 1940s Gamow added his own earlier work, which showed that the sun's nuclear furnace was driven by the conversion of hydrogen nuclei into helium. He used the mathematics of this model to determine what would happen to various atoms in a primordial fireball. He used research from the development of the atomic bomb and test data on high-energy radiation of various nuclei to describe what happened inside a fire of almost infinite temperature.

From these sources, he slowly built a model of the cosmic egg's explosion and of the chemical reactions that happened in the seconds thereafter. He called that explosion the "Big Bang" and mathematically showed how, at that moment, the universe had been composed primarily of densely packed neutrons. This allowed him to use available studies showing how neutrons, under extreme heat and pressure, combine into larger nuclei and also separate into protons and electrons, forming hydrogen and helium as they do.

Gamow was able to mathematically trace this cosmic explosion forward in time. This description included a detailed, second-by-second picture of the fireball explosion and showed, according to known physics and chemistry laws, how that explosion resulted in the composition and distribution of matter that makes up the present universe.

Gamow also showed that the Big Bang would have created a vast surge of energy that spread and cooled as the universe expanded. But this energy would still be "out there" and could be detected as a faint "afterglow" or echo of that great explosion. This echo would show up as a band of noise at 5°K.

This cosmic background radiation was finally detected in the late 1990s by advanced radio astronomers, which confirmed Gamow's Big Bang theory. Using physics, chemistry, and math, Gamow had discovered the birth of the universe, 15 billion years ago.

 **Fun Facts:** Gamow was an imposing figure at six feet, three inches and over 225 pounds but was known for his impish practical jokes. He was once described as "the only scientist in America with a real sense of humor" by a United Press International reporter.

## More to Explore

Alpher, Ralph. *Genesis of the Big Bang.* New York: Oxford University Press, 2001.

Barrow, John. *The Origin of the Universe.* New York: Basic Books, 1994.

Fox, Karen. *The Big Bang: What Is It, Where Does It Come From, and Why It Works.* New York: John Wiley & Sons, 2002.

Gribbin, John. *In Search of the Big Bang.* London: Heinemann, 1986.

Hawking, Stephen. *A Brief History of Time.* New York: Bantam Books, 1988.

Longair, Malcolm. *The Origins of the Universe.* New York: Cambridge University Press, 1990.

Munitz, Milton, ed. *Theories of the Universe: From Babylonian Myths to Modern Science.* New York: Free Press, 2001.

Rees, Martin. *Before the Beginning: Our Universe and Others.* Reading, MA: Addison-Wesley, 1997.

Silk, Joseph. *The Big Bang,* 3d ed. San Francisco: W. H. Freeman, 2001.

Weinberg, Steven. *The First Three Minutes.* New York: Basic Books, 1987.

# Definition of Information

> **What Is It?** Information can both follow all mathematical and physical laws created to describe matter and act like physical matter.
>
> **Who Discovered It?** Claude Shannon

## Why Is This One of the 100 Greatest?

Every time you surf the Net, download an article, print from your computer screen, use a cell phone, rent a DVD, or listen to a CD, you do so because of Claude Shannon's discovery. The whole digital revolution started with Claude Shannon's discovery that information can be turned into digital bits (single blocks) of information and treated like any physical flow of matter.

Shannon made information physical. His discovery allowed physicists and engineers to switch from analog to digital technologies and opened the door to the Information Age. His 1948 article describing the digital nature of information has been called the Magna Carta of the Information Age.

## How Was It Discovered?

Claude Shannon was born in rural Michigan in 1916 and grew up with a knack for electronics—turning long fences of barbed wire into his private telephone system, and earning money rebuilding radios. He studied for his doctorate in mathematics at the Massachusetts Institute of Technology (MIT). His professors described him as brilliant, but not terribly serious as a student, spending his time designing rocket-powered Frisbees and juggling machines.

However, his 1938 master's thesis (written as part of his studies) startled the world of physics. In it Shannon described the perfect match between electronic switching circuits and the mathematics of nineteenth-century British genius George Boole. Shannon showed that a simple electronic circuit could carry out all of the operations of Boolean symbolic logic. This was the first time anyone had showed that more than simple mathematics could be embodied in electronic circuits. This student thesis opened the door to digital computers, which followed a decade later.

After graduation Shannon was hired by Bell Telephone Laboratories in New Jersey. Engineers there faced a problem: how to stuff more "information" into a noisy wire or microwave channel. They gave the job to Claude Shannon, even though he was best known for riding a unicycle through the lab hallways.

Shannon bypassed others' attempts to work with specific kinds of information—text, numbers, images, sounds, etc. He also decided not to work on any single way of transmitting information—along a wire, sound waves through the air, radio waves, microwaves, etc. Instead, Shannon decided to focus on a question so basic, no one had thought to study it: What is information? What happened when information traveled from sender to receiver?

Shannon's answer was that information consumed energy and, upon delivery, reduced uncertainty. In its simplest form (an atom or a quantum of energy), information answered a simple yes/no question. That answer reduced (or eliminated) uncertainty. Flip a coin. Will it be heads or tails? You don't know. You are uncertain. When it lands, you get information: yes or no. It was heads or it wasn't. Uncertainty is gone. That's information.

Shannon realized that he could convert *all* information into a long string of individual simple yes/no bits of information and that electrical circuits were ideal for processing and transmitting this kind of digital information. In this way, he converted information—in any form—into a string of digital yeses and nos: ones and zeros.

Shannon was then able to apply the laws of physics to information streams. He showed that there was a limit to the amount of information that could be pushed through any communications channel—just as there was a limit to the amount of water that can be pushed through a hose no matter how great the pressure. He also derived a mathematical equation to describe the relationship between the range of frequencies available to carry information and the amount of information that can be carried. This became what we call "bandwidth."

Shannon's discovery made information as physical and easy to work with as water flowing through a pipe or air pumped through a turbine. In this way, Shannon discovered what information is and opened the door to our modern digital age.

 **Fun Facts:** There are 6,000 new computer viruses released every *month*.

# More to Explore

Adler, Robert. *Science Firsts*. New York: John Wiley & Sons, 2003.

Horgan, John. "Claude Shannon: Unicyclist, Juggler, and Father of Information Theory." *Scientific American* 262, no. 1 (1995): 22–22B.

Liversidge, Anthony. "Claude Shannon." *OMNI* (August 1997): 61.

Riordan, Michael. *Crystal Fire: The Birth of the Information Age*. New York: W. W. Norton, 1997.

Shannon, Claude. *The Mathematical Theory of Communication*. Urbana: University of Illinois Press, 1999.

Sloane, N., and Aaron Wyner. *Claude Elwood Shannon: Collected Papers*. Piscataway, NJ: IEEE Press, 1997.

# Jumpin' Genes

## Year of Discovery: 1950

> **What Is It?** Genes are not permanently fixed on chromosomes, but can jump from position to position.
>
> **Who Discovered It?** Barbara McClintock

## Why Is This One of the 100 Greatest?

Every researcher in the world accepted that genes were strung along chromosomes in fixed positions like pearls on a necklace. Working alone in a small, windswept cornfield at Cold Springs Harbor, Long Island, Barbara McClintock proved every other genetic scientist in the world wrong.

Carefully studying wild corn, Barbara McClintock found that genes not only *can* jump, but regularly *do* jump from one position to another on a chromosome. She found that a few controlling genes direct these jumping messenger genes to shift position and turn on, or turn off, the genes next to them in their new location.

Barbara McClintock's work became the building block for a dozen major medical and disease-fighting breakthroughs. The 1983 Nobel Prize Committee called Barbara McClintock's pioneering work "one of the two great discoveries of our time in genetics."

## How Was It Discovered?

With a Ph.D. in genetics, Barbara McClintock lived in a trim two-room apartment over the bright-green-painted garage of the Carnegie Institute's Cold Spring Harbor Research Facility.

A small, slight woman, Barbara stood barely five feet tall and weighed less than 90 pounds. Her face and hands were worn and wrinkled from long exposure to wind and sun.

Cold Spring Harbor is an isolated spot on northeastern Long Island characterized by wind, rolling sand dunes, and waving shore grass. Stooping in a small half-acre cornfield tucked between the facility's cluster of buildings and the choppy waters of the Long Island Sound, Barbara planted corn seeds by hand one-by-one in carefully laid out rows.

The year 1950 was Barbara's sixth year of planting, growing, and studying the genes of these corn plants as they passed from generation to generation. She often felt more like a farmer than a genetics researcher.

How Barbara spent her days depended on the season. In summer, most of her time was spent in the cornfield, nurturing the plants that would produce her data for the year, weeding, checking for pests and disease that could ruin her experiments. In the fall she harvested each ear by hand, carefully labeled it, and began her lab analysis of each gene's location and structure on the chromosomes of each ear. Her lab consisted of one powerful microscope, chemical lab trays, and stacks of journals to record her findings. This work consumed the long hours of winter.

In the spring she split her time between numerical analysis of the previous year's data and field planning and preparation for the next generation of corn plants.

She carefully tracked color mutations, patterns, and changes year after year and discovered that genes are not fixed along chromosomes as everyone thought. Genes could move. They *did* move. Some genes seemed able to direct other genes, telling them where to go and when to act. These genetic directors controlled the movement and action of other genes that jumped positions on command and then turned on—or turned off—the genes next to them in their new location.

It sounded like scientific heresy. It contradicted every genetics textbook, every genetics research paper, and the best minds and most advanced research equipment on Earth. At the end of the 1950 harvest season Barbara debated about releasing her results and finally decided to wait for one more year's data.

McClintock presented her research at the 1951 national symposium on genetic research. Her room had seats for 200. Thirty attended. A few more straggled in during her talk.

She was not asked a single question. Those few left in the room when she finished simply stood up and left.

As so often happens with radically new ideas, Barbara McClintock was simply dismissed by the audience with a bored and indifferent shrug. She was ignored. They couldn't understand the implications of what she said.

Feeling both helpless and frustrated, Barbara returned to harvest her cornfield and start her analysis of the seventh year's crop.

It took another 25 years for the scientific community to understand the importance of her discovery.

 **Fun Facts:** Barbara McClintock became the first woman to receive an unshared Nobel Prize in Physiology or Medicine. When she died in 1992, one of her obituaries suggested that she might well be ranked as the greatest figure in biology in the twentieth century.

# More to Explore

Dash, Joan. *The Triumph of Discovery.* New York: Simon & Shuster, 1991.

Heiligman, Deborah. *Barbara McClintock: Alone in Her Field.* New York: W. H. Freeman, 1998.

Keller, Evelyn. *A Feeling for the Organism: The Life and Work of Barbara McClintock.* San Francisco: W. H. Freeman, 1993.

Maranto, Gina. "At Long Last—A Nobel for a Loner." *Discover* (December 1983): 26.

Opfell, Olga. *The Lady Laureates: Women Who Have Won the Nobel Prize.* Metuchen, NJ: Scarecrow Press, 1993.

Shields, Barbara. *Winners: Women and the Nobel Prize.* Minneapolis, MN: Dillon Press, 1999.

# Fusion

**What Is It?** The opposite of fission, fusion fuses two atomic nuclei into one, larger atom, releasing tremendous amounts of energy.

**Who Discovered It?** Lyman Spitzer

## Why Is This One of the 100 Greatest?

Fusion energy is the power of the sun. It is a virtually unlimited power source that can be created from hydrogen and lithium—common elements in the earth's crust. Fusion is clean, environmentally friendly, and nonpolluting. Fusion was theorized in the late 1910s and the 1920s. It was mathematically described in the 1930s. It was finally discovered (demonstrated in the lab) in 1951. Fusion's technology was turned into the hydrogen bomb shortly thereafter.

But fusion has not yet been converted into its promised practical reality. It still works only in the lab. If this discovery can be converted into a working reality, it will end energy shortages for thousands of years.

## How Was It Discovered?

Scientists had always thought that the sun produced heat and light by actually burning its own matter through normal combustion. In the nineteenth century, a few scientists (most notably British Lord Kelvin) argued that the sun could create heat from its own gravitational collapse—but that such a process could only last for a few million years.

Einstein's famous 1905 equation ($E = mc^2$) allowed scientists to realize that even tiny amounts of matter could be turned into tremendous amounts of energy. In 1919 American astronomer Henry Russell described the physics and mathematical processes that would allow the sun to fuse hydrogen atoms into helium atoms and release vast amounts of energy in the process. The process was called fusion. This theory of how the sun works was confirmed in 1920 by astronomer Francis Aston's measurements.

The *theory* of fusion existed. But was fusion something that could be practically developed on Earth? In 1939 German physicist Hans Bethe described—in mathematical detail—the theory of how to create a fusion reaction on Earth. But there was a problem. Bethe's equations said that hydrogen atoms had to be raised to a temperature of over 100 *million* degrees C (180 million°F) and had to be squeezed into a small space so that the protons in hydrogen nuclei would collide and fuse into helium nuclei. There was no known material or force that could accomplish such a feat.

Dr. Lyman Spitzer founded the Princeton University Plasma Physics Lab in 1948. He soon realized that the only way to contain a fusion reaction was with a high-energy magnetic field. He surrounded a donut-shaped tube that contained hydrogen gas with coils of wire to create a magnetic field that kept hydrogen atoms trapped while lasers heated them many millions of degrees.

But there was a problem. When he looped thousands of loops of wire down through the middle of the donut and up along the outside, it naturally packed the wires more densely on the *inside* of the donut than on the *outside*. That created a stronger magnetic field on the inside (center) of the donut-shaped tube than on the outside. Hydrogen atoms were pushed to the outside and flung at near light speed out of the tube. The fusion generator didn't work.

Then Spitzer discovered a marvelous remedy. He twisted the donut containing his hydrogen gas into a figure eight. As hydrogen sped through this looping tube, it spent part of each lap near the inside of the figure eight and part near the outside and so was kept from being pulled out of the tube by variations in the magnetic field

In 1951 Spitzer completed work on this first hydrogen plasma fusion generator. He called it a *stellarator*—since it was like creating a star—and fired it for the first time for only a small fraction of a second, still not sure that superheated hydrogen plasma wouldn't turn into a hydrogen bomb.

For one glorious half-second the donut-shaped mass of gas blazed supernova bright, like a blinding sun burning at 70 million degrees Fahrenheit. Unimaginably bright and hot, the gas became a two-foot diameter, seething, explosively powerful pool of hydrogen plasma. Then it faded to dull purple, and, two seconds after it first ignited, turned back to black.

For one flickering moment, Lyman Spitzer had created a new star—almost. More important, he had discovered that fusion was possible on Earth.

 **Fun Facts:** As an alternative energy source, fusion has many advantages, including worldwide long-term availability of low-cost fuel, no contribution to acid rain or greenhouse gas emissions, no possibility of a runaway chain reaction, by-products that are unusable for weapons, and minimum problems of waste disposal.

## More to Explore

Fowler, T. *The Fusion Quest*. New York: Johns Hopkins University Press, 1997.

Heiman, Robin. *Fusion: The Search for Endless Energy*. London: Cambridge University Press, 1990.

Peat, F. *Cold Fusion*. New York: Contemporary Books, 1999.

Richardson, Hazel. *How to Split the Atom*. New York: Franklin Watts, 2001.

# Origins of Life

## Year of Discovery: 1952

> **What Is It?** The first laboratory re-creation of the process of originally creating life on Earth.
>
> **Who Discovered It?** Stanley Miller

## Why Is This One of the 100 Greatest?

One of the greatest mysteries has long been: How did life first form on this planet? Theories abound. Bacteria not naturally found on Earth have been found in meteorites recovered in Antarctica. Possibly life *here* came from some other planet.

For over a hundred years, the most popular scientific theory has been that DNA molecules (life) first evolved from amino acids that were somehow spontaneously created in the soupy chemical mix of the primordial seas. It was just a theory—albeit a popular one—until Stanley Miller re-created the conditions of the early oceans in his lab and showed that amino acids could, indeed, form from this chemical soup.

This was the first laboratory evidence, the first scientific discovery, to support the theory that life on Earth evolved naturally from inorganic compounds in the oceans. It has been a cornerstone of biological sciences ever since.

## How Was It Discovered?

By 1950 scientists had used a variety of methods to determine that the earth was 4.6 billion years old. However, the oldest fossil records of even tiny bacterial cells were no older than 3.5 billion years. That meant that Earth had spun through space for over a billion years as a lifeless planet before life suddenly emerged and spread across the globe.

How, then, did life start? Most agreed that life had to have emerged from inorganic chemicals. While this theory made sense, no one was sure if it could really have happened.

Through the late 1940s Harold Urey, a chemist at the University of Chicago, teamed with astronomers and cosmologists to try to determine what Earth's early environment looked like. They determined that Earth's early atmosphere would chemically resemble the rest of the universe—90 percent hydrogen, 9 percent helium, with the final 1 percent made up of oxygen, carbon, nitrogen, neon, sulfur, silicon, iron, and argon. Of these helium, argon, and neon don't react with other elements to form compounds.

Through experiments, Urey determined that the remaining elements, in their likely composition in Earth's early atmosphere, would have combined to form water, methane, ammonia, and hydrogen sulfide.

Enter Stanley Miller. In 1952 this 32-year-old chemist decided to test the prevailing theory and see if life could be produced from Urey's mix of chemical compounds. Miller carefully sterilized long sections of glass tubing, flasks, and beakers. He built what looked like a sprawling erector set of support poles in his lab and clamped flasks, beakers, and connecting glass tubes to this structure. He filled one large beaker with sterilized water. He filled other flasks with the three gasses Urey had identified as part of Earth's early atmosphere—methane, ammonia, and hydrogen sulfide.

Miller slowly boiled the beaker of water so that water vapor would rise into his enclosed "atmosphere" of a labyrinth of glass tubes and beakers. There it mixed with the three other gasses in swirling clouds in a beaker labeled "atmosphere."

Miller realized he needed an energy source to start his life-creating chemical reaction. Since other scientists had determined that the early atmosphere contained almost continual rolling thunder and lightning storms, Miller decided to create artificial lightning in his atmosphere. He hooked a battery to two electrodes and zapped lightning bolts across the "atmosphere" chamber. A glass pipe led from this chamber and past a cooling coil. Here water vapor recondensed and dripped into a collection beaker that was connected to the original water beaker.

After one week of continual operation of his closed-cycle atmosphere, Miller analyzed the residue of compounds that had settled in the collection beaker of his system. He found that 15 percent of the carbon in his system had now formed into organic compounds. Two percent had formed actual amino acids (the building blocks of proteins and of DNA). In just one short week, Miller had created the building blocks of organic life! Virtually all scientists were amazed at how easy it was for Miller to create amino acids—the building blocks of life.

In 1953 the structure of the DNA molecule was finally discovered. Its structure fit well with how Miller's amino acid molecules would most likely combine to create longer chains of life. This was another bit of evidence to support the idea that Stanley Miller had discovered of how life on Earth began.

 **Fun Facts:** There are 20 types of amino acids. Eight are "essential amino acids" that the human body cannot make and must therefore obtain from food.

# More to Explore

Davies, Paul. *Fifth Miracle: The Search for the Origin and Meaning of Life.* New York: Simon & Schuster, 2000.

Gallant, Roy. *The Origins of Life.* New York: Benchmark Books, 2000.

Jenkins, Steve. *Life on Earth: the Story of Evolution.* New York: Houghton Mifflin, 2002.

MacDougall, J. D. *Short History of Planet Earth: Mountains, Mammals, Fire, and Ice.* New York: John Wiley & Sons, 1998.

Morgan, Jennifer. *From Lava to Life: The Universe Tells Our Earth Story.* Nevada City, CA: Dawn Publications, 2003.

# DNA

> **What Is It?** The molecular structure of, and shape of, the molecule that carries the genetic information for every living organism.
>
> **Who Discovered It?** Francis Crick and James Watson

## Why Is This One of the 100 Greatest?

British biochemist Francis Crick, and his American partner, James Watson, created the first accurate model of the molecular structure of deoxyribonucleic acid, or DNA, the master code to the building and operation of all living organisms. That discovery has been called by many "the most significant discovery of the century."

This discovery of the details of the DNA molecule's structure allowed medical scientists to understand, and to develop cures for, many deadly diseases. Millions of lives have been saved. Now DNA evidence is commonly used in court. This discovery has also led to the unraveling of the human genome and promises to lead to cures for a wide variety of other serious aliments and birth defects.

Crick's discoveries relating to DNA structure and function reshaped the study of genetics, virtually created the field of molecular biology, and gave new direction to a host of endeavors in various fields of medicine.

## How Was It Discovered?

The room looked like a tinker toy party gone berserk, like the playroom of overactive second-grade boys. Complex mobiles of wire, colored beads, strips of sheet metal, cardboard cutouts, wooden dowels, and wooden balls dangled from the ceiling like a forest of psychedelic stalactites. Construction supplies, scissors, and tin snips were strewn about the desks and floor, as were pages of complex equations, stacks of scientific papers, and photographic sheets of fuzzy X-ray crystallography images.

The room was really the second-floor office shared by graduate students Francis Crick and James Watson in a 300-year-old building on the campus of Cambridge University. The year was 1953. The mobiles were not the idle toys of students with too much free time. Rather, they were a frantic effort to win the worldwide race to unravel the very core of life and decipher the shape of the DNA molecule.

By 1950 biochemists had already deduced that DNA in a cell's nucleus carried genetic information. The key mystery was how the huge DNA molecule reproduces itself to physically pass this information to a new cell, a new organism, and a new generation. To answer that question, someone had to first figure out what this giant DNA molecule looked like.

At Cambridge, Crick teamed with American biologist James Watson. The two agreed to pool their efforts to construct a model of the DNA molecule while they pursued their separate studies and thesis research.

By 1951 bits and pieces of information about the DNA molecule were emerging from across the globe. Erwin Chargaff discovered that a definite ratio of nucleotide sequences could be detected in the DNA bases, suggesting a paired relationship. Oswald Avery conducted experiments on bacteria DNA showing that DNA carried genetic information. Linus Pauling conceptualized the alpha helix configuration for certain chains of proteins.

Crick and Watson attempted to combine these separate clues into a single physical structure. Using bits of wire, colored beads, sheet metal, and cardboard cutouts, Crick and Watson hung possible spiral models across their shared office. They correctly surmised that a linking chain of sugar and phosphate formed the backbone of the DNA spiral. They correctly linked base pairs of peptides. Still the model did not fit with available atomic data.

Also at Cambridge, but independent of Crick and Watson's efforts, Rosalind Franklin used X-ray crystallography to create two-dimensional images of the DNA molecule. In mid-January 1953, Rosalind had redesigned the X-ray cameras she used. X-ray film from these cameras showed the now-famous "X" shape that suggested a helix shape for the DNA molecule.

Tipped off that Franklin had new information, Crick stole one of Rosalind's X-shaped X-rays. This stolen insight finally put Crick and Watson ahead in the race to solve the structure of DNA. By mid-February they had constructed the first complete physical model of a DNA molecule, using the now-familiar double helix shape, like two intertwined spiral chains.

 **Fun Facts:** If you straightened each strand of DNA from each cell in your body and lined them end-to-end, you'd have about nine million kilometers of DNA. That's enough to reach to the moon and back 13 times!

# More to Explore

Crick, Francis. *Life Itself: Its Origins and Nature.* New York: Simon & Schuster, 1981.

———. *Of Molecules and Men.* Washington, DC: Washington University Press, 1966.

Judson, Horace. *The Eighth Day of Creation: Makers of the Revolution in Biology.* London: S & S Trade Books, 1999.

Maitland, Edey, and Donald Johanson. *BLUEPRINTS: Solving the Mystery of Evolution.* New York: Penguin Books, 1996.

More, Ruth. *The Coil of Life: The Story of the Great Discoveries of the Life Sciences.* New York: Knopf, 1991.

Olby, Robert. *The Path to the Double Helix*. Seattle: University of Washington Press, 1994.

Sayre, Anne. *Rosalind Franklin and DNA*. New York: Norton, 1991.

Stille, Darlene R. *Extraordinary Women Scientists*. Chicago: Children's Press, 1995.

Ulf, Lagerkvist. *DNA Pioneers and Their Legacy*. New Haven, CT: Yale University Press, 1998.

Watson, James. *The Double Helix: A Personal Account of the Discovery of the Structure of DNA*. New York: Atheneum, 1985.

# Seafloor Spreading

## Year of Discovery: 1957

> **What Is It?** The ocean floors slowly move, spreading from central rifts, and carry the continents on their backs as they do.
>
> **Who Discovered It?** Harry Hess

## Why Is This One of the 100 Greatest?

We now know that Earth's continents move. Over hundreds of millions of years, they drift across Earth's surface. You have likely seen pictures of what Earth looked like 500 million years ago. But just 60 years ago, no one believed that it was possible for massive continents to move. There was no force great enough to move vast continents weighing trillions of tons.

Then Harry Hess discovered the theory of ocean-floor spreading. That discovery suddenly not only made continental movement plausible, but made drifting continents a fact. Hess's discovery was the key evidence that confirmed early theories on continental drift by Wegener. Hess's work launched the study of plate tectonics and created new understanding of the history and mechanics of Earth's crust and started the serious study of the past motion of Earth's continents.

## How Was It Discovered?

Standing on the bridge of a mammoth deep-ocean drilling ship in the mid-Atlantic in 1957, Navy Commander Harry Hess watched as a crane operator maneuvered the drilling pipe sections from atop the drilling derrick mounted high above the deck. This was the first time a ship had been able to drill and collect core samples from the ocean floor 13,000 feet below. Hess had designed and managed the operation. He should have been pleased and proud. But test after test showed the ocean bottom below them was less than 50 million years old—disproving every theory about the ocean floor that Harry Hess had created and promoted.

A geology professor before he joined the navy, Hess had been given command of the transport U.S.S. *Cape Johnson* operating in the Pacific in 1945. Using Navy sonar systems, Hess made the first systematic echo-sounding surveys of the Pacific Ocean floor over a two-year period as he steamed back and forth on navy assignments. He discovered over 100 submerged, flat-topped seamounts 3,000 to 6,000 feet under water between the Hawaiian and Mariana islands. Hess described these seamounts as "drowned ancient islands" and named them guyots (to honor Arnold Guyot, a geology professor at Princeton).

Hess theorized that guyots had originally been islands dating back to 800 million years ago, a period before coral existed. His argument rested, in part, on his hypothesis that continual deposits of sediment on the seafloor had made the sea level rise.

When, in 1956, fossils only 100 million years old were found in guyots, Hess changed his theory to say that guyots had originally been volcanoes that had eroded to flat tops by wave action. He abandoned this theory when erosion rate calculations showed that the guyots couldn't have eroded enough to reach their current depth.

Then his 1957 oceanic core samples showed that the Atlantic Ocean floor was much younger than the continents and that oceanic sedimentation rates were slower than previously thought. Hess—again—had to search for a new theory.

Luckily, his 1957 survey allowed him to collect core samples from more than 20 sites across the Atlantic. These tests showed that the age of the ocean bottom grew progressively older as it moved away from the mid-oceanic ridge and toward either continent.

The seafloor wasn't fixed and motionless as everyone had thought. It had to be spreading, moving as if on a giant conveyor belt, inching year by year away from the mid-oceanic ridge. Hess argued that magma rose from the earth's mantle up through oceanic rifts and spread out laterally across the ocean floor. As the magma cooled, it formed new oceanic crust. He estimated the oceanic crust to be spreading apart along the mid-oceanic ridge by one to two inches a year.

Hess's discovery became known as seafloor spreading and was the foundation of the plate tectonics revolution in the late 1960s and early 1970s.

 **Fun Facts:** The Pacific Ocean is slowly shrinking as the Americas slide west. Two hundred million years ago, the Atlantic Ocean didn't exist. South America and Africa were joined, as were North America and Europe. The Atlantic is still spreading and growing. So is the Red Sea. In 150 million years, that currently skinny sea will be as wide as the Atlantic is now.

# More to Explore

Bermen, Howard, ed. *The National Cyclopedia of American Biography, Volume N-63.* Clifton, NJ: James T. White & Co., 1984.

Daintith, John, ed. *Biographical Encyclopedia of Science.* 2d ed. Philadelphia: Norton Scientific, 1994.

Gillispie, Charles Coulston, ed. *Dictionary of Scientific Biography.* New York: Charles Scribner's Sons, 1998.

Hess, Harry. "History of the Ocean Basins." In *Petrological Studies,* edited by A. Engle and H. James. New York: Harper, 1992.

Rubey, William. "Harry Hammond Hess." In *Yearbook of the American Philosophical Society (1995).* New York: American Philosophical Society, 1996.

# The Nature of the Atmosphere

## Year of Discovery: 1960

> **What Is It?** The atmosphere is chaotic and unpredictable.
>
> **Who Discovered It?** Ed Lorenz

## Why Is This One of the 100 Greatest?

Ed Lorenz uncovered a nonlinear, complex, interdependent system of equations that describe the real movement of the atmosphere. He showed that atmospheric models are so dependent on initial and boundary conditions (starting data supplied to the model) that even seemingly infinitesimal changes in them create major changes in the system. In other words, when a butterfly flaps its wings over Beijing, the models might well predict that it will change the weather in New York. But everyone admitted that just couldn't happen.

Lorenz discovered not how to make long-range predictions, but rather the forces that make such predictions impossible. He then developed chaos theory—the study of chaotic and unpredictable systems. Scientists are discovering that many natural, biological, and environmental systems are best described and better understood under chaos theory than through traditional forms of analysis.

## How Was It Discovered?

Having a computer was enough of a novelty in 1958 to entice many MIT faculty and students to make the trip to Ed Lorenz's office just to watch the thing work. But excitement quickly turned to despair for Lorenz.

Lorenz created a set of equations to act as a mathematical model of atmospheric storm movement and behavior. He noticed that tiny changes in the starting conditions of the model soon produced enormous changes in the outcome. Tiny starting differences always *amplified* over time, rather than damping, or normalizing out.

If the actual atmosphere acted like Lorenz's models, he had just proved that long-range weather forecasting was impossible since starting conditions were never known with enough precision to prevent chaotic, amplified error. It was an unsettling and sinking feeling to trade the excitement of finding a new research tool for the despair of proving that your field and work were both inherently flawed and impossible.

When Ed entered Dartmouth College in 1934, he had long ago made up his mind to be a mathematician. He graduated with a bachelor's degree in mathematics in 1938 and entered Harvard to continue his study of math. With the outbreak of World War II, Lorenz joined the Army Air Corps, who assigned him to attend army meteorology classes at MIT.

He learned to regard the weather as a combination of density, pressure, temperature, three-dimensional wind velocities, and the atmosphere's gaseous, liquid, and solid content. The equations that describe this host of variables define the current weather conditions. The rates of change in these equations define the changing weather pattern.

What Lorenz was not taught, and only much later discovered, was that no one knew how to use these nonlinear dynamic meteorology equations to actually predict weather and that most thought it could not be done. The equations were too complex and required too much initial and boundary data.

Lorenz tried to apply the dynamic equations to predict the motion of storms. As computers were not commonly available in the early 1950s, most of this work was carried out on blackboards and with slide rules and paper and pencil. Each calculation was tediously time-consuming. Lorenz was never able to reach any meaningful results while hand-calculating these equations.

In 1958 Lorenz obtained that Royal-McBee LGP-30 computer (about the size of a large desk) to develop his sets of dynamic, nonlinear model equations. The results of those computer simulations showed that tiny initial differences *amplified* over time, rather than gradually normalizing out. If the model was right, weather was chaotic and inherently unpredictable.

Several years of atmospheric testing convinced Lorenz and others in his department that he and his model were correct. The atmosphere was a chaotic rather than a predictable system (such as the system of interactions between inorganic chemicals, or the physical pull of gravity). A drive to use a new tool to complete an old project had turned into one of the most profound discoveries for the science of meteorology.

Lorenz will always be known as the person who discovered the true nature of the atmosphere and who thereby discovered the limits of accuracy of weather forecasting.

 **Fun Facts:** Actor Jeff Goldblum played the role of Ian Malcolm in the *Jurassic Park* movies. Malcolm is a mathematician who specializes in the study of the chaos theory and refers to himself as a "chaotician." A central theme of these movies is proving that Malcolm's chaos theories are right.

# More to Explore

Fuller, John. *Thor's Legions.* Boston: American Meteorological Society, 1990.

Gleick, James. *Chaos: Making a New Science.* New York: Viking, 1991.

Lorenz, Ed. *The Essence of Chaos.* Seattle: University of Washington Press, 1993.

———. "A Scientist by Choice." In *Proceedings of the Kyoto Prize for 1991.* Kyoto, Japan: The Inamori Foundation, 1991.

Parker, Berry. *Chaos in the Cosmos.* New York: Plenum Press, 1996.

# Quarks

## Year of Discovery: 1962

> **What Is It?** Subatomic particles that make up protons and neutrons.
>
> **Who Discovered It?** Murry Gell-Mann

## Why Is This One of the 100 Greatest?

First scientists identified plant *fibers*, then individual *cells*. Then scientists conceived of atoms and molecules. In the early twentieth century, scientists discovered electrons and then the existence of protons and neutrons. In each case, scientists believed that they had finally discovered the smallest possible particle of matter. Each time this belief proved wrong.

The discovery of quarks (fundamental particles that make up protons and neutrons) in 1962 led science into the bizarre and alien quantum world inside protons and neutrons, a world of mass with no mass and where mass and energy are freely exchanged. This discovery has taken science one giant step closer to answering one of the most basic questions of all: What *really* is matter made of? At each new level the answer and the world grows stranger.

## How Was It Discovered?

As the nineteenth century closed, Marie Curie broke open the atom and proved that it was not the smallest possible particle of matter. Soon scientists had identified two subatomic particles: electrons and protons. In 1932 James Chadwick discovered the neutron. Once again scientists thought they had uncovered the smallest particles of all matter.

When particle accelerators were invented in the mid-1930s, scientists could smash neutrons into protons, and protons into heavier nuclei to see what the collisions would produce. In the 1950s Donald Glaser invented the "bubble chamber." Subatomic particles were accelerated to near light speed and flung into this low-pressure, hydrogen-gas-filled chamber. When these particles struck a proton (a hydrogen nucleus), the proton disintegrated into a host of strange new particles. Each of these particles left a telltale trail of infinitesimally small bubbles as they sped away from the collision site. Scientists couldn't see the particles themselves. But they *could* see the trails of bubbles.

Scientists were both amazed and baffled by the variety and number of these tiny tracks on bubble chamber plots (each indicating the temporary existence of a previously unknown particle). They were unable to even guess at what these new subatomic particles were.

Murry Gell-Mann was born in Manhattan in 1929. A true prodigy, he could multiply large numbers in his head at age three. At seven, he beat twelve-year-olds in spelling bees. By age eight, his intellectual ability matched that of most college students. Gell-Mann, however, was bored and restless in school and suffered from acute writer's block. He rarely finished papers and project descriptions, even though they were easy for him to complete.

Still, he sailed through undergraduate school at Yale and then drifted through MIT, the University of Chicago (where he worked for Fermi) and Princeton (where he worked for Oppenheimer). By the age of 24, he had decided to focus on understanding the bizarre particles that showed up on bubble chamber plots. Bubble chamber plots allowed scientists to estimate the size, electrical charge, direction, and speed of each particle, but not its specific identity. By 1958 almost 100 names were in use to identify and describe this forest of new particles that had been detected.

Gell-Mann decided that he could make sense of these particles if he applied a few fundamental concepts of nature. He assumed that nature was simple and symmetrical. He also assumed that, like all other matter and forces in nature, these subproton sized particles had to be conservative. (Mass, energy, and electrical charge would be conserved—not lost—in all collision reactions.)

With these principles as his guides, Gell-Mann began to group and to simplify the reactions that happened when a proton split apart. He created a new measure that he called *strangeness* that he took from quantum physics. Strangeness measured the quantum state of each particle. Again he assumed that strangeness would be conserved in each reaction.

Gell-Mann found that he could build simple patterns of reactions as particles split apart or combined. However, several of these patterns didn't appear to follow the laws of conservation. Then Gell-Mann realized that he could make all of the reactions follow simple, conservative laws if protons and neutrons weren't solid things, but were, instead, built of three smaller particles.

Over the course of two years' work, Gell-Mann showed that these smaller particles had to exist inside protons and neutrons. He named them *k-works*, then *kworks* for short. Soon afterward he read a line by James Joyce that mentioned "three quarks." Gell-Mann changed the name of his new particles to quarks.

 **Fun Facts:** The James Joyce line mentioned above is "Three quarks for Muster Mark!" in *Finnegan's Wake*. Can you find that quote?

# More to Explore

Apfel, Necia. *It's All Elementary: From Atoms to the Quantum World of Quarks, Leptons, and Gluons*. New York: HarperColllins, 1997.

Berger, Melvin. *Atoms, Molecules and Quarks*. New York: Penguin Young Readers' Group, 1996.

Bortz, Fred. *Quarks*. Cherry Hill, NJ: Rosen Publishing, 2004.

Gell-Mann, Murry. *The Quark and the Jaguar*. New York: Abacus Books, 1995.

Kidd, Jerry. *Nuclear Power: The Study of Quarks and Sparks*. New York: Facts on File, 2006.

Schwartz, David. *Q Is for Quark: A Science Alphabet Book*. Berkeley, CA: Ten Speed Press, 2001.

# Quasars and Pulsars

## Years of Discovery: 1963 and 1967

**What Is It?** The discovery of super-dense, distant objects in space.

**Who Discovered It?** Allan Rex Sandage (quasar) and Antony Hewish and Jocelyn Bell (pulsar)

## Why Is This One of the 100 Greatest?

Quasars and pulsars represent a new class of objects in space, a new kind of massive, extraordinarily bright object. Massive, exceedingly dense, and producing powerful radio and light transmissions, quasars and pulsars radically expanded and altered scientists' view of space and space structures.

Quasars are some of the brightest and most distant objects in the universe. Pulsars provide hints of the life path and life expectancy of stars. Their discovery led to a greater understanding of the life and death of stars and opened up new fields of study in astronomy, super-dense matter, gravitation, and super-strong magnetic fields.

## How Was It Discovered?

In the fall of 1960, American astronomer Allan Rex Sandage noticed a series of dim objects that looked like stars. He cross checked them with a radio telescope to see if they transmitted radio signals as well as dim light.

Each of these dim objects produced amazingly powerful radio signals. No known object could do that. Maybe they weren't really stars—at least not stars like other stars. Sandage called these mystery objects *quasi-stellar radio sources*. Quasi-stellar quickly shortened to *quasar*.

Sandage studied the spectrographic lines of these strange objects (lines that identify the chemical makeup of a distant star). The lines didn't match any known chemical elements and could not be identified.

Sandage and Dutch-born American astronomer Maarten Schmidt finally realized that the spectral lines *could* be identified as normal and common elements *if* they were viewed as spectrograph lines that normally occurred in the ultraviolet range and had been displaced by a tremendous red shift (Doppler shift) into the visible range. (Doppler shifts are changes in the frequency of light or sound caused by the motion of an object.)

While that explanation solved one mystery, it introduced another. What could cause such a giant Doppler shift? In 1963 they decided that the only plausible answer was distance and that the quasars must be over a billion light years away—the most distant objects ever detected!

But now the dim light of the quasars was too bright for a single star at that distance —often 1,000 times as bright as whole galaxies. Sandage and Schmidt proposed that each quasar must really be a distant galaxy. However, the measured radio signals varied too much (on the order of days and hours) to be a galaxy of separate stars. That indicated a compact mass, not a galaxy.

Quasars remained a perplexing mystery until, in 1967, it was proposed that they were really the material surrounding massive black holes. Quasars instantly became the most interesting and important objects in distant space.

That same year (in July 1967) Cambridge University Astronomy professor Antony Hewish completed a 4.5-acre radio antenna field to detect radio frequency transmissions from the farthest corners of space. This gargantuan maze of wire would be the most sensitive radio frequency receiver on Earth.

The radio telescope printed 100 feet of output chart paper each day. Graduate assistant Jocelyn Bell had the job of analyzing this chart paper. She compared the chart's squiggly lines to the position of known space objects and then compared the known electromagnetic emissions of these bodies to the chart's squiggles and spikes in order to account for each mark on the chart.

Two months after the telescope started up, Bell noticed an unusual, tight-packed pattern of lines that she called a "bit of scruff"—a squiggling pattern she couldn't explain. She marked it with a question mark and moved on.

Four nights later, she saw the same pattern. One month later she found the same pattern of scruff and recognized that the antenna was focused on the same small slice of sky. She took the extra time to expand and measure the squiggles. Whatever it was, this radio signal regularly pulsed every 1 1/3 seconds. No natural body in the known universe emitted regular signals like that.

Before Hewish publicly announced their discovery, Bell found another bit of scruff on chart printouts from a different part of the sky. The pulses of this second signal came 1.2 seconds apart and at almost the exact same frequency.

Every theoretician at Cambridge was brought in to explain Jocelyn's scruff. After months of study and calculation the science team concluded that Bell had discovered super-dense, rotating stars. Astronomers had mathematically theorized that when a huge star runs out of nuclear fuel, all matter in the star collapsed inward, creating a gigantic explosion, called a supernova.

What remained became a hundred million times denser than ordinary matter —a neutron star. If the star rotated, its magnetic and electric fields would broadcast beams of powerful radio waves. From Earth, a rapidly rotating neutron star would appear to pulse and so these were named "pulsars."

 **Fun Facts:** The more distant the quasar is, the redder its light appears on Earth. The light from the most distant quasar known takes 13 billion light-years to reach Earth. Thirteen billion light-years is how far away that quasar was 13 billion years ago when the light we now see first left the star and headed toward where Earth is now. Quasars are the most distant objects in the universe.

# More to Explore

Asimov, Isaac. *Black Holes, Pulsars, and Quasars.* New York: Gareth Stevens, 2003.

McGrayne, Sharon. *Nobel Prize Women in Science: Their Lives, Struggles, and Momentous Discoveries.* New York: Carol Publishing Group, A Birch Lane Press Book, 1993.

Raymo, Chet. *365 Starry Nights: An Introduction to Astronomy for Every Night of the Year.* New York: Simon & Schuster, 1992.

Schaaf, Fred. *The Amateur Astronomer: Explorations and Investigations.* New York: Franklin Watts, 1994.

Stille, Darlene R. *Extraordinary Women Scientists.* Chicago: Children's Press, 1995.

# Complete Evolution

## Year of Discovery: 1967

> **What Is It?** Evolution is driven by symbiotic mergers between cooperating species.
>
> **Who Discovered It?** Lynn Margulis

## Why Is This One of the 100 Greatest?

Charles Darwin was the first to conceive that species evolved—changed—over time, and the first to identify a driving force for that change—survival of the fittest. Darwin's theories instantly became the bedrock of biological thinking and survived unchallenged for a century.

Lynn Margulis was the first to discover and prove modification to Darwin's theory of evolution. In so doing, she filled in the one, nagging gap in Darwin's theory. More than any scientist since Darwin, she has forced a radical revision of evolutionary thinking. Like Copernicus, Galileo, Newton, and Darwin before her, Margulis has uprooted and changed some of science's most deeply held theorems and assumptions.

## How Was It Discovered?

Born in 1938, Lynn Margulis was raised on the streets of Chicago. Called precocious as a child, she entered the University of Chicago when only 14 years old. There she studied genetics and evolution.

Since Darwin's time the field of evolution has struggled with a problem called "variation." Researchers assumed that variation in an individual's DNA provided the "trial balloons" that natural selection kept or discarded. Those mutations that nature kept would slowly spread through the entire species.

However, a nagging question could not be answered: What causes new variations in the individuals of a species? Theories centered on random errors that somehow rewrote sections of the DNA genetic code.

Even early in her career, it seemed obvious to Margulis that this was not what really happened. Margulis saw no hard evidence to support small, random mutations driving species evolution. Instead she found evidence for large, sudden jumps—as if evolution happened not as a slow, steady creep, but as sudden, dramatic adaptive advances. She saw that evolutionary change was not nearly so random as others believed.

Margulis focused on the concept of *symbiosis*—two organisms (or species) living cooperatively together for their mutual benefit. She found many elementary examples of two species choosing to live in intimate, interdependent existence. Lichens were composed of an algae and a fungus that, living as a single organism, survived better than either could alone. Cellulose-digesting bacteria lived in the gut of termites. Neither could survive without the other. Yet together they both thrived. Without a symbiotic merger, this arrangement could never have developed.

Margulis found symbiotic relationships abounding wherever she looked. Existing species sought out new cooperative, symbiotic relationships to improve their survivability. Human corporations did it. So did nature when, for example, a bacterium (a highly evolved life form) incorporated itself into another existing species to create a new symbiotic mutation and the species jumped forward in its capabilities.

Margulis studied Earth's early life forms and discovered four key symbioses that allowed the development of complex life on Earth: (1) a union between a heat-loving archae-bacterium and a swimming bacterium (a spirochete). Some of the original spirochete genes were then coopted (2) to produce the organizing centers and filaments that pull genetic material to opposite sides of a cell before it splits. This allowed the creation of complex life forms. This new creature engulfed (3) an oxygen-burning bacterium (once oxygen began to proliferate in the atmosphere). Finally, this swimming, complex, oxygen-processing one-celled organism engulfed (4) a photosynthesizing bacterium. The result of this four-step evolutionary merger was all modern algae and plants!

Margulis showed that the cells of plants, animals, fungi, and even humans evolved through specific series of symbiotic mergers that represented large, instant steps forward for the involved species.

She published her landmark work in 1967, but biologists were skeptical until it was shown that mitochondria in all human cells have their own DNA, thus establishing that even human cells are the result of at least one symbiotic merger. This discovery spurred a generation of scientists who have searched for, found, and studied symbiotic mergers. They have found them everywhere.

Nine out of ten plants survive because of symbiotic mergers with root fungi that process crucial nutrients from the soil. Humans and other animals have whole colonies of cooperating bacteria and other bugs living in our guts to process and digest the food we eat. Without them, we would not survive. Without Margulis's discovery, Darwin's theory would have remained incomplete.

 **Fun Facts:** Margulis and her writer/astronomer husband, Carl Sagan, are the ones who said: "Life did not take over the globe by combat, but by networking (cooperation), and Darwin's notion of evolution driven by the combat of natural selection is incomplete."

# More to Explore

Adler, Robert. *Science Firsts*. New York: John Wiley & Sons, 2002.

Brockman, John. *Curious Minds: How a Child Becomes a Scientist*. New York: Knopf, 2005.

Margulis, Lynn. *Diversity of Life: The Five Kingdoms*. Hillside, NJ: Enslow Publishers, 1996.

————. *Microcosmos: Four Billion Years of Evolution from Our Microbial Ancestors.* Berkeley: University of California Press, 1997.

————. *Symbiotic Planet: A New Look at Evolution.* New York: Basic Books, 1998.

————. What Is Life? Berkeley: University of California Press, 2000.

Sapp, Jan. *Evolution by Association: A History of Symbiosis.* New York: Oxford University Press, 1999.

# Dark Matter

## Year of Discovery: 1970

> **What Is It?** Matter in the universe that gives off no light or other detectible radiation.
>
> **Who Discovered It?** Vera Rubin

## Why Is This One of the 100 Greatest?

Calculations of the expansion of the universe didn't work. Calculations of the speed of stars in distant galaxies didn't match what astronomers observed. Calculations of the age of the universe (based on the speed of its expansion) didn't make sense. Something had to be wrong with the methods used for these calculations. With these major question marks hanging over the calculations, no one could dependably calculate the history of, present mass of, or future of, the universe. Much of physics research ground to a halt.

Vera Rubin only meant to test a new piece of equipment. What she discovered was that the *actual* motion of stars and galaxies appeared to prove that Newton's laws—the most fundamental principles of all of astronomy—were wrong. In trying to explain the difference between observations and Newtonian physics, Rubin discovered *dark matter*—matter that exists but gives off no light or other radiation that scientists could detect. Astronomers and physicists now believe that 90 percent of the mass of the universe is dark matter.

## How Was It Discovered?

In 1970 Vera Rubin worked at the Department of Terrestrial Magnetism (DTM) at the Carnegie Institute of Washington. DTM's director, astronomer Kent Ford, had just created a new high-speed, wide-band spectrograph that could complete eight to ten spectrographs (graphic images on chart paper of some spectrum—in this case of the energy emitted from distant stars at different frequencies along the frequency spectrum) in a single night while existing models were lucky to complete one in a day. Vera was itching to see what Ford's invention could do.

During the night of March 27, 1970, Rubin focused the DTM telescope on Andromeda, the nearest galaxy to our own. She planned to see whether Andromeda's millions of stars really moved as existing theory said they should.

When attached to powerful telescopes, spectrographs detect the presence of different elements in a distant star and display what they detect on chart paper. Rubin rigged a high-power microscope to read the charts created by Ford's spectrograph.

Rubin knew that the marks astronomers measured on a spectrograph shift a tiny bit higher or lower on the frequency chart paper depending on whether the star is moving toward Earth or away from it. This frequency shift is called a Doppler shift. The same kind of shift happens with sound waves as a car passes and the sound of its engine seems to change to a lower frequency. The greater that shift, the greater the object's speed. Rubin wanted to see if she could use Doppler shifts and Kent's new spectrograph to measure the speed of stars in distant galaxies.

She found that the stars near the outer edge of Andromeda moved just as fast as the stars near the galaxy's center. That wasn't the way it was supposed to be.

Over a period of two months she completed 200 spectrographs. For every galaxy it was the same. The velocities of stars she measured were all wrong. According to every known law of physics, some of those stars were moving too fast for gravity to hold them in their galaxies, and they should fly off into space. But they didn't.

Rubin was left with two possible explanations. Either Newton's equations were wrong (something the scientific world would not accept) or the universe contained extra matter no astronomer had detected.

She chose the second explanation and named this extra matter "dark matter" since it could not be seen or detected. Rubin calculated how much dark matter would be needed and how it would have to be distributed throughout the universe in order to make Newton's equations correct. She found that 90 percent of the universe had to be dark matter.

It took the rest of the scientific community a full decade to grudgingly accept Vera Rubin's results and the reality that most of the matter in the universe could not be seen or detected by any means available to humans.

However, Vera Rubin's work in that summer of 1970 changed every calculation and theory about the structure and origins of our universe. It vastly improved astronomers' ability to correctly calculate the distribution and motion of matter. Meanwhile—luckily—Newton's laws of motion still survive.

 **Fun Facts:** NASA has tried to take a photograph of dark matter (something no once can see or directly detect) by combining X-ray telescope images from the ROSAT satellite with other satellite imagery; the photo shown at http://heasarc.gsfc.nasa.gov/docs/rosat/gallery/display/darkmatter.html is the result. It could be the first photo of dark matter.

## More to Explore

Golway, James. *Where Is the Rest of the Universe?* (video). Los Angeles: KCET, 1991.

Kraus, Lawrence. *The Fifth Essence: The Search for Dark Matter.* New York: Basic Books, 1993.

———. *The Mystery of Missing Mass in the Universe.* New York: Basic Books, 2000.

Rubin, Vera. *Bright Galaxies, Dark Matter.* New York: American Institute of Physics, 1997.

St. Bartusiak, Marcia. *Through a Universe Darkly.* New York: HarperCollins, 1993.

Tucker, Wallace. *The Dark Matter.* New York: Morrow Books, 1998.

Yount, Lisa. *Contemporary Women Scientists.* New York: Facts on File, 1994.

# The Nature of Dinosaurs

## Year of Discovery: 1976

**What Is It?** How dinosaurs really acted, moved, and lived.

**Who Discovered It?** Robert Bakker

## Why Is This One of the 100 Greatest?

Dinosaurs were plodding, cold-blooded monsters. They were sluggish, dull-gray, and so dumb they weren't capable of decent parenting. That was the classical view of dinosaurs through the first half of the twentieth century. That was how dinosaurs were depicted in illustrations. That was what expert paleontologists believed. Robert Bakker shattered those beliefs.

Robert Bakker was the first to claim that dinosaurs were warm blooded, colorful, and quick, intelligent, and agile. He also first proposed that birds were descended from dinosaurs. The images we see of dinosaurs—from *Jurassic Park* to science museum displays—all owe their dinosaur concepts to Robert Bakker's discoveries. Robert Bakker completely rewrote the book on dinosaurs.

## How Was It Discovered?

A great revelation swept over Robert Bakker one night during his sophomore year at Yale University. As he walked through the darkened museum, faint bits of light caught the dinosaur skeletons and made them appear to move through the shadowed stillness. It occurred to Robert as he studied the familiar bones that these creatures had ruled the earth for 165 million years. They couldn't have been stupid, cold-blooded and sluggish. Intelligent mammals were around. They would have taken over unless the dinosaurs kept winning because they were fundamentally better.

Robert Bakker set out—all alone—to prove that the prevailing view of dinosaurs was completely wrong. Bakker turned to four sources of information to develop his case: comparative anatomy (comparing the size and shape of similar parts of different species), latitudinal zonation (where the animals live), the cumulative fossil record (all previously collected dinosaur bones and skeletons), and ecology (relationship of a species to its environment).

For three years Bakker exhaustively studied the bones of mammals and found that they, as were dinosaur bones, were rich in blood vessels and lacked growth rings—just the opposite of cold-blooded reptiles. He found that Cretaceous dinosaurs thrived in northern Canada where cold-blooded reptiles could not have survived. Finally he studied African and North American ecosystems and found that warm-blooded predators eat six to eight

**213**

times as much per pound of body weight as do reptile predators. By studying the fossil record, Bakker found that the ratio of predators to herbivores in dinosaur ecosystems matched what would be expected of a warm-blooded ecosystem.

Dinosaurs had to have been warm-blooded. Their bones, relative numbers, and locations proved it.

He studied the legs of zoo animals, comparing leg structure to how they moved. Did a chicken's leg bend differently than a zebra's? How did those differences relate to the different activity of each animal? How did form dictate function for each animal, and how did function dictate form? What did the shape of a dinosaur's joints and the size of its bones say about how it must have moved and functioned? He tried to account for this motion and the implied probable muscle masses to control and move each bone in his drawings.

He compared leg bone size, shape, and density for hundreds of modern animals with those of dinosaurs. He found that dinosaur leg bones closely matched the bone structure of running mammals—not those who sprint for 10 seconds when alarmed, but those who regularly run for 20 minutes.

Dinosaurs were runners. Their structure proved it. That also meant that they were agile. No sluggish, clumsy oaf would be a natural runner.

Bakker again turned to the fossil record and found that very few baby and juvenile dinosaur skeletons had been discovered. This meant that few died, which in turn meant that parent dinosaurs had to have been very successful at protecting, sheltering, and feeding their young. Dinosaurs were good parents.

The old myths were shattered. Bakker published his findings while still a graduate student at Harvard. But it took another 20 years of intense data collection and analysis for the tide of belief to turn in Bakker's direction. Even after Bakker's discoveries revolutionized science's views of dinosaurs, he was still viewed with suspicion as an untrustworthy radical.

 **Fun Facts:** Giant Brontosaurus became the most popular of all dinosaurs in the late nineteenth and early twentieth centuries. Its name means "thunder lizard." By 1970 some scientists claimed that "Brontosaurus" should not be used since it referred to three different species: Apatosaurus, Brachiosaurus, and Camarasaurus. The argument continues, though it's been 80 million years since any of the three thundered across the earth.

# More to Explore

Bakker, Robert. *The Dinosaur Heresies*. New York: Morrow Books, 1988.

———. "Unearthing the Jurassic." In *Science Year 1995*. New York: World Book, 1995.

Daintith, John. *Biographical Encyclopedia of Scientists, Volume 1*. Philadelphia: Institute of Physics Publishing, 1994.

Krishtalka, Leonard. *Dinosaur Plots*. New York: William Morrow, 1999.

Officer, Charles. *The Great Dinosaur Extinction Controversy*. Reading, MA, Addison Wasley, 1996.

Stille, Darlene. "Dinosaur Scientist." In *Science Year 1992*. New York: World Book, 1993.

# Planets Exist Around Other Stars

## Year of Discovery: 1995

---

**What Is It?** Planets—even planets like Earth—exist around other stars.

**Who Discovered It?** Michel Mayor and Didier Queloz

## Why Is This One of the 100 Greatest?

One of the great questions for humanity has always been: Are we alone? Science has long asked: Are we the only solar system with planets—and the only one with planets that could support life? The discovery of planets around other stars makes it likely that other planets exist capable of supporting life.

Of great importance to astronomers, the discovery of other solar systems lets them test their theories on the origin of planets and solar systems. The discovery of distant planets has fundamentally changed how we perceive our place in the universe.

## How Was It Discovered?

In the sixth century B.C., Greek scientist Anaximander was the first to theorize that other planets must exist. In 1600 Italian priest and astronomer Giordano Bruno was burned at the stake by the Catholic Church for professing the same belief. American astronomers were actively searching through giant telescopes for planets orbiting other stars by late the 1940s.

Michel Mayor was born in 1942 and even as a child was fascinated by stars and astronomy. With his collaborator, Antoine Duquennoy, he joined the many astronomers searching for small objects in the universe. But Mayor searched not for planets, but for brown dwarfs—cool, dim objects thought to form like stars, but which failed to grow massive enough to support hydrogen fusion and thus never lit up with starry furnace and fire. Too big for planets, too small to become stars, brown dwarfs were a galactic oddity.

Astronomers, however, had a problem: telescopes can't see planets and brown dwarfs because they don't give off light. Instead, astronomers searched for slight side-to-side wobbles in the motion of a star caused by the gravitational tug of a large planet (or brown dwarf).

Some tried to detect such wobble by carefully measuring the position of a star over the course of months or years. Others (Mayor included) looked for this wobble by using Doppler shift and measuring tiny shifts on a spectrograph in the color of the light coming from a star that would be the result of changes in the star's motion toward or away from Earth.

Following the death of Duquennoy in 1993, Mayor teamed with graduate student Didier Queloz and developed a new, more sensitive spectrograph to search for brown dwarfs. Their new spectrograph was capable of measuring velocity changes as small as 13 meters per second—about the same as the wobble in our sun's motion caused by Jupiter's gravitational tug.

But everyone assumed that such massive planets would take years to orbit a star (as they do in our system). Thus the wobble from a planet's tug would take *years* of data to notice. It never occurred to Mayor to use his new spectrograph and a few months' worth of time on a telescope to search for a planet.

Beginning in April 1994, using the Haute-Provence Observatory in southern France, Mayor and Queloz tested their new spectrograph on 142 nearby stars, hoping to detect a wobble that would indicate a massive nearby object like a brown dwarf. In January 1995 one star, 51 Peg (the fifty-first brightest star in the constellation Pegasus) caught Queloz's eye. It wobbled. It wobbled back and forth every 4.2 days.

They tested the star's light to make sure it didn't pulse. They tested to see if sun spots might create an apparent wobble. The tested to see if 51 Peg puffed up and contracted to create the appearance of wobble. Nothing could account for 51 Peg's wobble except for a sizable orbiting object.

From the amount of 51 Peg's wobble they calculated the mass of the object and knew it was too small to be a brown dwarf. It had to be a planet! They had discovered a planet outside our solar system.

By 2005, several hundred other planets had been located—gas giants speeding around Mercury-sized orbits; some rocky planets in cozy, not-too-hot-and-not-too-cold orbits; even some drifting free through space without a star to circle. Earth is certainly not alone. Mayor and Queloz were the first to discover proof of this spectacular reality.

 **Fun Facts:** If only one star in ten has planets (and current knowledge indicates that at least that many do), if the average star with planets has at least three, and if only one in every hundred are rocky planets in life-sustaining orbits (and recent discoveries indicate that to be the case), then there are at least 300,000 planets capable of supporting life in our galaxy alone!

# More to Explore

Adler, Robert. *Science Firsts.* New York: John Wiley & Sons, 2002.

Boss, Alan. *Looking for Earths: The Race to Find New Solar Systems.* New York: John Wiley & Sons, 1998.

Croswell, Ken. *Planet Quest: The Epic Discovery of Alien Solar Systems.* New York: Free Press, 2002.

Goldsmith, Donald. *Worlds Unnumbered: The Search for Extrasolar Planets.* Sausalito, CA: University Science Books, 2000.

Halpren, Paul. *The Quest for Alien Planets: Exploring Worlds Outside the Solar System.* New York: Plenum, 1999.

Lemonick, Michael. *Other Worlds: The Search for Life in the Universe.* New York: Simon & Schuster, 2001.

# Accelerating Universe

## Year of Discovery: 1998

---

**What Is It?** Our universe is not only expanding; the rate at which it expands is speeding up, not slowing down as had been assumed.

**Who Discovered It?** Saul Perlmutter

---

## Why Is This One of the 100 Greatest?

A great debate began after Edwin Hubble discovered that the universe is expanding: Is that expansion slowing so that it will eventually stop and the universe will begin to collapse? Saul Perlmutter discovered that the expansion of the universe is actually *accelerating*, shattering all existing scientific models of the motion of the universe. The universe is expanding faster now than it ever has before. It is tearing itself apart. Gravity is not slowing the expansion as it is supposed to.

This discovery has created a monumental shift in how scientists view the universe, its past, and its future. It has affected the calculations of the Big Bang and even scientists' view of what makes up the universe. The *Journal of Science* called this discovery the 1998 "Breakthrough of the Year."

## How Was It Discovered?

Edwin Hubble discovered that the universe was expanding in 1926. Scientists built new models that assumed that the expansion was slowing down as gravity tugged on stars and galaxies, pulling them back toward each other.

This model seemed logical. However, a few, highly technical problems existed with the mathematics associated with this model. Einstein tried to explain these problems by creating something he called the "cosmological constant"—a force that opposed gravity. But he then rejected the idea as his greatest scientific blunder.

After receiving a Ph.D. in physics in 1986, Saul Perlmutter worked at Lawrence Berkeley National Laboratory and headed the Supernova Cosmology Project (SCP). This group used the Hubble Space Telescope to find and study distant supernovae (exploding stars). They chose supernovae because they are the brightest objects in the universe. Type Ia supernovae produce a constant amount of light, and it is believed that all Ia supernovae shine at about the same brightness. This made them ideal for Perlmutter's study.

Over the 10-year period from 1987 to 1997, Perlmutter developed a technique to identify supernovae in distant galaxies and to analyze the light they produce. His team searched tens of thousands of galaxies to find a half dozen type Ia supernovae.

When Perlmutter found an Ia supernova, he measured its brightness to determine its distance from Earth. (The brighter it is, the closer it is.) Perlmutter also measured the red shift of the supernova's light. This is a technique based on Doppler shifts. If a star is moving toward Earth, its light is compressed and its color shifts a little toward blue. If the star is moving away, its light is stretched and the color shifts toward red. The faster the star is moving, the greater its color shift. By measuring the supernova's red shift, Perlmutter could calculate the star's velocity away from Earth.

Now came the hard part. Other factors could account for a red shift, and Perlmutter had to prove that the red shifts he measured were the result of only the star's motion away from Earth. Space dust can absorb some light and shift its color. Some galaxies have an overall color hue that could distort the color of the light coming from a supernova. Each of a dozen possible sources of error had to be explored, tested, and eliminated.

Finally, in early 1998, Perlmutter had collected reliable distance and velocity data for a dozen Ia supernovae spread across the heavens. All were moving at tremendous speeds *away* from Earth.

Perlmutter used mathematical models to show that these galaxies couldn't have been traveling at their current speeds ever since the Big Bang. If they had, they would be much farther away than they really are. The only way Perlmutter's data could be correct was for these galaxies to now be traveling outward faster than they had in the past.

The galaxies were *speeding up*, not slowing down. The universe had to be expanding at an accelerating rate!

Perlmutter's discovery showed that some new and unknown force (named "dark energy" by Michael Turner in 2000) must be pushing matter (stars, galaxies, etc.) *outward*. More recent research using new specially designed satellites has shown that the universe is filled with this "dark energy." (Some estimates say that two-thirds of all energy in the universe is dark energy.) Over the next few years this new discovery will rewrite human theories of the origin and structure of the universe.

 **Fun Facts:** A new $20 million telescope is being built at the South Pole to study and explain why the universe is accelerating, since this discovery violates all existing theories about the birth and expansion of the universe. The telescope will become operational in 2007.

## More to Explore

Adair, Rick. *Scientific Information about the Universe and the Scientific Theories of the Evolution of the Universe: An Anthology of Current Thought.* Cherry Hill, NJ: Rosen Central, 2005.

Anton, Ted. *Bold Science: Seven Scientists Who Are Changing Our World.* New York: W. H. Freeman, 2001.

Couper, Heather. *DK Space Encyclopedia.* New York: DK Publishers, 2001.

Gribbin, John. *The Birth of Time: How Astronomers Measured the Age of the Universe.* New Haven, CT: Yale University Press, 2001.

———. *EYEWITNESS: Time and Space.* New York: DK Publishers, 2000.

Kerrod, Robin. *The Way the Universe Works.* New York: DK Publishers, 2006.

# Human Genome

## Year of Discovery: 2003

**What Is It?** A detailed mapping of the entire human DNA genetic code.

**Who Discovered It?** James Watson and J. Craig Venter

## Why Is This One of the 100 Greatest?

Deciphering the human genetic code, the human genome, has been called the first great scientific discovery of the twenty-first century, the "Holy Grail" of biology. DNA is the blueprint for constructing, operating, and maintaining a living organism. It directs the transformation of a fertilized egg into a complete and complex human being. Deciphering that code is the key to understanding how cells are instructed to develop and grow, the key to understanding the development of life itself.

Because the human genome is unimaginably complex, it seemed impossible to decipher the three billion elements of this molecular code. Yet this Herculean effort has already led to medical breakthroughs in genetic defects, disease cures, and inherited diseases. It is the key to future discoveries about human anatomy and health. Understanding this genome vastly increased our appreciation of what makes us unique and what connects us with other living species.

## How Was It Discovered?

Austrian monk Gregor Mendel discovered the concept of heredity in 1865, launching the field of genetics. In 1953 Francis Crick and James Watson discovered the double helix shape of the DNA molecule that carried all genetic instructions.

The problem was that there were billions of genetic instructions carried on the complete human genetic code, or genome. Understanding it all seemed a physically impossible task. Sequencing the entire human genome was a project 20,000 times bigger and harder than any biological project attempted to that time.

Charles De Lisi at the U.S. Department of Energy (DOE) was the first to gain government funds to begin this monumental process, in 1987. By 1990, the DOE had joined with the National Institutes of Health (NIH) to create a new organization, the International Human Genome Sequencing Consortium (IHGSC). James Watson (of DNA discovery fame) was asked to head the project and was given 15 years to accomplish this monumental task.

At that time, scientists believed that human DNA contained about 100,000 genes spread along 23 chromosomes locked onto DNA's double helix, held together by over 3 billion base pairs of molecules. Watson's task was to identify, interpret, and sequence every gene on every chromosome, as well as every one of those billions of base pairs.

Certainly, the ability to identify and sequence individual pairs existed. Watson's problem was one of size. Using the existing (1990) technology, it would take thousands of years for all existing labs to complete the identification and sequencing of three *billion* pairs.

Watson decided to start with large-scale maps of what was known about chromosomes and work down toward the details of individual pairs. He directed all IHGSC scientists to work toward creating physical and linking maps of the 23 chromosomes. These maps would provide an overview of the human genome and would include only those few "snippets" of actual gene sequences that were already known.

By 1994 this first effort was complete. Watson ordered IHGSC scientists to map the complete genome of the simplest and best-known life forms on Earth to refine their technique before attempting to work on the human genome. IHGSC scientists chose fruit flies (studied extensively since 1910), *e. coli* (the common intestinal bacterium), bread molds, and simple nematodes (tiny oceanic worms). In the mid-1990s, work began on mapping the tens of millions of base pairs in these simple genomes.

However, not all biologists agreed with this approach. J. Craig Venter (a gene sequencer at the Institutes of Health) believed that scientists would waste precious years focusing on Watson's "big picture" and should instead sequence as many specific parts of the genome as they could and piece these individual sequences together later.

A war began between Watson (representing the "top down" approach) and Venter (representing the "bottom up" approach). Accusations and ugly words erupted from both sides at congressional hearings, at funding meetings, and in the press.

Venter quit his government position and formed his own company to develop as much of the genome sequence as he could ahead of IHGSC's effort. In 1998 Venter shocked the world by announcing that he would use linked supercomputers to complete his sequencing of the entire human genome by 2002, three years ahead of IHGSC's timetable.

In early 2000 President Clinton stepped in to end the war and merged both sides into a unified genome effort. In 2003 this merged team released their preliminary report, detailing the entire sequence of the human genome. In written form, that genome would fill 150,000 printed pages (500 books, each 300 pages long).

Surprisingly, these scientists found that humans have only 25,000 to 28,000 genes (down from the previously believed 100,000). A human's genetic sequence is only a few percent different from that of many other species.

Even though the information on this genetic sequence is only a few years old, it has already helped medical researchers make major advances on dozens of diseases and birth defects. Its full value will be seen in medical breakthroughs over the next 20 to 50 years.

 **Fun Facts:** If the DNA sequence of the human genome were compiled in books, the equivalent of 200 volumes the size of a Manhattan telephone book (at 1,000 pages each) would be needed to hold it all.

# More to Explore

Boon, Kevin. *Human Genome Project: What Does Decoding DNA Mean for Us?* Berkeley Heights, NJ: Enslow, 2003.

Brooks, Martin. *Get a Grip on Genetics.* New York: Time-Life Books, 1999.

Marshall, Elizabeth. *The Human Genome Project: Cracking the Code Within Us.* New York: Scholastic Library, 2001.

Sloan, Christopher. *The Human Story: Our Evolution from Prehistoric Ancestors to Today.* Washington, DC. National Geographic Society, 2004.

Toriello, James. *Human Genome Project.* Cherry Hill, NJ: Rosen Publishing, 2003.

# References

These book and Internet sources are good general references on scientific discovery, on the process of scientific investigation, on the history of scientific discoveries, and on important scientists.

## Book Sources

Aaseng, Nathan. *Twentieth-Century Inventors.* New York: Facts on File, 1996.

Adler, Robert. *Science Firsts,* New York: John Wiley & Sons, 2002.

———. *Medical Firsts.* New York: John Wiley & Sons, 2004.

Anton, Ted. *Bold Science: Seven Scientists Who Are Changing Our World.* New York: W. H. Freeman, 2001.

Ashby, Ruth. *Herstory.* New York: Penguin Books, 1995.

Asimov, Isaac. *Asimov's Chronology of Science and Discovery.* New York: Harper & Row, 1994.

Atkins, Peter, *Galileo's Finger: The Ten Great Ideas of Science.* New York: Random House, 2004.

Aubrey, John. *Brief Lives, Volumes I and II.* New York: Clarendon Press, 1998.

Badger, Mark. *Two-Fisted Science.* New York: G. T. Labs, 2001.

Berlinski, David. *Newton's Gift.* New York: Free Press, 2000.

Beshore, George. *Science in Ancient China.* New York: Franklin Watts, 1996.

Boorstin, Daniel. *The Discoverers: A History of Man's Search to Know His World and Himself.* New York: Random House, 1997.

Brockman, John. *Curious Minds: How a Child Becomes a Scientist.* New York: Knopf, 2005.

Brodie, James. *Created Equal: The Lives and Ideas of Black American Inventors.* New York: William Morrow, 1999.

Bryan, Jenny. *The History of Health and Medicine.* Florence, KY: Thompson Learning, 1999.

Bunch, Bryan. *The History of Science and Technology.* New York: Houghton Mifflin, 2004.

Chang, Laura, ed. *Scientists at Work.* New York: McGraw-Hill, 2000.

Clark, Donald. *Encyclopedia of Great Inventors and Discoveries*. London: Marshall Cavendish Books, 1991.

Cohen, Bernard. *Revolutions in Science*. Cambridge, MA: Harvard University Press, 1995.

Collins, H., and T. Pinch. *What You Should Know About Science*. New York: Cambridge University, 1998.

Conrad, Lawrence, et al. *The Western Medical Tradition: 800 BC to 1900 AD*. New York: Cambridge University Press, 1999.

Cropper, William. *Great Physicists*. New York: Oxford University Press, 2001.

Day, Lance, ed. *Biographical Dictionary of the History of Technology*. New York: Routledge, 1996.

Diagram Group. *Facts on File Chemistry Handbook*. New York: Facts on File, 2000.

———. *Facts on File Physics Handbook*. New York: Facts on File, 2006.

Downs, Robert. *Landmarks in Science*. Englewood, CO: Libraries Unlimited, 1993.

Dreyer, J. *A History of Astronomy from Thales to Kepler*. New York: Dover, 1993.

Ferguson, Keith. *Measuring the Universe: The Historical Quest to Quantify Space*. New York: Headline Books, 1999.

Fox, Ruth. *Milestones in Medicine*. New York: Random House, 1995.

Francis, Raymond. *The Illustrated Almanac of Science, Technology, and Invention*. New York: Plenum Trade, 1997.

Frontier Press Co. *Great Masters of Achievement in Science and Discovery*. Whitefish, MT: Kessinger, 2005.

Gallant, Roy. *The Ever-Changing Atom*. New York: Benchmark Books, 2000.

Garwin, Laura. *A Century of Nature: Twenty-One Discoveries That Changed Science and the World*. Chicago: University of Chicago Press, 2003.

Gibbs, C.R. *Black Inventors from Africa to America*. Silver Springs, MD: Three Dimensional, 1999.

Gratzer, Walter. *Eurekas and Euphorias*. New York: Oxford University Press, 2004.

Greenstein, George. *Portraits of Discovery: Profiles in Scientific Genius*. New York: John Wiley & Sons, 1997.

Gribbin, John. *The Scientists: A History of Science Told through the Lives of Its Greatest Inventors*. New York: Random House, 2002.

Hall, Ruppert. *A Brief History of Science*. Iowa City: Iowa State Press, 1999.

Hammond, Allen, ed. *A Passion to Know: 20 Profiles in Science*. New York: Scribner's, 1995.

Hatt, Christine. *Scientists and Their Discoveries*. New York: Franklin Watts, 2001.

Haven, Kendall. *Amazing American Women*. Englewood, CO: Libraries Unlimited, 1996.

————. *Marvels of Science.* Englewood, CO: Libraries Unlimited, 1994.

————. *The 100 Greatest Science Inventions of All Time.* Westport, CT: Libraries Unlimited, 2005.

————. *That's Weird! Awesome Science Mysteries.* Boulder, CO: Fulcrum Resources, 2000.

————. *Women at the Edge of Discovery.* Englewood, CO: Libraries Unlimited: 2003.

Haven, Kendall, and Donna Clark. *The 100 Most Popular Scientists for Young Adults.* Westport, CT: Libraries Unlimited, 2001.

Hawking, Steven. *A Brief History of Time.* New York: Bantam, 1996.

Hawley, John, and Katherine Holcomb. *Foundations of Modern Cosmology.* New York: Oxford University Press, 1998.

Hayden, Robert. *9 African American Inventors.* New York: Twenty-First Century Books, 1992.

Heilbron, John. *The Oxford Companion to the History of Modern Science.* New York: Oxford University Press, 2003.

Hooft, G. *In Search of the Ultimate Building Blocks.* New York: Cambridge University Press, 1997.

Huff, Toby. *The Rise of Early Modern Science.* New York: Cambridge University Press, 1993.

Irwin, Keith. *The Romance of Chemistry.* New York: Viking Press, 1996.

Jones, Alexander, ed. *Cambridge History of Science: Ancient Science.* New York: Cambridge University Press, 2006.

Jungk, R. *Brighter Than a Thousand Suns: A Personal History of the Atomic Scientists.* New York: Harcourt Brace, 1998.

Kass-Simon, Amy. *Women of Science: Righting the Record.* Bloomington: Indiana University Press, 1996.

Koestler, Arthur. *The Sleepwalkers: A History of Man's Changing Vision of the Universe.* London: Hutchinson & Co., 1999.

Levere, Trevor. *Transforming Matter : A History of Chemistry from Alchemy to the Buckyball.* Baltimore, MD: Johns Hopkins University Press, 200

Lomask, Milton. *Invention and Technology Great Lives.* New York: Charles Scribner's Sons, 1994.

Maddox, John. *What Remains to Be Discovered.* New York: Free Press, 1998.

Mather, John, and John Boslough. *The Very First Light: The True Inside Story of the Scientific Journey Back to the Dawn of the Universe.* New York: Basic Books, 1996.

McGrayne, Sharon. *Nobel Prize Women of Science.* New York: Birch Lane Press, 1997.

McNeil, Ian. *An Encyclopedia of the History of Technology.* New York: Routledge, 1996.

Messadie, Gerald. *Great Scientific Discoveries.* New York: Chambers, 2001.

Nader, Helen. *Rethinking the World: Discovery and Science in the Renaissance.* Bloomington: Indiana University Press, 2002.

National Geographic Society. *Inventors and Discoveries: Changing Our World.* Washington, DC: National Geographic Society, 1998.

Nelson, Clifford. *Discoveries in Science.* New York: Harcourt Brace, 1994.

North, John. *The Norton History of Astronomy and Cosmology.* New York: Norton, 1995.

Pais, Abraham. *The Genius of Science: A Portrait Gallery.* New York: Oxford University Press, 2000.

Palmer, Eric. *Philosophy of Science and History of Science.* New York: Xlibris Corp., 2000.

Parker, Steve. *Galileo and the Universe.* New York: HarperCollins Children's Books, 1996.

Perkowitz, Sidney. *Empire of Light: A History of Discovery in Science.* New York: National Academies Press, 1998.

Philbin, Tom. *The 100 Greatest Inventions of All Time.* New York: Citadel Press, 2003.

Porter, Theodore. *The Cambridge History of Science.* New York: Cambridge University Press, 2003.

Pullman, Bernard. *The Atom in the History of Human Thought.* New York: Oxford University Press, 1999.

Pyenson, Lewis, and Susan Pyenson. *Servants of Nature,* New York: HarperCollins, 1999.

Rattanski, P. M. *Pioneers of Science and Discovery.* Charleston, WV: Main Line Books, 1997.

Schlessinger, Bernard, and June Schlessinger. *The Who's Who of Nobel Prize Winners 1901–1999.* New York: Oryx Press, 2001.

Shepherd, Linda. *Lifting the Veil: The Feminine Face of Science.* Boston: Shambala, 2000.

Sherrow, Victoria. *Great Scientists.* New York: Facts on File, 1998.

Silvers, Robert. *Hidden Histories of Science.* New York: New York Review of Books, 2003.

Singh, Simon. *The Science Book: 250 Milestones in the History of Science.* London: Cassell, 2001.

Smith, Roger. *The Norton History of Human Sciences.* New York. W. W. Norton, 1997.

Snedden, Robert. *Scientists and Discoveries.* Portsmouth, NH: Heinemann, 2001.

Stille, Darlene. *Extraordinary Women Scientists.* Chicago: Children's Press, 1999.

Sturtevant, A. H. *A History of Genetics.* Cold Spring Harbor, NY: Cold Spring Harbor Laboratory Press, 2001.

Suplee, Curt. *Milestones of Science.* Washington, DC: National Geographic Society, 2000.

Temple, Robert. *The Genius of China: 3,000 Years of Science, Discovery, and Invention.* New York: Simon & Schuster, 2000.

Veglahn, Nancy. *Women Scientists.* New York: Facts on File, 1997.

Whitfield, Peter. *Landmarks in Western Science.* London: British Library, 1999.

Yenne, Bill. *100 Inventions That Shaped World History.* New York: Bluewood Books, 1993.

Yuval, Neeman, and Yoram Kirsh. *The Particle Hunters.* Cambridge, MA: Harvard University Press, 1999.

## Internet Web Site Sources

These sites focus on the history of science and discoveries in general. Conduct your own searches for specific scientific topics, fields, or periods.

www.echo.gmu.edu/center
www.hssonline.org/
www.depts.washington.edu/hssexec/
www.bshs.org.uk
www2.lib.udel.edu/subj/hsci/internet.htm
www.fordham.edu/halsall/science/sciencesbook.html
www2.sjsu.edu/elementaryed/ejlts/archives/diversity/hampton.htm
www.aip.org/history/web-link.htm
www.fas.harvard.edu/~hsdept/
www.mpiwg-berlin.mpg.de
www.hps.cam.ac.uk/whipple/
www.mdx.ac.uk/www/study/sshtim.htm
hos.princeton.edu
www.astro.uni-bonn.de/~pbrosche/hist_sci/hs_general.html
www.mhs.ox.ac.uk/exhibits/
www.smithsonianeducation.org/
www.hstm.imperial.ac.uk/rausingschol.htm
www.clas.ufl.edu/users/rhatch/pages/10-HisSci/links/index.htm
hpst.stanford.edu/
www.library.ualberta.ca/subject/historyscience/guide/index.cfm
www.sil.si.edu/Libraries/Dibner/index.htm
www.physlink.com/Education/History.cfm
www.si.edu/history_and_culture/history_of_science_and_technology/
www.mla-hhss.org/histlink.htm

# Appendix 1: Discoveries by Scientific Field

These tables list the 100 greatest science discoveries divided into their appropriate fields of science so that readers can easily identify the individual discoveries that relate to the same area. Within each field inventions are listed chronologically.

## Physical Sciences

| Discovery | Discovering Scientist | Year | Page |
|---|---|---|---|
| *Astronomy* | | | |
| Sun-centered universe | Copernicus, Nicholaus | 1520 | 5 |
| Planets' true orbits | Kepler, Johannes | 1609 | 11 |
| Other planets have moons | Galilei, Galileo | 1610 | 13 |
| Distance to the sun | Cassini, Giovanni | 1672 | 27 |
| Galaxies | Herschel, William | 1750 | 36 |
| | Wright, Thomas | 1750 | 36 |
| Black hole | Schwarzschild, Karl | 1916 | 140 |
| | Wheeler, John | 1971 | 141 |
| Expanding universe | Hubble, Edwin | 1926 | 150 |
| The Big Bang | Gamow, George | 1948 | 185 |
| Quasar | Sandage, Allan | 1963 | 205 |
| Pulsar | Bell, Jocelyn | 1967 | 205 |
| | Hewish, Antony | 1967 | 205 |
| Dark matter | Rubin, Vera | 1970 | 211 |
| Planets around other stars | Mayor, Michel | 1995 | 215 |
| | Queloz, Didier | 1995 | 215 |
| Universe is accelerating | Perlmutter, Saul | 1998 | 218 |
| | | | |
| *Chemistry* | | | |
| Boyle's Law | Boyle, Robert | 1662 | 19 |
| Oxygen | Priestley, Joseph | 1774 | 43 |
| Electrochemical bonding | Davy, Humphrey | 1806 | 61 |
| Molecules | Avogadro, Amedeo | 1811 | 63 |
| Atomic light signatures | Bunsen, Robert | 1859 | 81 |
| | Kirchhoff, Robert | 1859 | 81 |

| Discovery | Discovering Scientist | Year | Page |
|---|---|---|---|
| Periodic Table | Mendeleyev, Dmitri | 1880 | 90 |
| Radioactivity | Curie, Marie and Pierre | 1901 | 105 |
| Radioactive dating | Boltwood, Bertram | 1907 | 119 |
| Isotopes | Soddy, Frederick | 1913 | 133 |

## *Physics*

| | | | |
|---|---|---|---|
| Levers and buoyancy | Archimedes | 260 B.C. | 3 |
| Law of falling objects | Galilei, Galileo | 1598 | 9 |
| Air pressure | Torricelli, Evangelista | 1640 | 17 |
| Universal gravitation | Newton, Isaac | 1666 | 23 |
| Laws of motion | Newton, Isaac | 1687 | 31 |
| Nature of electricity | Franklin, Benjamin | 1752 | 38 |
| Conservation of matter | Lavoisier, Antoine | 1789 | 47 |
| Nature of heat | Rumford, Count | 1790 | 49 |
| Infrared | Herschel, Frederick | 1800 | 55 |
| Ultraviolet | Ritter, Johann | 1801 | 55 |
| Atoms | Dalton, John | 1802 | 59 |
| Electromagnetism | Oersted, Hans | 1820 | 65 |
| Calorie | Joule, James | 1843 | 71 |
| Conservation of energy | Helmholtz, H. von | 1847 | 73 |
| Doppler effect | Doppler, Christian | 1848 | 75 |
| Electromagnetic radiation | Maxwell, James | 1864 | 83 |
| X-rays | Roentgen, Wilhelm | 1895 | 95 |
| Energy equation | Einstein, Albert | 1905 | 111 |
| Relativity | Einstein, Albert | 1905 | 114 |
| Superconductivity | Onnes, Heike | 1911 | 128 |
| Atomic bonding | Bohr, Niels | 1913 | 131 |
| Quantum theory | Born, Max | 1925 | 148 |
| Uncertainty Principle | Heisenberg, Werner | 1927 | 153 |
| Speed of light | Michelson, Albert | 1928 | 155 |
| Antimatter | Dirac, Paul | 1929 | 160 |
| Neutron | Chadwick, James | 1932 | 163 |
| Strong force | Yukawa, Hideki | 1937 | 171 |
| Nuclear fission | Meitner, Lise | 1939 | 178 |
| | Hahn, Otto | 1939 | 178 |
| Semiconductor transistor | Bardeen, John | 1947 | 183 |
| Definition of information | Shannon, Claude | 1948 | 188 |
| Nuclear fusion | Bethe, Hans | 1951 | 192 |
| | Spitzer, Lyman | 1951 | 192 |
| Quarks | Gell-Mann, Murry | 1962 | 203 |
| Weak force | Rubbia, Carlo | 1983 | 171 |

# Earth Sciences

| Discovery | Discovering Scientist | Year | Page |
|---|---|---|---|
| Gulf Stream | Franklin, Benjamin | 1770 | 40 |
|  | Humbolt, A. von | 1814 | 41 |
| Erosion (weathering) | Hutton, James | 1792 | 51 |
| Ice ages | Agassiz, Louis | 1837 | 69 |
|  | Milankovich, Milutin | 1920 | 70 |
| Atmospheric layers | de Bort, L. Teisserenc | 1902 | 107 |
| Fault lines | Reid, Harry | 1911 | 126 |
| Earth's core | Gutenberg, Beno | 1914 | 136 |
| Continental drift | Wegener, Alfred | 1915 | 138 |
| Ecosystem | Tansley, Arthur | 1935 | 169 |
| Seafloor spreading | Hess, Harry | 1957 | 199 |
| Chaos theory | Lorenz, Ed | 1960 | 201 |

# Life Sciences

| Discovery | Discovering Scientist | Year | Page |
|---|---|---|---|
| *Biology* |  |  |  |
| Cells | Hooke, Robert | 1665 | 21 |
| Fossils | Steno, Nicholas | 1669 | 25 |
| Bacteria | Leeuwenhoek, Anton van | 1680 | 29 |
| Taxonomy system | Linnaeus, Carl | 1735 | 33 |
| Photosynthesis | Ingenhousz, Jan | 1779 | 45 |
| Dinosaur fossils | Buckland, William | 1824 | 67 |
|  | Mantell, Gideon | 1824 | 67 |
| Germ theory | Pasteur, Louis | 1856 | 77 |
| Deep-sea life | Thomson, Charles | 1870 | 88 |
| Cell division | Flemming, Walther | 1882 | 92 |
| Virus | Beijerinick, Martinus | 1898 | 101 |
|  | Ivanovsky, Dmitri | 1898 | 101 |
| Cell structure | Claude, Albert | 1933 | 165 |
| Origins of life | Miller, Stanley | 1952 | 194 |
| Nature of dinosaurs | Bakker, Robert | 1976 | 213 |

| Discovery | Discovering Scientist | Year | Page |
|---|---|---|---|
| ***Evolution and Human Anatomy*** | | | |
| Human anatomy | Vesalius, Andreas | 1543 | 7 |
| Evolution | Darwin, Charles | 1858 | 79 |
| Heredity | Mendel, Gregor | 1865 | 86 |
| Mitochondria | Benda, Carl | 1898 | 103 |
| Genetic mutations | Morgan, Thomas | 1909 | 121 |
| Neurotransmitters | Loewi, Otto | 1921 | 144 |
| | Walder-Hartz, Heinrich | 1921 | 144 |
| Human evolution | Dart, Raymond | 1924 | 146 |
| Coelacanth | Smith, J. L. B | 1938 | 176 |
| Jumping genes | McClintock, Barbara | 1950 | 190 |
| DNA | Crick, Francis | 1953 | 196 |
| | Watson, James | 1953 | 196 |
| | Franklin, Rosalind | 1953 | 197 |
| Complete evolution | Margulis, Lynn | 1967 | 208 |
| Human genome | Venter, Craig | 2003 | 220 |
| | Watson, James | 2003 | 220 |
| | | | |
| ***Medical Science*** | | | |
| Human circulatory system | Harvey, William | 1628 | 15 |
| Vaccinations | Montagu, Lady Mary Wortley | 1798 | 53 |
| | Jenner, Edward | 1794 | 53 |
| Anesthesia | Davy, Humphry | 1801 | 57 |
| Chloroform (anesthesia) | Simpson, Young | 1801 | 57 |
| Ether (anesthesia) | Long, Crawford | 1801 | 58 |
| Blood types | Landsteiner, Karl | 1897 | 97 |
| Hormones | Bayliss, William | 1902 | 109 |
| | Starling, Ernest | 1902 | 109 |
| Vitamins | Hopkins, Frederick | 1906 | 117 |
| | Eijkman, Christiaan | 1906 | 117 |
| Antibiotics | Ehrlich, Paul | 1910 | 124 |
| Insulin | Banting, Frederick | 1921 | 142 |
| Penicillin | Flemming, Alexander | 1928 | 158 |
| Genes | Beadle, George | 1934 | 167 |
| Metabolism (Krebs Cycle) | Krebs, Hans | 1938 | 174 |
| Blood plasma | Drew, Charles | 1940 | 181 |

# Appendix 2: Scientists

This table is an alphabetical list of the scientists featured in the discussions of the 100 greatest discoveries. Each is listed with his or her discovery and the year the discovery was made.

| Name | Discovery | Year | Page |
|------|-----------|------|------|
| Abel, John | Hormones | 1898 | 109 |
| Agassiz, Louis | Ice ages | 1837 | 69 |
| Archimedes | Levers and buoyancy | 260 B.C. | 3 |
| Avogadro, Amedeo | Molecules | 1811 | 63 |
| Bakker, Robert | Nature of dinosaurs | 1976 | 213 |
| Banting, Frederick | Insulin | 1921 | 142 |
| Bardeen, John | Semiconductor transistor | 1947 | 183 |
| Bayliss, William | Hormones | 1902 | 109 |
| Beadle, George | Genes | 1934 | 167 |
| Beijerinick, Martinus | Virus | 1898 | 101 |
| Bell, Jocelyn | Pulsar | 1967 | 205 |
| Benda, Carl | Mitochondria | 1898 | 103 |
| Bethe, Hans | Nuclear fusion | 1939 | 192 |
| Bohr, Niels | Atomic bonding | 1913 | 131 |
| Boltwood, Bertram | Radioactive dating | 1907 | 119 |
| Born, Max | Quantum theory | 1925 | 148 |
| Boyle, Robert | Boyle's law | 1662 | 19 |
| Buckland, William | Dinosaur fossils | 1824 | 67 |
| Bunsen, Robert | Atomic light signatures | 1859 | 81 |
| Cassini, Giovanni | Distance to the sun | 1672 | 27 |
| Chadwick, James | Neutron | 1932 | 163 |
| Claude, Albert | Cell structure | 1933 | 165 |
| Copernicus, Nicholaus | Sun-centered universe | 1520 | 5 |
| Courtenay-Latimer, M. | Coelacanth | 1938 | 176 |
| Crick, Francis | DNA | 1953 | 196 |
| Curie, Marie and Pierre | Radioactivity | 1901 | 105 |
| Dalton, John | Atoms | 1802 | 59 |
| Dart, Raymond | Human evolution | 1924 | 146 |
| Darwin, Charles | Evolution | 1858 | 79 |
| Davy, Humphry | Anesthesia | 1801 | 57 |
| Davy, Humphry | Electrochemical bonding | 1806 | 61 |
| de Bort, Leon Teisserenc | Atmospheric layers | 1902 | 107 |

| Name | Discovery | Year | Page |
|---|---|---|---|
| Dirac, Paul | Antimatter | 1929 | 160 |
| Doppler, Christian | Doppler effect | 1848 | 75 |
| Drew, Charles | Blood plasma | 1940 | 181 |
| Ehrlich, Paul | Antibiotics | 1910 | 124 |
| Eijkman, Christiaan | Vitamins | 1906 | 117 |
| Einstein, Albert | Energy equation | 1905 | 111 |
| Einstein, Albert | Relativity | 1905 | 114 |
| Galilei, Galileo | Law of falling objects | 1598 | 9 |
| Galilei, Galileo | Other planets have moons | 1609 | 11 |
| Gamow, George | The Big Bang | 1948 | 185 |
| Gell-Mann, Murry | Quarks | 1962 | 203 |
| Gutenberg, Beno | Earth's core | 1914 | 136 |
| Fermi, Enrico | Nuclear fission | 1939 | 178 |
| Flemming, Alexander | Penicillin | 1928 | 158 |
| Flemming, Walther | Cell division | 1882 | 92 |
| Franklin, Benjamin | Nature of electricity | 1752 | 38 |
| Franklin, Benjamin | Gulf Stream | 1770 | 40 |
| Franklin, Rosalind | DNA | 1953 | 197 |
| Hahn, Otto | Nuclear fission | 1939 | 178 |
| Harvey, William | Human circulatory system | 1628 | 15 |
| Heisenberg, Werner | Uncertainty Principle | 1927 | 153 |
| Helmholtz, Hermann von | Conservation of energy | 1847 | 73 |
| Herschel, Frederick | Infrared | 1800 | 55 |
| Herschel, William | Galaxies | 1750 | 36 |
| Hess, Harry | Seafloor spreading | 1957 | 199 |
| Hewish, Antony | Pulsar | 1967 | 205 |
| Hodgkin, Dorothy | Penicillin | 1942 | 159 |
| Hooke, Robert | Cells | 1665 | 21 |
| Hopkins, Frederick | Vitamins | 1906 | 117 |
| Hubble, Edwin | Expanding universe | 1926 | 150 |
| Humbolt, Alexander von | Gulf Stream | 1814 | 41 |
| Hutton, James | Erosion (weathering) | 1792 | 51 |
| Ingenhousz, Jan | Photosynthesis | 1779 | 45 |
| Ivanovsky, Dmitri | Virus | 1898 | 101 |
| Jenner, Edward | Vaccinations | 1794 | 53 |
| Joule, James | Calorie | 1843 | 71 |
| Kepler, Johannes | Planets' true orbits | 1609 | 11 |
| Kirchhoff, Robert | Atomic light signatures | 1859 | 81 |
| Krebs, Hans | Metabolism (Krebs Cycle) | 1938 | 174 |
| Landsteiner, Karl | Blood types | 1897 | 97 |
| Lavoisier, Antoine | Conservation of matter | 1789 | 47 |

| Name | Discovery | Year | Page |
|------|-----------|------|------|
| Lehman, Inge | Earth's core | 1938 | 137 |
| Leeuwenhoek, Anton van | Bacteria | 1680 | 29 |
| Linnaeus, Carl | Taxonomy system | 1735 | 33 |
| Long, Crawford | Ether (anesthesia) | 1801 | 58 |
| Loewi, Otto | Neurotransmitters | 1921 | 144 |
| Lorenz, Ed | Chaos theory | 1960 | 201 |
| Mantell, Gideon | Dinosaur fossils | 1824 | 67 |
| Margulis, Lynn | Complete evolution | 1967 | 208 |
| Mayor, Michel | Planets around other stars | 1995 | 215 |
| Maxwell, James | Electromagnetic radiation | 1864 | 83 |
| McClintock, Barbara | Jumping genes | 1950 | 90 |
| Meitner, Lise | Nuclear fission | 1939 | 178 |
| Mendel, Gregor | Heredity | 1865 | 86 |
| Mendeleyev, Dmitri | Periodic Table | 1880 | 90 |
| Michelson, Albert | Speed of light | 1928 | 155 |
| Milankovich, Milutin | Ice ages | 1920 | 70 |
| Miller, Stanley | Origins of life | 1952 | 194 |
| Montagu, Lady Mary | Vaccinations | 1798 | 53 |
| Morgan, Thomas | Genetic mutations | 1909 | 121 |
| Newton, Isaac | Universal gravitation | 1666 | 23 |
| Newton, Isaac | Laws of motion | 1687 | 31 |
| Oersted, Hans | Electromagnetism | 1820 | 65 |
| Onnes, Heike | Superconductivity | 1911 | 128 |
| Pasteur, Louis | Germ theory | 1856 | 77 |
| Perlmutter, Saul | Universe is accelerating | 1998 | 218 |
| Priestley, Joseph | Oxygen | 1774 | 43 |
| Queloz, Didier | Planets around other stars | 1995 | 215 |
| Reid, Harry | Fault lines | 1911 | 126 |
| Ritter, Johann | Ultraviolet` | 1801 | 55 |
| Roentgen, Wilhelm | X-rays | 1895 | 95 |
| Rubbia, Carlo | Weak force | 1983 | 171 |
| Rubin, Vera | Dark matter | 1970 | 211 |
| Rumford, Count | Nature of heat | 1790 | 49 |
| Sandage, Allan | Quasar | 1963 | 205 |
| Schwarzschild, Karl | Black hole | 1916 | 140 |
| Shannon, Claude | Definition of information | 1948 | 188 |
| Sharpey-Schafer, Edward | Hormones | 1894 | 109 |
| Simpson, Young | Chloroform (anesthesia) | 1801 | 57 |
| Smith, J. L. B. | Coelacanth | 1938 | 176 |
| Soddy, Frederick | Isotopes | 1913 | 133 |
| Spitzer, Lyman | Nuclear fusion | 1951 | 193 |

| **Name** | **Discovery** | **Year** | **Page** |
|---|---|---|---|
| Starling, Ernest | Hormones | 1902 | 109 |
| Steno, Nicholas | Fossils | 1669 | 25 |
| Takamine, Jokichi | Hormones | 1900 | 109 |
| Tansley, Arthur | Ecosystem | 1935 | 169 |
| Tatum, Edward | Genes | 1934 | 167 |
| Thomson, Charles | Deep-sea life | 1870 | 88 |
| Torricelli, Evangelista | Air pressure | 1640 | 17 |
| Venter, Craig | Human genome | 2003 | 220 |
| Vesalius, Andreas | Human anatomy | 1543 | 7 |
| Walder-Hartz, Heinrich | Neurotransmitters | 1888 | 144 |
| Watson, James | DNA | 1953 | 196 |
| Watson, James | Human genome | 2003 | 220 |
| Wegener, Alfred | Continental drift | 1915 | 138 |
| Wheeler, John | Black holes | 1971 | 141 |
| Wright, Thomas | Galaxies | 1750 | 36 |
| Yukawa, Hideki | Strong force | 1937 | 171 |

# Appendix 3: The Next 40

This table is a list of 40 important discoveries that *almost* made the final list of the greatest 100. Each is worthy of consideration, honor, and study. Pick one or more of these to research and describe.

| | | |
|---|---|---|
| Earth is a sphere | Aristotle | 387 B.C. |
| The heavens are not fixed and unchanging | Brahe | 1574 |
| The nature of light | Galileo, Newton, Young, Einstein | various years |
| Compressibility of gasses | Boyle | 1688 |
| Lift/fluid pressure | Bernoulli | 1738 |
| Comets have predictable orbits | Halley | 1758 |
| Hydrogen | Cavendish | 1776 |
| Origin of the solar system | Laplace | 1796 |
| Mass of the earth | Cavendish | 1798 |
| Liquification of gasses | Faraday | 1818 |
| Fingerprints, uniqueness of | Purkinje | 1823 |
| Magnetic induction | Faraday | 1831 |
| Age of the sun | Helmholtz | 1853 |
| Sun is a gas | Carrington | 1859 |
| Age of the earth | Lyell (first), Holmes (accurate) | 1860, 1940 |
| Antiseptics | Lister | 1863 |
| Plastics | Hyatt | 1869 |
| Alternating current | Tesla | 1883 |
| Bacteriology | Koch | 1890 |
| Earth's magnetic field reversals | Brunhes | 1906 |
| Chemotherapy | Ehrlich | 1906 |
| Cosmic radiation | Hess | 1911 |
| Electroencephalogram | Berger | 1924 |
| adjustrightBrucellosis bacterium | Evans | 1925 |
| Exclusion principle | Pauli | 1926 |
| Neutrino | Pauli | 1926 |
| Galaxies emit radio waves | Jansky | 1932 |
| Artificial radioactivity | Curie and Joliot | 1934 |
| Cortisone | Kendall | 1935 |
| Sulfa drugs | Domagk | 1936 |
| Radiation therapy | Priore | 1950 |
| Laser | Townes and Gould | 1954/1957 |

| | | |
|---|---|---|
| Global warming | Many | late twentieth century |
| First cloning | Gurden | 1967 |
| Laetoli footprints (3.5 million years old) | Mary Leakey | 1973 |
| "Lucy" (3.2 million-year-old skull) | Donald Johnson | 1974 |
| Non-oxygen-based deep sea life | Ballard | 1977 |
| Dinosaur extinction (K-T asteroid) | Alvarez | 1979 |
| Human retrovirus HIV | Gallo and Montagnier | 1982 |
| Toumai skull (6 to 7 million years old) | Michel Brunet | 2002 |

# Index

Absolute zero temperature
  superconductivity, 128–29
Accelerating universe
  importance of, 218
  origins of discovery, 218–19
Acetylcholine
  neurotransmitters, 145
Achromatic microscope
  mitochondria, 103
Adrenaline, 109
Agassiz, Louis
  ice ages, 69–70
Agglutination, 99
Air pressure
  importance of, 17
  origins of discovery, 17–18
Algae
  complete evolution, 209
Amino acids. *See also* Tryptophan
  origins of life, 194–95
  vitamins, 118
Anaerobic process
  metabolism, 174–75
Anatomy. *See* Comparative anatomy; Human
    anatomy
Anesthesia
  definition of, 57
  importance of, 57
  origins of discovery, 57–58
Animals. *See also* Ecosystems; Plants
  coelacanth, 176–77
  continental drift, 138
  deep-sea life, 88–89
  order in nature, 33–34
  theory of evolution, 79–80
Anthropology
  theory of evolution, 79
Antibiotics
  importance of, 124
  origins of discovery, 124–25
  penicillin, 158–59

Antimatter. *See also* Matter
  $E = mc^2$, 112
  importance of, 160
  origins of discovery, 160–61
Apes
  human evolution, 146
Archimedes
  levers and buoyancy, 3–4
Aristotle
  Jupiter's moons, 13
  law of falling objects, 9–10
  laws of motion, 31
Arteries
  circulatory system, 15–16
Astrology
  distance to the sun, 27
Astronomy. *See also* Big Bang theory; Black
    holes; Expanding universe; Galaxies;
    Origins of life; Solar system; Speed
    of light; Sun-centered universe
  dark matter, 211–12
  distance to the sun, 27–28
  Doppler Effect, 75–76
  electromagnetic radiation/radio waves, 83
  existence of planets around other stars,
    215–16
  Infrared (IR) and ultraviolet (UV) light,
    55–56
  planetary motion, 11–12
  quasars and pulsars, 205–6
Atmosphere. *See also* Ice ages; Nature of the
    atmosphere; Oceans, effects on
    weather; Oxygen; Weather
  air pressure, 17–18
  matter, 47–48
  origins of life, 194–95
  photosynthesis, 45
Atmospheric layers
  importance of, 107
  origins of discovery, 107–8
Atomic bonding
  importance of, 131
  origins of discovery, 131–32

Atomic energy
  fusion, 192–93
  isotopes, 133–34
Atomic light signatures
  importance of, 81
  origins of discovery, 81–82
Atomic weight
  isotopes, 133–34
  Periodic Chart of the Elements, 90–91
Atoms. *See also* Big Bang theory;
    Electrochemical bonding; Electrons;
    Existence of cells; Hydrogen bomb;
    Isotopes; Molecules; Neutrons; Nuclear
    bomb; Nuclear fission; Radioactivity;
    Subatomic particles; Uncertainty
    Principle
  Boyle's Law, 19
  importance of, 59
  origins of discovery, 59–60
  weak and strong force, 171–72
ATP
  metabolism, 175
Avogadro, Amedeo
  Avogadro's Number, 63
  molecules, 63–64

Bacteria. *See also* Antibiotics; Origins of life;
    Penicillin; Viruses
  complete evolution, 209
  germ theory, 77–78
  importance of, 29
  origins of discovery, 29–30
Bakker, Robert
  nature of dinosaurs, 213–14
Balloons
  atmospheric layers, 107
Bandwidth
  definition of information, 189
Banting, Frederick
  insulin, 142–43
Bardeen, John
  semiconductor transistor, 183–84
Barium
  nuclear fission, 178–79
Barometer. *See also* Atmosphere; Weather
  air pressure, 17
  atmospheric layers, 107–8
Batteries
  electrochemical bonding, 62
  electricity, 38
  "Voltaic Pile," 62

Bayliss, William
  hormones, 109–10
Beadle, George
  genes, function of, 167–68
Beijerinick, Martinus
  viruses, 101–2
Bell, Jocelyn. *See also* Sandage, Allan Rex
  pulsars, 205–6
Benda, Carl
  mitochondria, 103–4
Beryllium
  neutrons, 164
Big Bang theory. *See also* Accelerating
    universe
  expanding universe, 150
  importance of, 185
  origins of discovery, 185–86
Binomial system, 34
Biochemical genetics
  genes, function of, 167–68
Biology. *See also* Complete evolution;
    Existence of cells; Microbiology;
    Molecular biology; Origins of life
  cell division, 92–93
  cell structure, 165–66
  chromosomes, function of, 121–22
  coelacanth, 176–77
  ecosystems, 169–70
  "jumping genes," 191
  order in nature, 33–34
  theory of evolution, 79–80
Birds
  nature of dinosaurs, 213
"Bit of scruff," 206
Black holes
  importance of, 140
  origins of discovery, 140–41
  quasars and pulsars, 206
"Black reaction," 103
Blood cells, 29
Blood plasma
  importance of, 181
  origins of discovery, 181–82
Blood sugar
  insulin, 142–43
Blood transfusions
  plasma, 181–82
Blood types
  importance of, 97
  origins of discovery, 97–98

Bohr, Niels
  atomic bonding, 131–32
Boltwood, Bertram
  radioactive dating, 119–20
Bonding. *See* Atomic bonding; Electrochemical
    bonding
Bone structure
  nature of dinosaurs, 214
Boolean logic
  definition of information, 188
Born, Max
  quantum theory, 148–49
Botany
  order in nature, 33–34
Boyle, Robert
  Boyle's Law, 19–20
Boyle's Law
  importance of, 19
  origins of discovery, 19–20
Brahe, Tycho
  planetary motion, 11–12
Brain function
  neurotransmitters, 144–45
Brown dwarfs
  existence of planets around other stars,
    215–16
Bubble chamber, 203–4
Buckland, William
  dinosaur fossils, 67–68
Bunsen, Robert
  atomic light signatures, 81–82
  Bunsen burner, 82
Buoyancy. *See also* Levers
  definition of, 3
  importance of, 4
  origins of discovery, 3–4

Calculus, 31–32
Caloric, 49–50
Calories
  as units of energy, 71
  importance of, 71
  origins of discovery, 71–72
  vitamins, 117–18
Cancer research
  cell structure, 165–66
Capillaries, 29
Carbon
  metabolism, 175
  radioactive dating, 120

Carbon dioxide. *See also* Oxygen;
    Photosynthesis
  electrochemical bonding, 61–62
  metabolism, 175
Cassini, Giovanni
  Cassini gaps, 27
  distance to the sun, 27–28
Catastrophism
  erosion of Earth's surface, 51
Cathode rays
  electrons, 101–2
Cell division
  importance of, 92
  origins of discovery, 92–93
Cell structure
  importance of, 165
  origins of discovery, 165–66
Cells. *See* Blood cells; Complete evolution;
    Existence of cells; Genes;
    Microbiology; Mitochondria;
    Neurotransmitters; Viruses
Centrifuge
  cell structure, 166
Chadwick, James
  neutrons, 163–64
Chaos theory
  nature of the atmosphere, 201–2
Chart of the Elements. *See* Periodic Chart of
    the Elements
Chemical compounds
  antibiotics, 124–25
  isotopes, 133–34
  vitamins, 117–18
Chemical messengers. *See* Hormones;
    Neurotransmitters
Chemistry. *See also* Electrochemical
    bonding; Electrochemistry;
    Neurotransmitters; Periodic Chart of
    the Elements; Photochemistry
  atoms, 59–60
  Big Bang theory, 186
  Boyle's Law, 19
  isotopes, 133–34
  matter, 47
Chemotherapy
  antibiotics, 124–25
Chloroform, 57
Chromatic aberration, 103
Chromatin, 93

Chromosomes
  cell division, 92–93
  cell structure, 166
  function of, 121–23
  heredity, 86
  human genome, 221
  "jumping genes," 190–91
Circulatory system
  importance of, 15
  origins of discovery, 15–16
Citric acid
  metabolism, 175
Claude, Albert
  cell structure, 165–66
Climate. *See* Atmospheric layers; Oceans,
    effects on weather
Clouds
  atmospheric layers, 107
Coelacanth
  importance of, 176
  origins of discovery, 176–77
Combustion, 43–44, 49
Communication
  neurotransmitters, 144–45
Comparative anatomy
  nature of dinosaurs, 213
Complete evolution
  importance of, 208
  origins of discovery, 208–9
Compounds. *See* Chemical compounds;
    Inorganic compounds
Computers
  definition of information, 188–89
  human genome, 221
Conductivity. *See* Semiconductor transistor;
    Superconductivity
Conservation of energy
  contradictions, 112
  importance of, 73
  origins of discovery, 73–74
Conservation of mass
  contradictions, 112
Continental drift. *See also* Earth's core and
    mantle; Plate tectonics; Seafloor
    spreading
  importance of, 138
  origins of discovery, 138–39
Copernicus, Nicholaus
  Jupiter's moons, 13–14
  planetary motion, 11
  sun-centered universe, 5–6

Core and mantle. *See* Earth's core and
    mantle
Corn research
  "jumping genes," 190–91
Corpuscular theory of matter
  fossils, 26
Cortisone, 110
"Cosmic egg," 185
"Cosmological constant," 218
Council of Cardinals
  Jupiter's moons, 14
Courtroom evidence
  DNA, 196
Crick, Francis
  DNA, 196–97
Crookes' tube
  X-rays, 95–96
Curie, Marie
  radioactivity, 105–6
"Curvature of space, the"
  black holes, 140
Cytoplasm
  mitochondria, 103–4

Dalton, John
  atoms, 59–60
"Dark energy," 219
Dark matter
  importance of, 211
  origins of discovery, 211–12
Dart, Raymond
  human evolution, 146–47
Darwin, Charles. *See also* Complete evolution
  dinosaur fossils, 67
  heredity, 86
  human evolution, 146–47
  theory of evolution, 79–80, 121
Dating. *See* Radioactive dating
Davy, Humphry
  anesthesia, 57–58
  electrochemical bonding, 61–62
Decay. *See* Radioactive decay
Decomposers
  ecosystems, 170
Deep-sea life
  importance of, 88
  origins of discovery, 88–89
Definition of information
  importance of, 188
  origins of discovery, 188–89

Democritus
Boyle's Law, 19
Density
atmospheric layers, 107–8
Big Bang theory, 185–86
black holes, 140–41
buoyancy, 4
Earth's core and mantle, 136–37
nature of the atmosphere, 202
quasars and pulsars, 205–6
Deoxyribonucleic Acid (DNA). *See also*
Human genome; mDNA; Origins of life;
Ribonucleic Acid (RNA)
chromosomes, function of, 121
complete evolution, 208
genes, function of, 167–68
heredity, 86–87
importance of, 196
mitochondria, 103–4
origins of discovery, 196–97
*Depths of the Sea, The,* 89
Detritus, 89
Diabetes
insulin, 142–43
Dietary health. *See also* Nutrition
vitamins, 117–18
Diffraction patterns
Earth's core and mantle, 137
Digestive juices
insulin, 142–43
Digital technology. *See also* Computers
definition of information, 188
Dinosaur fossils. *See also* Nature of dinosaurs
importance of, 67
origins of discovery, 67–68
Dirac, Paul
antimatter, 160–62
Diseases. *See* Antibiotics; Bacteria;
Deoxyribonucleic Acid (DNA); Human
genome; "Jumping genes"; Penicillin;
Vaccinations; Viruses; Vitamins
Dissections
circulatory system, 15
human anatomy, 7–8
Distance to the sun
importance of, 27
origins of discovery, 27–28
DNA. *See* Deoxyribonucleic Acid (DNA)
Doppler, Christian
Doppler Effect, 75–76

Doppler Effect
Doppler shift, 76
importance of, 75
origins of discovery, 75–76
Doppler shift, 76
accelerating universe, 219
dark matter, 212
existence of planets around other stars, 215–16
quasars and pulsars, 205
Double helix model
DNA, 197
human genome, 220–21
Drew, Charles
blood plasma, 181–82

$E = mc^2$
black holes, 140
fusion, 192
importance of, 111
origins of discovery, 111–12
speed of light, 155
Earth's core and mantle. *See also*
Continental drift; Plate tectonics;
Seafloor spreading
importance of, 136
origins of discovery, 136–37
Earthquakes. *See* Fault lines
Ecology
nature of dinosaurs, 213
theory of evolution, 79–80
Ecosystems
importance of, 169
nature of dinosaurs, 213
order in nature, 33
origins of discovery, 169–70
"Eddington's equations," 160
Ehrlich, Paul
antibiotics, 124–25
Eijkman, Christiaan
vitamins, 117–18
Einstein, Albert
$E = mc^2$, 111–13
theory of relativity, 114–16
Electrical currents
antimatter, 160–61
neurotransmitters, 144–45
neutrons, 163
semiconductor transistor, 183–84
Electrical energy
semiconductor transistor, 183–84
superconductivity, 128–29

Electrical fields
  electromagnetic radiation/radio waves, 84
Electrical resistance
  semiconductor transistor, 183–84
  superconductivity, 128–29
Electricity. *See also* Superconductivity
  conservation of energy, 74
  electromagnetic radiation/radio waves,
    83–84
  electromagnetism, 65–66
  electrons, 101
  importance of, 38
  origins of discovery, 38–39
Electrochemical bonding
  importance of, 61
  origins of discovery, 61–62
Electrochemistry
  infrared (IR) and ultraviolet (UV) light, 56
  metabolism, 175
Electrodes, 62
Electrolytes, 62
Electromagnetic radiation/radio waves
  importance of, 83
  origins of discovery, 83–84
  quasars and pulsars, 206
Electromagnetism
  electrons, 102
  importance of, 65
  origins of discovery, 65–66
  weak and strong force, 171–72
Electron microscope
  atoms, 59
  cell structure, 165–66
  viruses, 97–98
Electronic circuits
  definition of information, 188
Electrons. *See also* Atomic bonding;
    Proton-electrons; Protons;
    Superconductivity; Uncertainty Principle
  antimatter, 160–61
  atoms, 59–60
  Big Bang theory, 186
  electrochemical bonding, 61–62
  importance of, 101
  isotopes, 134
  neutrons, 163
  origins of discovery, 101–2
  quantum theory, 148–49
Elementary particles
  antimatter, 161
  Uncertainty Principle, 153

Elements. *See* Periodic Chart of the
    Elements; Isotopes; Radioactive
    dating; Trace elements
Ellipses. *See also* Epi-circles
  definition of, 12
  laws of motion, 31
  planetary motion, 11–12
Endocrinology
  hormones, 109–10
Energy. *See* Antimatter; Calories;
    Conservation of energy; "Dark
    energy;" Fission; Fusion; Kinetic
    energy; Metabolism; Nuclear fission;
    Solar energy
Energy and matter
  antimatter, 161
  $E = mc^2$, 111–12
  theory of relativity, 115
Enzymes
  genes, function of, 167–68
  metabolism, 175
Epi-circles. *See also* Ellipses
  planetary motion, 11–12
  sun-centered universe, 5–6
Epinephrine, 109
Erosion of Earth's surface
  importance of, 51
  origins of discovery, 51–52
Escape velocity
  black holes, 141
Ether, 58
Event horizon
  black holes, 141
Evolution. *See* Complete evolution; Human
    evolution; Theory of evolution
Existence of cells
  cell, definition of, 22
  importance of, 21
  origins of discovery, 21–22
Existence of planets around other stars
  importance of, 215
  origins of discovery, 215–16
Expanding universe
  Big Bang theory, 185–86
  importance of, 150
  origins of discovery, 150–51
*Experiments Upon Vegetables,* 46

Falling objects. *See* Law of falling objects;
    Laws of motion

Fault lines. *See also* San Andreas fault
  importance of, 126
  origins of discovery, 126–27
Field data
  ice ages, 69
Fission. *See also* Fusion; Nuclear fission
  radioactive dating, 119
Fixed-order lines
  chromosomes, function of, 122
Fleming, Alexander
  penicillin, 158–59
Flemming, Walther
  cell division, 92–94
"Fly Room, The," 121
Food
  metabolism, 174–75
  vitamins, 117–18
Force. *See also* Weak and strong force
  laws of motion, 31–32
Fossils. *See also* Coelacanth; Continental drift;
    Dinosaur fossils; Geology; Human
    evolution; Nature of dinosaurs; Origins
    of life
  definition of, 25
  importance of, 25
  "living fossil," 176–77
  origins of discovery, 25–26
  seafloor spreading, 200
Fractionation
  cell structure, 165–66
Franklin, Benjamin
  electricity, 38–39
  oceans, effects on weather, 40–42
Friction
  nature of heat, 49–50
*Fundamentals of Ecology,* 170
Fusion. *See also* Fission
  importance of, 192
  origins of discovery, 192–93

Galaxies
  accelerating universe, 218–19
  atomic light signatures, 81–82
  dark matter, 212
  Doppler Effect, 75–76
  expanding universe, 150–51
  existence of planets around other stars, 216
  importance of, 36
  origins of discovery, 36–37
  quasars and pulsars, 206
  weak and strong force, 171–72

Galen
  circulatory system, 15
  human anatomy, 7–8
Galilei, Galileo
  air pressure, 17
  Jupiter's moons, 13–14
  law of falling objects, 9–10
  laws of motion, 31
  sun-centered universe, 6
Gamma rays. *See also* X-rays
  electromagnetic radiation/radio waves, 83
  infrared (IR) and ultraviolet (UV) light,
    55
  isotopes, 134
Gamow, George
  Big Bang theory, 185–86
Gas. *See also* Nitrous oxide; Oxygen
  anesthesia, 58
  atomic light signatures, 81–82
  Boyle's Law, 19–20
  electrochemical bonding, 61
  matter, 47
  molecules, 63–64
  nature of the atmosphere, 202
  origins of life, 195
Geiger counter, 120
Gell-Mann, Murry
  quarks, 203–4
Generators
  electricity, 38
Genes. *See also* "Jumping genes"
  chromosomes, function of, 121
  function of, 167–68
  importance of, 167
  origins of discovery, 167–68
Genetics. *See* Biochemical genetics;
    Chromosomes; Complete evolution;
    Heredity
Genome. *See* Human genome
Geology, 26, 52. *See also* Continental drift;
    Fault lines; Fossils; Ice ages;
    Isotopes; Radioactive dating
Geophysics
  Earth's core and mantle, 136–37
Germ theory. *See also* Viruses
  importance of, 77
  origins of discovery, 77–78
Germanium, 183–84
Glaciers
  ice ages, 69–70

Gravitation. *See* Accelerating universe; Air
    pressure; Conservation of energy; Law
    of falling objects; Laws of motion;
    Quasars and pulsars; Theory of
    relativity; Universal gravitation; Weak
    and strong force
Gravitational pull
    accelerating universe, 218–19
    black holes, 140–41
    existence of planets around other stars, 215
Gravitons
    weak and strong force, 172
Gulf Stream, 40–41
Gutenberg, Beno
    Earth's core and mantle, 136–37
Guyots, 199–200

Half-life
    radioactive dating, 119
Harvey, William
    circulatory system, 15–16
Health. *See* Dietary health
Heart
    circulatory system, 15
Heat. *See also* Nature of heat;
    Thermodynamics
    atomic light signatures, 81–82
    calories, 71–72
    conservation of energy, 74
    fusion, 192–93
    metabolism, 174
    semiconductor transistor, 183–84
Heisenberg, Werner
    Uncertainty Principle, 153–54
Helium. *See* Liquid helium
Heredity. *See also* Genes; Human genome
    cell division, 92–93
    importance of, 86
    origins of discovery, 86–87
Herschel, Frederick
    Infrared (IR) light, 55–56
Herschel, William
    galaxies, 36–37
Hess, Harry
    seafloor spreading, 199–200
Hewish, Antony. *See also* Bell, Jocelyn
    pulsars, 205–6
Hooke, Robert
    existence of cells, 21–22

Hopkins, Frederick
    vitamins, 117–18
Homo sapiens, 33
Hormones. *See also* Insulin
    importance of, 109
    origins of discovery, 109–10
Hubble, Edwin
    expanding universe, 150–52
Human anatomy. *See also* Circulatory
    system; Existence of cells; Fossils
    genes, function of, 168
    importance of, 7
    metabolism, 174–75
    origins of discovery, 7–8
    vitamins, 117–18
Human evolution
    importance of, 146
    origins of discovery, 146–47
Human genome
    DNA, 196
    importance of, 220
    origins of discovery, 220–21
Human species
    DNA, 196–97
    order in nature, 33
Humanoids
    human evolution, 147
Humidity
    atmospheric layers, 107–8
Hutton, James
    erosion of Earth's surface, 51–52
Hydrogen bomb
    fusion, 192–93

Ice ages
    importance of, 69
    origins of discovery, 69–70
Iguanodon, 68
Immune system
    antibiotics, 124–25
Infections. *See* Antibiotics; Bacteria;
    Diseases; Penicillin; Vaccinations;
    Viruses
Influenza
    penicillin, 159
Information. *See* Definition of information
Information Age
    definition of information, 188
Information streams
    definition of information, 189

Infrared (IR) and ultraviolet (UV) light
    importance of, 55
    origins of discovery, 55–56
Ingenhousz, Jan
    photosynthesis, 45–46
Ingrafting, 53
Inorganic compounds
    origins of life, 194–95
Insulin
    importance of, 142
    origins of discovery, 142–43
Isotopes
    importance of, 133
    origins of discovery, 133–34
    radioactive dating, 119–20
Ivanovsky, Dmitri
    viruses, 101–102

Jenner, Edward. *See also* Montagu, Lady Mary
        Wortley
    vaccinations, 53–54
Joule, James
    calories, 71–72
"Jumping genes"
    importance of, 190
    origins of discovery, 190–91
Jupiter's moons
    importance of, 13
    origins of discovery, 13–14

Kelvin, Lord
    fusion, 192
    superconductivity, 128
Kepler, Johannes
    distance to the sun, 27
    laws of motion, 31
    planetary motion, 11–12
    sun-centered universe, 6
Kinetic energy
    conservation of energy, 73–74
Kirchhoff, Gustav
    atomic light signatures, 81–82
Krebs, Hans Adolf
    metabolism, 174–75

Lactic acid
    metabolism, 174–75
Landsteiner, Karl
    blood types, 97–98

Latitudinal zonation
    nature of dinosaurs, 213
Lavoisier, Antoine
    matter, 47–48
Law of falling objects. *See also* Planetary
        motion; Universal gravitation
    importance of, 9
    origins of discovery, 9–10
Laws of motion. *See also* Dark matter;
        Planetary motion; Universal
        gravitation
    importance of, 31
    origins of discovery, 31–32
Lead. *See also* Uranium
    radioactive dating, 120
Leeuwenhoek, Anton van
    bacteria, 29–30
Levers. *See also* Buoyancy
    definition of, 3
    importance of, 3
    origins of discovery, 3–4
Life. *See* Origins of life
Light. *See also* Dark matter; $E = mc^2$;
        Infrared (IR) and ultraviolet (UV)
        light; Speed of light
    accelerating universe, 218–19
    atomic light signatures, 81
    black holes, 140–41
    conservation of energy, 74
    deep-sea life, 88–89
    electricity, 38
    existence of planets around other stars,
        215–16
    quasars and pulsars, 205–6
    semiconductor transistor, 183–84
Light, space, and time
    black holes, 140–41
    $E = mc^2$, 111–12
    theory of relativity, 114–15
Light waves
    Doppler Effect, 75–76
Light years
    quasars and pulsars, 206
    speed of light, 155–56
Lightning
    electricity, 38–39
    lightning rod, 39
Linnaeus, Carl
    order in nature, 33–35
Liquid helium
    superconductivity, 129

Liquid mercury
    air pressure, 17
    Boyle's Law, 20
    superconductivity, 129
Loewi, Otto
    neurotransmitters, 144–45
Logarithms
    planetary motion, 12
Lorenz, Ed
    nature of the atmosphere, 201–2
Lungs
    circulatory system, 15

"Magic bullet," 125
Magma
    seafloor spreading, 200
Magnetic fields
    fusion, 193
Magnetism. See also Electromagnetic
        radiation/radio waves; Electromagnetism
    conservation of energy, 74
    electrons, 101–2
Mantell, Gideon
    dinosaur fossils, 67–68
Mantle. See Earth's core and mantle
Margulis, Lynn
    complete evolution, 208–9
Marine science
    coelacanth, 177
Mathematics. See also Nonlinear model
        equations
    accelerating universe, 218–19
    antimatter, 160–61
    Big Bang theory, 186
    definition of information, 188–89
    $E = mc^2$, 111–12
    fusion, 192–93
    nature of the atmosphere, 201–2
    quantum theory, 148
    superconductivity, 129
    theory of relativity, 114
    Uncertainty Principle, 153–54
Matrix mechanics
    Uncertainty Principle, 153–54
Matter. See also Antimatter; Dark matter; E =
        $mc^2$; Energy and matter
    atoms, 59–60
    Big Bang theory, 185–86
    conservation of, 47–48
    definition of information, 188–89
    fusion, 192–93

importance of, 47
laws of motion, 31–32
origins of discovery, 47–48
oxygen, 43
photosynthesis, 46
quarks, 203–4
Maxwell, James Clerk
    electromagnetic radiation/radio waves, 83–85
Mayor, Michel
    existence of planets around other stars,
        215–16
McClintock, Barbara
    "jumping genes," 190–91
mDNA
    mitochondria, 104
Measurement
    accelerating universe, 219
    antimatter, 161
    Big Bang theory, 185–86
    Doppler Effect, 76
    $E = mc^2$, 112
    existence of planets around other stars,
        215–16
    fusion, 192–93
    matter, 47–48
    speed of light, 155–56
Medicine
    anesthesia, 57–58
    human anatomy, 7–8
Megalosaurus, 68
Meitner, Lise
    nuclear fission, 178–80
Mendel, Gregor
    heredity, 86–87
Mendeleyev, Dmitri
    Periodic Chart of the Elements, 90–91
Mercury. See Liquid mercury
Mesons. See also Pi-mesons
    weak and strong force, 172
Metabolism
    importance of, 174
    origins of discovery, 174–75
Meteorology. See Atmosphere; Atmospheric
        layers; Barometer; Oceans, effects on
        weather; Weather
Michelson, Albert
    speed of light, 155–56
Microbiology
    bacteria, 29–30
    mitochondria, 103–4
    germ theory, 78

Microorganisms
    antibiotics, 124–25
    germ theory, 77–78
Microscopes. *See also* Achromatic microscope;
    Antibiotics; Electron microscope;
    Telescopes
    bacteria, 29–30
    cell division, 92–93
    existence of cells, 21
    dark matter, 211
    fossils, 26
    "jumping genes," 191
    mitochondria, 103
    quantum theory, 148–49
    viruses, 97–98
Microscopic organisms
    antibiotics, 124
    germ theory, 77–78
Microwaves
    infrared (IR) and ultraviolet (UV) light, 55
Milky Way, 36
Miller, Stanley
    origins of life, 194–95
"Mind (or thought) experiments"
    Einstein, Albert, 111, 115
"Missing link," 147
Mitochondria. *See also* Cell structure; Complete
    evolution
    importance of, 103
    origins of discovery, 103–4
Mitosis. *See* Cell division
Mold
    genes, function of, 168
    penicillin, 159
Molecular biology
    DNA, 196–97
Molecules. *See also* Atoms; Protein molecules
    definition of, 64
    DNA, 196–97
    importance of, 63
    origins of discovery, 63–64
    X-rays, 95
Momentum
    conservation of energy, 74
Montagu, Lady Mary Wortley. *See also* Jenner,
    Edward
    vaccinations, 53–54
Moons. *See* Jupiter's moons
Morgan, T. H.
    chromosomes, function of, 121–23

Motion. *See also* Black holes; Dark matter;
    Law of falling objects; Laws of
    motion; Momentum; Uncertainty
    Principle
    accelerating universe, 218–19
    nature of heat, 50
    nature of the atmosphere, 202
    quasars and pulsars, 205–6
    seafloor spreading, 199–200
Motors
    electricity, 38
    electromagnetism, 65
Muscles
    metabolism, 174–75
Mutations
    chromosomes, function of, 121–22
    complete evolution, 208–9
    genes, function of, 168
    "jumping genes," 191

Napier, John
    planetary motion, 12
Natural selection
    complete evolution, 208–9
    theory of evolution, 80
*Naturalist's Voyage on the Beagle, A*
    theory of evolution, 80
Nature. *See* Order in nature
Nature of dinosaurs
    importance of, 213
    origins of discovery, 213–14
Nature of heat
    importance of, 49
    origins of discovery, 49–50
Nature of the atmosphere
    importance of, 201
    origins of discovery, 201–2
Neosalvarsan
    antibiotics, 125
Neurons, 144–45
Neurospora
    genes, function of, 167
Neurotransmitters
    importance of, 144
    origins of discovery, 144–45
Neutrinos
    antimatter, 161
Neutron star, 206

Neutrons. *See also* Electrons; Protons; Quarks
    antimatter, 161
    Big Bang theory, 186
    importance of, 163
    isotopes, 134
    origins of discovery, 163–64
    weak and strong force, 172
Newton, Isaac
    air pressure, 17
    law of falling objects, 9
    laws of motion, 31–32
    universal gravitation, 23–24
Nitrogen cycle
    ecosystems, 169
Nitrous oxide
    anesthesia, 58
    electrochemical bonding, 61
Nonlinear model equations
    nature of the atmosphere, 202
Nuclear bomb
    Big Bang theory, 186
    E = mc², 111–12
    fission, 179
    neutrons, 163
Nuclear energy
    E = mc², 111–12
    fission, 178–79
    fusion, 192–93
    quantum theory, 148–49
    speed of light, 156
Nuclear fission
    importance of, 178
    origins of discovery, 178–79
Nucleus. *See also* Atomic bonding; Cell
        structure; Cells
    isotopes, 133–34
    mitochondria, 103
    neutrons, 163–64
    Uncertainty Principle, 153
Nutrition
    vitamins, 117–18

Oceans, effects on weather. *See also* Deep-sea
        life
    importance of, 40
    origins of discovery, 40–41
Oersted, Hans
    electromagnetism, 65–66
Onnes, Heike Kamerlingh
    superconductivity, 128–30

Order in nature
    importance of, 33
    origins of discovery, 33–34
Organelles
    cell structure, 166
    mitochondria, 103
*Origin of Species*
    theory of evolution, 80
Origins of life
    importance of, 194
    origins of discovery, 194–95
*Original Theory on New Hypothesis of the
        Universe, An,* 37
Oxidation
    nature of heat, 49
Oxygen. *See also* Gas; Photosynthesis
    atmospheric layers, 107
    importance of, 43
    metabolism, 174–75
    origins of discovery, 43–44

Paleontology. *See also* Anthropology;
        Nature of dinosaurs
    dinosaur fossils, 67
    theory of evolution, 79
Pancreas
    insulin, 142
Pangaea, 139
Particle physics. *See also* Elementary
        particles; Subatomic particles
    electrons, 101–2
Pasteur, Louis
    bacteria, 30
    germ theory, 77–78
Pasteurization, 77–78
Penicillin
    antibiotics, 124
    importance of, 158
    origins of discovery, 158–59
Periodic Chart of the Elements
    importance of, 90
    isotopes, 133
    origins of discovery, 90–91
Perlmutter, Saul
    accelerating universe, 218–19
Pharmacology
    antibiotics, 124–25
    neurotransmitters, 145
Phlogiston, 49
Phosphates
    metabolism, 175

Photochemistry
  atomic light signatures, 82
Photons
  $E = mc^2$, 111
Photosynthesis. *See also* Oxygen; Plants
  importance of, 45
  origins of discovery, 45–46
Physics. *See also* Atomic bonding; $E = mc^2$;
    Energy and matter; Geophysics; Particle
    physics; Quantum physics; Quantum
    theory; Speed of light; Theory of
    relativity; Uncertainty Principle
  antimatter, 160–61
  atoms, 59–60
  Big Bang theory, 185–86
  dark matter, 211–12
  electromagnetic radiation/radio waves,
      83–84
  isotopes, 133–34
  nuclear fission, 178–79
  radioactivity, 105–6
  superconductivity, 128–29
  weak and strong force, 171–72
Physiology. *See* Antibiotics; Circulatory
    system; Hormones; Human anatomy;
    Vitamins
Pi-mesons
  weak and strong force, 172
Pistons
  Boyle's Law, 19–20
Pitchblende, 105
Plague
  vaccinations, 53–54
Planetary motion. *See also* Galaxies; Law of
    falling objects; Laws of motion
  importance of, 11
  origins of discovery, 11–12
  tables of calculations, 12
Planets. *See* Existence of planets around other
    stars
Plants. *See also* Algae; Animals; Ecosystems;
    Photosynthesis
  bacteria, 29
  complete evolution, 209
  continental drift, 138
  deep-sea life, 88–89
  order in nature, 33–34
  radioactive dating, 119–20
  theory of evolution, 79–80
Plasma. *See* Blood plasma

Plate tectonics. *See also* Continental drift;
    Seafloor spreading
  fault lines, 126–27
Polonium, 105–6
Positrons
  antimatter, 161
Potassium
  electrochemical bonding, 61–62
Priestley, Joseph
  oxygen, 43–44
*Principia,* 32
Prism
  atomic light signatures, 82
Protein molecules
  vitamins, 118
Proton-electrons
  neutrons, 163–64
Protons. *See also* Electrons; Quarks
  antimatter, 160–61
  Big Bang theory, 186
  isotopes, 133–34
  nuclear fission, 178–79
  quantum theory, 148–49
  Uncertainty Principle, 153
  weak and strong force, 171–72
Protozoa, 29
Ptolemy
  Jupiter's moons, 13
  law of falling objects, 9
  Ptolemy's model, 5–6
Pulsars. *See* Quasars and pulsars
Pure air. *See also* Oxygen
  matter, 47

Quanta
  atomic bonding, 132
  $E = mc^2$, 111
Quantum electrodynamics
  antimatter, 160
Quantum mechanics
  antimatter, 160–61
  quantum theory, 148–49
Quantum physics
  antimatter, 160
  *strangeness,* 204
  weak and strong force, 171
Quantum theory
  Big Bang theory, 186
  importance of, 148
  origins of discovery, 148–49
  superconductivity, 129

Quarks
    importance of, 203
    origins of discovery, 203–4
    weak and strong force, 172
Quasars and pulsars
    importance of, 205
    origins of discovery, 205–6
Queloz, Didier
    existence of planets around other stars,
        215–16

Radiation. See Atomic bonding; Big Bang
        theory; Dark matter; Electromagnetic
        radiation/radio waves; Infrared (IR) and
        ultraviolet (UV) light; Solar radiation
Radiation sickness, 105
Radioactive dating. See also Isotopes
    importance of, 119
    origins of discovery, 119–20
Radioactive decay
    nuclear fission, 178
    weak and strong force, 171
Radioactivity
    importance of, 105
    origins of discovery, 105–6
    polonium, 105–6
    radium, 105–6
    splitting of the atom, 105–6
Radio signals
    quasars and pulsars, 205–6
Radio waves. See Electromagnetic
        radiation/radio waves
Radium, 105–6
Recyclers
    ecosystems, 170
Reid, Harry
    fault lines, 126–27
Relativity. See Theory of relativity
Reproduction. See Sexual reproduction
Ribonucleic Acid (RNA)
    cell structure, 166
Ribosomes
    cell structure, 166
Ricci, Ostilio
    law of falling objects, 10
Richer, Jean
    distance to the sun, 28
Ritter, Johann
    ultraviolet (UV) light, 56
Roentgen, Wilhelm
    X-rays, 95–96

Rubbia, Carlo
    weak force, 171–72
Rubin, Vera
    dark matter, 211–12
Rumford, Count
    nature of heat, 49–50

San Andreas fault, 127
Sandage, Allan Rex
    quasars, 205–6
Schwarzschild, Karl
    black holes, 140–41
Seafloor spreading
    importance of, 199
    origins of discovery, 199–200
Secretin, 110
Sedimentation
    fossils, 26
Seismic waves
    Earth's core and mantle, 137
Seismology. See also Fault lines; Geology
    Earth's core and mantle, 136–37
Semiconductor transistor
    importance of, 183
    origins of discovery, 183–84
Sexual reproduction
    order in nature, 34
Shadow zone, 136
Shannon, Claude
    definition of information, 188–89
Shipping
    oceans, effects on weather, 41
Smith, J. L. B.
    coelacanth, 176–77
Soddy, Frederick
    isotopes, 133–35
Sodium
    electrochemical bonding, 61–62
Solar energy
    fusion, 192–93
Solar radiation
    atomic light signatures, 81–82
Solar system. See also Distance to the sun;
        Galaxies
    existence of planets around other stars,
        215–16
    planetary motion, 11–12
Sonar
    seafloor spreading, 199–200
Sound
    conservation of energy, 74

Sound waves
    Doppler Effect, 75–76
Space. *See* Light, space, and time
Spectrographs
    dark matter, 211–12
    distance to the sun, 27
    existence of planets around other stars, 216
    expanding universe, 151
    quasars and pulsars, 205
Spectrography
    atomic light signatures, 81
    isotopes, 134
    quasars and pulsars, 205
    radioactive dating, 120
Speed of light
    black holes, 141
    distance to the sun, 27
    $E = mc^2$, 111–12
    electromagnetic radiation/radio waves, 84
    importance of, 155
    origins of discovery, 155–56
    quarks, 203–4
Sperm, 29
Spitzer, Lyman
    fusion, 192–93
Starling, Ernst
    hormones, 109–10
Stars. *See* Atomic light signatures; Black holes;
    Distance to the sun; Doppler Effect;
    Existence of planets around other stars;
    Expanding universe; Galaxies; Neutron
    star; Quasars and pulsars; Solar system;
    Stellarator; Supernovae
Static
    electricity, 38–39
Stellarator
    fusion, 193
Steno, Nicholas
    fossils, 25–26
*Strangeness*
    quarks, 204
Stratosphere
    atmospheric layers, 108
Strong force. *See* Weak and strong force
Subatomic particles. *See also* Atomic bonding;
    Quantum theory; Quarks
    antimatter, 160–61
    electrons, 101–2
    isotopes, 133
    neutrons, 163

    radioactivity, 105–6
    weak and strong force, 172
Sugar
    metabolism, 174–75
Sun-centered universe. *See also* Distance to
    the sun; Galaxies
    importance of, 5
    origins of discovery, 5–6
    Ptolemy's model, 5–6
Sunlight
    photosynthesis, 46
Superconductivity
    importance of, 128
    origins of discovery, 128–29
    semiconductor transistor, 184
Supernovae
    accelerating universe, 218
    quasars and pulsars, 206
Supplements. *See* Vitamins
Symbiosis
    complete evolution, 208–9
Synchrotron
    weak and strong force, 172
*Systema Naturae,* 34

Tansley, Arthur
    ecosystems, 169–70
Taung skull
    human evolution, 146–47
Taxonomy. *See also* Order in nature
    definition of, 33
Teisserenc de Bort, Leon Philippe
    atmospheric layers, 107–8
Telescopes. *See also* Microscopes
    atmospheric layers, 108
    dark matter, 211–12
    definition of, 14
    distance to the sun, 27–28
    Doppler Effect, 76
    existence of planets around other stars,
      215–16
    expanding universe, 150–51
    planetary motion, 13
    radio, 205
Temperature. *See also* Absolute zero temperature
    atmospheric layers, 107–8
    Big Bang theory, 186
    Earth's core and mantle, 136–37
    fusion, 192–93
    infrared (IR) and ultraviolet (UV) light, 55

Temperature (*Cont.*)
  nature of heat, 50
  nature of the atmosphere, 202
  oceans, effects on weather, 40–41
  superconductivity, 128–29
Theory of evolution. *See also* Heredity
  chromosomes, function of, 121
  importance of, 79
  origins of discovery, 79–80
Theory of relativity
  black holes, 140
  $E = mc^2$, 112
  importance of, 114
  origins of discovery, 114–15
Thermodynamics
  calories, 71
  conservation of energy, 73
Thermometer
  atmospheric layers, 107
  superconductivity, 129
Thompson, Benjamin. *See* Rumford, Count
Thomson, Charles
  deep-sea life, 88–89
Thomson, J. J.
  electrons, 101–2
Thorium
  isotopes, 134
  radioactive dating, 119
Time. *See* Light, space, and time
Torricelli, Evangelista
  air pressure, 17–18
Trace elements
  vitamins, 117–18
Traits. *See also* Genes
  chromosomes, function of, 121
  heredity, 86–87
Transfer resistors
  semiconductor transistor, 184
Transfusions
  blood types, 100
Transistor. *See* Semiconductor transistor
Transverse waves
  Earth's core and mantle, 137
Troposphere
  atmospheric layers, 108
Tryptophan
  vitamins, 118

Ultraviolet (UV) light. *See* Infrared (IR) and
  ultraviolet (UV) light

Uncertainty Principle
  importance of, 153
  origins of discovery, 153–54
Universal gravitation. *See also* Law of
    falling objects; Laws of motion
  importance of, 23
  origins of discovery, 23–24
Universe. *See* Accelerating universe; Dark
    matter; Existence of planets around
    other stars; Expanding universe;
    Quasars and pulsars
Uranium. *See also* Lead
  isotopes, 134
  radioactive dating, 119
  radioactivity, 105–6
*Urkraft*
  electromagnetism, 65–66
  infrared (IR) and ultraviolet (UV) light,
    56

Vaccinations
  importance of, 53
  origins of discovery, 53–54
Vacuum
  air pressure, 17–18
  matter, 48
Vagus nerve
  neurotransmitters, 145
Vagusstoff. *See* Acetylcholine
van Helmholtz, Hermann
  conservation of energy, 73–74
"Variation," 208
Vegetation zones
  ecosystems, 169
Veins
  circulatory system, 15–16
Venter, J. Craig
  human genome, 220–21
Vesalius, Andreas
  human anatomy, 7–8
Viruses. *See also* Antibiotics; Bacteria; Cell
    structure
  importance of, 97
  origins of discovery, 97–98
"Vital force" theory
  conservation of energy, 73
Vitamins
  definition of, 118
  importance of, 117
  origins of discovery, 117–18

Volume
  Boyle's Law, 20
  buoyancy, 4
  gas, 19–20
  oceans, effects on weather, 41

Water
  air pressure, 17
Watson, James
  DNA, 196–7
  human genome, 220–21
Weak and strong force
  definitions of, 171–72
  importance of, 171
  origins of discovery, 171–72
Weapons advancement
  E = mc², 112
  isotopes, 133
  nuclear fission, 178–79
  speed of light, 156
Weather. *See also* Atmosphere; Barometer;
      Oceans, effects on weather; Troposphere
  air pressure, 17–18
  atmospheric layers, 107–8
  forecasting, 201–2
  ice ages, 69–70
  nature of the atmosphere, 202
Wegener, Alfred
  continental drift, 138–39

Weight. *See also* Atomic weight; Matter
  air pressure, 17–18
  atoms, 60
  Boyle's Law, 20
  law of falling objects, 9–10
  levers, 3
Wind
  atmospheric layers, 107
Wobble effect
  existence of planets around other stars,
      215–16
Wright, Thomas
  galaxies, 36–37

X-ray crystalography
  penicillin, 159
X-rays. *See also* Gamma rays
  dark matter, 212
  DNA, 196–97
  electromagnetic radiation/radio waves, 83–84
  genes, function of, 167–68
  importance of, 95
  infrared (IR) and ultraviolet (UV) light, 55
  origins of discovery, 95–96

Yukawa, Hideki
  strong force, 171–72

Zonation. *See* Latitudinal zonation

# About the Author

**Kendall Haven.** The only West Point graduate and only senior oceanographer to become a professional storyteller, Haven has performed for four million. He has won numerous awards for his story writing and his storytelling and has conducted story writing and storytelling workshops for 40,000 teachers and librarians and 200,000 students. Haven has published five audiotapes and twenty-five books, including three award-winning books on story: *Write Right* and *Get It Write* on writing, and *Super Simple Storytelling*, on doing, using, and teaching storytelling. Through this work he has become a nationally recognized expert on the architecture of narratives and on teaching creative and expository writing.

Haven served on the National Storytelling Association's Board of Directors and founded the International Whole Language Umbrella's Storytelling Interest Group. He served as co-director of the Sonoma and Bay Area Storytelling Festivals, was an advisor to the Mariposa Storytelling Festival, and is founder of Storytelling Festivals in Las Vegas, Nevada, and Boise, Idaho. He lives with his wife in the rolling Sonoma County grape vineyards in rural Northern California.